Gift to:

_____

From:

_____

Date:

_____

Message:

_____

_____

_____

_____

Gift to:

From:

Date:

Message:

Precious in the Father's Sight

Catherine Marshall

Fleming H. Revell
A Division of Baker Book House Co
Grand Rapids, Michigan 49516

PRECIOUS IN THE FATHER'S SIGHT

© 1997 by Marshall-LeSourd L.L.C
Originally published under the title
Day by Day with Catherine Marshall
by Chosen Books, a division of Baker Book House
Company, Grand Rapids, Michigan, 49516, U.S.A.

Scripture quotations are from the New American Standard
Bible, © the Lockman Foundation 1960, 1962, 1963, 1968,
1971, 1973, 1975, 1977.

© 1996: Christian Art, P O Box 1599, Vereeniging, 1930,
South Africa

Designed by: Christian Art

ISBN 0-8007-7158-3

Printed in Hong Kong

JANUARY

JANUARY 1

GOD'S SOVEREIGNTY

> *"... He knows the way I take;*
> *When He has tried me,*
> *I shall come forth as gold."*
> Job 23:10

Our God is the Divine Alchemist.
He can take junk from the rubbish
heap of life, and melting this base
refuse in the pure fire of His love,
hand us back – gold.

JANUARY 2

GOD'S SOVEREIGNTY

*"'Do I not fill the heavens and
the earth?' declares the LORD."*
Jeremiah 23:24

Like a great bell tolling over all
the land, the consistent voice of the
sovereign power of God reverberates
throughout Old Testament and New.
He is omnipotent, omnipresent, omniscient in this life and the next. We cannot
believe this and also think that our God
is no match for the evil of the world.

JANUARY 3

GOD'S SOVEREIGNTY

"I am like a luxuriant cypress;
From Me comes your fruit."
Hosea 14:8

The Gospel truly is good news. The news is that there is no situation — no breakage, no loss, no grief, no sin, no mess — so dreadful that out of it God cannot bring good, total good, not just "spiritual" good, if we will allow Him to.

JANUARY 4

SURRENDER

"And why do you call Me, 'Lord, Lord,' and do not do what I say?"
Luke 6:46

Any human physician requires the surrender of a given case into his care; he can do nothing unless the patient agrees to follow his orders. Common sense told me that exactly the same was true of the Great Physician.

JANUARY 5

THE KINGDOM

*"... seek first His kingdom
and His righteousness ..."*
Matthew 6:33

*"J*ohn is a great man, the greatest,"
Jesus was saying. "Yet the humblest
disciple in the Kingdom has riches and
privileges and authority of which John
never dreamed." How could that be?
Because man's efforts were at an end.
In the new era of the Kingdom it would
be God's Spirit *in* man doing the work.

JANUARY 6

ASKING

"Ask, and it shall be given to you ..."
Matthew 7:7

God insists that we ask, not because He needs to know our situation, but because *we* need the spiritual discipline of asking.

PRAYER

"For I, the LORD, do not change ..."
Malachi 3:6

The reason many of us retreat into vague generalities when we pray is not because we think too highly of God, but because we think too little.

JANUARY 8

PRAYER

...Jesus said to the centurion, "Go your way;
let it be done to you as you have believed."
Matthew 8:13

*I*n order to make sure that we are
not retreating from the tension of faith,
it is helpful to ask ourselves as we pray,
"Do I really expect anything to happen?" This will prevent us from
going window-shopping in prayer.

OUR WILL AND GOD'S

... according to the kind intention of His will.
Ephesians 1:5

Because God loves us so much, He often guides us by planting His own lovely dream in the barren soil of a human heart. When the dream has matured, and the time for its fulfillment is ripe, to our astonishment and delight, we find that God's will has become our will, and our will, God's.

HUMOR

*"You blind guides, who strain out
a gnat and swallow a camel!"*
Matthew 23:24

Jesus' humor was always for a
purpose. Sometimes it was His bridge
to an individual He would otherwise
have had trouble reaching. Most often
it was to illuminate a truth.

HUMOR

"For it is easier for a camel to go through the eye of a needle, than for a rich man to enter the kingdom of God."
Luke 18:25

To awaken people at every level of their being, Jesus used every weapon of language and communication to achieve His goals; most effective were the humorous thrusts and banter about those who put on airs. Jesus sees all our incongruities and absurdities, and He laughs along with us.

JANUARY 12

GOD'S OMNISCIENCE

*"Look at the birds of the air, that
they do not sow ... and yet your
heavenly Father feeds them. Are you
not worth much more than they?"*
Matthew 6:26

Each of us is infinitely precious in
the Father's sight, so much so that He
knows every detail about us, even to
the number of hairs on our heads.

JANUARY 13

REWARDS

"... and your reward will be great ..."
Luke 6:35

Jesus spoke often of heaven's rewards. If that offends us by seeming too material-istic, perhaps we should be wary of being more "spiritual" than our Lord.

JANUARY 14

LIFE AFTER DEATH

*"For in the resurrection they ...
are like angels in heaven."*
Matthew 22:30

I guessed that ... the one who has
stepped over into the next life still
remembers every tender moment
on earth, still cares what happens to
those left behind, still wants to help
them – but that the emotion of his
love is intensified and purified.

LIFE AFTER DEATH

Love never fails ...
1 Corinthians 13:8

We have the apostle Paul, in his famous love poem, setting love at the summit of all spiritual gifts, describing for us in gladsome detail what it will be like someday. It was on this conception of a new kind of love, on a different kind of relationship that I had to fix my mind.

LIFE AFTER DEATH

When my anxious thoughts multiply within me,
Thy consolations delight my soul.
Psalm 94:19

I remembered how often before Peter died that he had said from his pulpit, "Death has no scissors with which to cut the cords of love." Of course he had been right. Yet it is difficult for us to imagine love without possessiveness.

JANUARY 17

GUIDANCE

*... we are the people of His pasture,
and the sheep of His hand.*
Psalm 95:7

Often God has to shut a door in our face
so that He can subsequently open the
door through which He wants us to go.

JANUARY 18

ANSWERED PRAYER

He will bring me out to the light,
And I will see His righteousness.
Micah 7:9

My Teacher had yet to show me the difference between the presumption that masquerades as faith and real faith. The dividing line between the two lies at the point of one's motive.

HEAVENLY FATHER

"… how much more shall your heavenly Father give the Holy Spirit to those who ask Him?"
Luke 11:13

Jesus delighted in comparing earthly fathers to His heavenly Father, and then in adding, "But how much more God!" The riches of heaven and earth all belong to our Father, and He loves to shower them upon us. In Jesus' eyes, though, the most precious of all gifts is this one of the Holy Spirit.

JANUARY 20

GOD'S CARE

*"... his father saw him ... and
ran and embraced him ..."*
Luke 15:20

God deals differently with each of us.
He knows no "typical" case. He seeks
us out at a point in our own need and
runs down the road to meet us. This
individualized treatment should delight
rather than confuse us, because it so
clearly reveals the highly personal
quality of God's love and concern.

JANUARY 21

GOD'S CARE

*"And he who beholds Me beholds
the One who sent Me."*
John 12:45

Jesus' ringing response leaves no
doubt: "I do choose. Be cleansed."
And Jesus is the portrait of God. By
every word and deed, Jesus made it
clear that His Father not only cares,
but that no detail of any life is too
insignificant for His loving providence.

JANUARY 22

JOYFULNESS

*"[God] ... hath anointed Thee
with the oil of gladness ..."*
Hebrews 1:9

As I read through the Gospels I see
that Jesus had quite a bit to say
about joy. We are not invited to a
relationship that will take away our
fun but asked to "enter into the joy
of the Lord." The purpose of His
coming to earth, Jesus said, was in
order that our joy might be full!

JANUARY 23

JOYFULNESS

*"In the world you have tribulation, but
take courage; I have overcome the world."*
John 16:33

I can see that Jesus drew men
and women into the Kingdom by
promising them two things: first,
trouble – hardship, danger; and
second, joy. But what curious alchemy
is this that He can make even danger
and hardship seem joyous?

DAILY DEVOTIONS

In the morning, O LORD,
Thou wilt hear my voice;
In the morning I will order my
prayer to Thee and eagerly watch.
Psalm 5:3

It is wise to give God a chance to speak to us each day, perhaps the first thing in the morning when the mind is freshest. A few minutes of quietness help us focus on the areas where we most need God's help.

JANUARY 25

TRUST

*"(A)nd He gave Him authority ...
because He is the Son of Man."*
John 5:27

You are not really trusting God until
you are trusting Him for the ultimates
of life. And what are the ultimates? Life
and death, health, economic necessities,
the need to find one's own place in the
world, to love and to be loved.

JANUARY 26

DOING FOR OURSELVES

*Not that we are adequate in ourselves
to consider anything as coming from
ourselves, but our adequacy is from God.*
2 Corinthians 3:5

I believe that the old cliché, "God
helps those who help themselves," is
not only misleading but often dead
wrong. My most spectacular answers
to prayers have come when I was so
helpless, so out of control as to be
able to do nothing at all for myself.

THE WORD

*All things came into being by Him,
and apart from Him nothing came
into being that has come into being.*
John 1:3

Jesus stands sentinel over His Book
to show us that we can use His word
in Scripture with real power only as
He Himself energizes it and speaks
to us personally through it.

JANUARY 28

THE WORD

(H)ow shall the ministry of the Spirit
fail to be even more with glory?
2 Corinthians 3:8

*R*hema is that part of the logos to which
the Holy Spirit points us personally,
which He illuminates and brings to life
for us in our particular situations.

PRAYERS

*"For whoever wishes to save his life
shall lose it; but whoever loses his
life for My sake shall find it."*
Matthew 16:25

God cannot get His word through
to us when our prayers are limited
to self-centered monologues.

JANUARY 30

BIBLE VERSES

... He [Jesus] entered the synagogue on the Sabbath, and stood up to read. And the book of the prophet Isaiah was handed to Him.
Luke 4:16-17

By saturating my mind with Bible verses I find that the grayness lifts, the spirit is infused with spiritual food and I am ready to meet any difficulty that comes along.

THE KING

*... "When He ascended on high,
He led captive a host of captives ..."*
Ephesians 4:8

Until we catch a glimpse of the full glory of this crowned Christ, of the honors heaped upon Him, of the extent of the power the Father has placed in His hands, we can never grasp the significance of Jesus' question, "Who do you say that I am?" For Christ is the King of kings and the Lord of lords.

FEBRUARY

FEBRUARY 1

PRAISE

*At that time Jesus answered and said, "I praise
Thee, O Father, Lord of heaven and earth ..."*
Matthew 11:25

My first discovery was that I knew
almost nothing about praise. The
subject is mentioned occasionally as
a nice worship exercise, a sort of icing
on the cake as a gesture to God, but
praise as the key to answered prayer,
no. That was a new concept altogether.

PRAISE

Yet Thou art holy, O Thou who
art enthroned upon the praises of Israel.
Psalm 22:3

*T*he quickest way to go to meet Him is
through praise. No wonder we meet
Him there, for Scripture goes on to
teach us that God actually "inhabits"
(lives in) the praises of His people.

FEBRUARY 3

PRAISE

Through Him then, let us continually offer up a sacrifice of praise to God ...
Hebrews 13:15

The fact that the word "sacrifice" is used regarding praise tells us that the writers of Scripture understood well that when we praise God for trouble, we're giving up something. What we're sacrificing is the right to the blessings we think are due to us.

FEBRUARY 4

PRAISE

*Thou art my God, and I
give thanks to Thee ...*
Psalm 118:28

Even as God asked praise of Jehoshaphat
and of Paul and Silas, so He asks it of
each one of us. And the longer one
ponders this matter of praise and
experiments with it, the more evidence comes to light that here is
the most powerful prayer of all, a
golden bridge to the heart of God.

PRAISE

The cords of the wicked have encircled me,
But I have not forgotten Thy law.
At midnight I shall rise
to give thanks to Thee...
Psalm 119:61-62

We must begin to praise by obeying Jesus' injunction "Resist not evil." So we stop fighting whatever form evil is at the moment taking.

FEBRUARY 6

PRAISE

*For Thy righteousness, O God, reaches
to the heavens, Thou who hast done
great things; O God, who is like Thee?*
Psalm 71:19

*P*raise is the swiftest,
surest route to faith.

SOUL SEARCHING

*And everyone who has this hope fixed
on Him purifies himself, just as He is pure.*
1 John 3:3

*H*e is always Light, so I too must walk in
the light. All closet doors, every shut-
tered room in me must be thrown open.
So began months of soul searching.

FEBRUARY 8

THE BIBLE

Thy word is a lamp to my feet ...
Psalm 119:105

I wanted authoritative answers. Therefore, I went directly to the most authoritative source I knew – the Scriptures. And I discovered what I should have known before – that when you and I go to the Bible out of great need to learn what it has to say to us, it is then that we get real help.

FEBRUARY 9

PRAYER

Worship the LORD with reverence,
And rejoice with trembling.
Psalm 2:11

God, who created heaven and earth, will hear *my* voice? The King of the universe will consider *my* meditation? Oh, thank You, Lord, for the undreamed-of opportunity of this audience with the King!

FAITH

*Now faith is ... the conviction
of things not seen.*
Hebrews 11:1

Faith is not hocus-pocus, opposed to knowledge and reality. In fact, faith does not go against experience at all; rather it appeals to experience, just as science does. The difference is that it appeals to experience in a realm where our five senses are not supreme rulers.

FAITH

*By faith Abraham, when he was called,
obeyed by going out to a place which he
was to receive for an inheritance; and he
went out, not knowing where he was going.*
Hebrews 11:8

Faith in God is simply trusting Him
enough to step out on that trust.

FAITH

*By faith Moses, when he was born, was
hidden for three months by his parents,
because they saw he was a beautiful child;
and they were not afraid of the king's edict.*
Hebrews 11:23

Faith is strengthened only as we
ourselves exercise it. We have to
apply it to our problems: poverty,
bodily ills, bereavement, job troubles,
tangled human relationships.

FEBRUARY 13

FAITH

*"To give to His people the
knowledge of salvation
By the forgiveness of their sins,
Because of the tender mercy of our God ..."*
Luke 1:77-78

We cannot have faith and a
guilty conscience at the same time.
Every time faith will fade away.

FEBRUARY 14

FAITH

" *... blessed is she who believed that there
would be a fulfillment of what had
been spoken to her by the Lord.*"
Luke 1:45

*F*aith has to be in the present
tense – now. A vague prospect
that what we want will transpire
in the future is not faith, but hope.

FEBRUARY 15

FAITH

The LORD is our lawgiver,
The LORD is our king;
He will save us.
Isaiah 33:22

Faith means that we must let Him do the work. Almost always it takes longer than we think it should. When we grow impatient and try a deliverance of our own, through friends or circumstances, we are taking God's work out of His hands.

FEBRUARY 16

FAITH

... "Do you believe that I am able to do this?"
Matthew 9:28

Once I thought that faith was
believing this or that specific thing
in my mind with never a doubt. Now
I know that faith is nothing more
or less than actively trusting God.

FEBRUARY 17

A PURPOSE

*And the Lord said to him, "Arise and
go to the street called Straight ..."*
Acts 9:11

*T*he idea that He might have a
particular purpose for any one of us —
a reason why we are here on earth —
boggles the mind. So as He begins
to unfold that bigger design into
which we fit, it is up to us to take
the first step forward in obedience.

FREE IN CHRIST

*But know that the LORD has set
apart the godly man for Himself;
The LORD hears when I call to Him.*
Psalm 4:3

The psalmist says that when he is
hemmed in on every side, the Lord
frees him. Gradually I have learned
to recognize this hemming-in as one
of God's most loving devices for teaching us that He is real and gloriously
adequate for our problems.

OBEDIENCE

... as a result of the works, faith was perfected.
James 2:22

Nor can trust ever end in just intellectual faith or lip service to faith. When it is the real thing, it will spill over into action — and that will mean obedience.

OBEDIENCE

*(F)or it is God who is at work in you, both to
will and to work for His good pleasure.*
Philippians 2:13

*H*ow can we *not* want to obey
when we begin to comprehend the
magnitude or the Holy Spirit's love
and complete good will for us?

IMPURITIES

*... let us keep living by that same
standard to which we have attained.*
Philippians 3:16

I knew that anything unloving in
me, any resentment, unforgiveness
or impurity would shut out God,
just as a muddy windowpane
obscures the sunlight.

CONVICTION

And he said, "Who art Thou, Lord?" And He said, "I am Jesus whom you are persecuting ..."
Acts 9:5

*H*ere we have Jesus telling us that convicting one another is not, and never was, our work: It's the Holy Spirit's business. Each of us must receive illumination about his guilt from the inside.

FORGIVENESS

*... and if he has committed sins,
they will be forgiven him.*
James 5:15

Long ago we had learned the principle that it is necessary to get the past confessed and straightened out (as far as is possible) before we can live abundantly in the present.

FORGIVENESS

For Thou, Lord, art good,
and ready to forgive,
And abundant in loving-
kindness to all who call upon Thee.
Psalm 86:5

Forgiveness is the precondition of love.

WEALTH

The earth is the Lord's and all it contains ...
Psalm 24:1

*I*f I truly believe that I am a child of a
King, then my fear will disappear.
Worrying would be the sure sign that I
did not believe God's ownership of
earth's resources. To think myself a
pauper is to deny either the King's
riches or my being His beloved child.

FEBRUARY 26

FAMILIES

*"Just as the Father has loved Me, I
have also loved you; abide in My love."*
John 15:9

There's no way to get our
world back together again except
as each of us begins with himself
and with his own family.

FEAR

The LORD is the defense of my life;
Whom shall I dread?
Psalm 27:1

Fear is like a screen erected between us and God so that His power cannot get through to us.

FEAR

*Thou hast removed all the wicked
of the earth like dross;
Therefore I love Thy testimonies.*
Psalm 119:119

Sometimes it helps to write down one's fears, then hold them up one by one to the light of Christ's clear understanding. Never is Jesus as the Light of the world more clear than in these murky areas of our semiconscious fears, most of them unreal and psychotic.

FEAR

*... "Why are you troubled, and why
do doubts arise in your hearts?"*
Luke 24:38

*T*he time came when I realized that,
in Jesus' eyes, fear is a sin since it is
acting out a lack of trust in God.

MARCH

FEAR

> *"And there is no other*
> *God besides Me,*
> *A righteous God and a Savior;*
> *There is none except Me."*
> Isaiah 45:21

Faith is the strong tower into which we can run for protection today. It isn't a physical place but the light of a protecting Presence. It makes the unreal fears vanish and gives us literal protection against the real ones.

MARCH 2

HELPLESSNESS

What then shall we say to these things? If God is for us, who is against us?
Romans 8:31

Sometimes life finds us powerless before facts that cannot be changed. Then we can only stand still at the bottom of the pit and claim for our particular trouble that best of all promises, that God will make even this to "work together for good."

MARCH 3

HELPLESSNESS

*"... For the LORD GOD is
my strength and song,
And He has become my salvation."*
Isaiah 12:2

Why would God insist on
helplessness as a prerequisite to
answered prayer? One obvious
reason is because our human
helplessness is bedrock fact.
God is a realist and insists
that we be realists too.

HELPLESSNESS

*"Call to Me, and I will answer you,
and I will tell you great and mighty
things, which you do not know."*
Jeremiah 33:3

It should not surprise us that creativity arises out of the pit of life rather than the high places. For creativity is the ability to put old material into new form. And it is only when old molds are broken up by need or suffering, compelling us to regroup, that the creative process starts to flow.

MARCH 5

INHERITED TRAITS

So rejoice, O sons of Zion,
And be glad in the LORD your God ...
Joel 2:23

Just as we can inherit either a fortune
or debts, so in the spiritual realm we
can inherit either spiritual blessings or
those liabilities (unabashedly called
"sins" in Scripture) that hinder our
development into mature persons.

GIVING

*"There is a lad here who has five
barley loaves and two fish, but what
are these for so many people?" Jesus
said, "Have the people sit down."*
John 6:9-10

The secret of receiving is to give —
even out of poverty. In fact, the more
sunk we are in visions of lack, the
greater need we have to start giving.

MARCH 7

IMMORTALITY

He heals the brokenhearted ...
Psalm 147:3

My first discovery was that reading
what the Bible has to say about
death and immortality immediately
bathes the subject in the sunlight of
normalcy. What a grave injustice we
do ourselves when we fail to take
advantage of this help and go on
through life fearing and wondering!

MARCH 8

IMMORTALITY

*For now we see in a mirror
dimly, but then face to face ...*
1 Corinthians 13:12

*T*he New Testament reassures
us that the next life is not only a
fully conscious one with every intellectual and spiritual faculty intact, but
that these faculties are heightened.

IMMORTALITY

*"In my Father's house are many
dwelling places; if it were not so,
I would have told you ..."*
John 14:2

We shall be able to remember, to
think, to will, to love, to worship and
to understand so much more on the
other side of the barrier of death.
Our new life will be no sleeping,
non-conscious or unfeeling existence.

MARCH 10

IMMORTALITY

*... "Truly I say to you, today you
shall be with Me in Paradise."*
Luke 23:43

Christ's words to the dying thief would
have been nonsense had He not meant
that after death on that very day, both
He and the thief would know themselves to be themselves, would remember that they had suffered together,
would recognize each other.

MARCH 11

THE SUBCONSCIOUS

*For all who are being led by the Spirit
of God, these are sons of God.*
Romans 8:14

The Christian may be permitted to
wonder whether somewhere in the deeps
of personality – still beyond the reach of
our scientific probing and measuring –
there is not a place where the Spirit that
is God can impress upon the spirit that
is man a thought, a direction, a solution.

MARCH 12

BORN OF THE SPIRIT

*" ... this is the one who
baptizes in the Holy Spirit."*
John 1:33

Scripture makes it clear that
Jesus Himself is the only One who
can baptize us with the Spirit. That
is why there must always be the
first step of commitment to Jesus
(being "born again") before we can
receive the fullness of His Spirit.

THE BATTLE

> " ... *do not resist him who is evil* ..."
> Matthew 5:39

*T*he way to win out when I feel evil at work in my life and the lives of those I love is not to fight it in the ordinary sense, but to give over those I love completely into the Father's hands, knowing that I am helpless to cope with evil, but that He is able.

MARCH 14

ILLNESS

The LORD is my shepherd ...
Psalm 23:1

*T*he unforgettable truth of David's
Psalm 23 came alive in my experience:
"He *maketh* me to lie down in green
pastures" – thus sometimes using
illness to get our full attention.

HUMAN RESOURCES

... examine yourselves!
2 Corinthians 13:5

So long as we are deluding ourselves that human resources can supply our heart's desires, we are believing a lie. And it is impossible for prayers to be answered out of a foundation of self-deception and untruth.

MARCH 16

REDEMPTION

... in Him you have been made complete, and He is the head over all rule and authority.
Colossians 2:10

God is not going to drop into our laps, as a package commodity, unselfishness or a loving disposition or any virtue. Instead, He has promised me Jesus' resurrection life in me. Thus it will be Jesus' selflessness and patience and love manifested in my life – not my own.

FAITHFULNESS

Great is Thy faithfulness.
Lamentations 3:23

Reading through the journals of my college years makes me aware as never before how tender God was with me, never intruding on my willfull self-centeredness, but always there when the heart hungers inside me cried out.

DIVIDENDS

*"For even the Son of Man did not
come to be served, but to serve ..."*
Mark 10:45

Jesus told His disciples to tarry until
they received the Holy Spirit's power
to become His witnesses. Note that
Jesus did not say that this gift is for our
own spiritual development or perfection
or happiness. All of those results will
follow provided we accept Jesus' top
priority – witnessing to the world.

MARCH 19

GUIDANCE

" ... O LORD, be Thou my helper."
Psalm 30:10

Apparently the surrender of self is
necessary groundwork for receiving
guidance, since not even God can lead
us until we want to be led. It is as if we
are given an inner receiving set at birth,
but the set is not tuned in until we
actively turn our lives over to God.

GUIDANCE

"(F)or where your treasure is,
there will your heart be also."
Matthew 6:21

Most of us think of our lives in compartments – home life, business life, social
life. Actually the various aspects of a
truly creative life must dovetail. God
will not direct a man's business life, for
example, when the man insists on
running his family his own way.

GUIDANCE

Commit your works to the LORD,
And your plans will be established.
Proverbs 16:3

In seeking guidance, I discovered that it was important to concentrate on one or two questions on which I needed light, and ask God for directions on those. This selectivity proved more effective than trying to make my mind blank, ready to receive any message on any subject.

GUIDANCE

*These all with one mind were
continually devoting themselves to prayer ...*
Acts 1:14

One reason the first Christians received
so much guidance was that they had
koinonia, a corporate fellowship that
made them "of one heart and soul." It
was in this setting that illumination,
inspiration and guidance flourished.

GUIDANCE

He who is holy, who is true ...
who opens and no one will shut,
and who shuts and no one opens ...
Revelation 3:7

*T*hen there is the check of providential circumstances. We are most fortunate in having this test. When we have asked God to guide us, we have to accept by faith the fact that He is doing so. This means that when He closes a door in our faces, we do well not to try to crash that door.

MARCH 24

GUIDANCE

*The mind of man plans his way,
But the LORD directs his steps.*
Proverbs 16:9

I found in the matter of guidance that I had to be willing to obey — no matter what. Otherwise no directions would be forthcoming. Receiving guidance is definitely not a matter of telling God what we want and hoping that He will approve.

GUIDANCE

"Sanctify them in the truth;
Thy word is truth."
John 17:17

I have found that the inner Voice is more likely to speak to me at the first moment of consciousness upon awakening, or during some odd moment of the day as I go about routine tasks, than while I wait expectantly with pad and pencil in hand.

GIFTS

*Pursue love, yet desire
earnestly spiritual gifts ...*
1 Corinthians 14:1

So far as the virtues and graces we
need for victory in our lives – faith,
joy, patience, peace of mind, the
ability to love the wretched and the
unlovely – there is no way we can
work up such qualities. Paul tells us
that these are gifts of the Holy Spirit.
They can be had in no other way.

MINISTRY

> ... *whoever wishes to become great*
> *among you shall be your servant.*
> Mark 10:43

Are we ready to give ourselves
to others? He will accept no
excuses about our inadequacy
in this way or that. Giving us
adequacy is His business. That's
what His coming to us is all about.

FREE WILL

And He said to them, "What do you want Me to do for you?"
Mark 10:36

Jesus had told me what to do. At that moment I understood as never before the totality of His respect for the free will He has given us and the fact that He will *never* violate it. His attitude said, "The decision is entirely yours."

SELF-SUFFICIENCY

For by grace you have been saved through faith; and ... not as a result of works ...
Ephesians 2:8-9

We want salvation from our sins and we yearn for eternal life. We think that we can earn these things. Then we find out, as Paul did, that we cannot pile up enough good marks and merits to earn anything from God. No, salvation "is the gift of God; not as a result of works, that no one should boast."

MARCH 30

OUT OF CONTROL

*... be strong in the Lord, and
in the strength of His might.*
Ephesians 6:10

Sometime in life every one of us finds
himself out of control, caught in circumstances that he is helpless to change.
We are to welcome such times. Often it
is only then that we lesser spirits enter
into the truth of Jesus' statement from
the fifteenth chapter of John: "Apart
from Me you can do nothing."

SEEKING APPROVAL

*(F)or they loved the approval of men
rather than the approval of God.*
.John 12:43

Certainly there is enormous pressure
on all of us to be accepted and approved
by others. But God wants us to resist
this pressure. Consider the tragedy of
the religious leaders of Jesus' day.

APRIL

APRIL 1

TWO WINGS

... be renewed in the spirit of your mind.
Ephesians 4:23

In order to fly we must have two wings. One wing is the realization of our human helplessness, the other is the realization of God's power. Our faith in God's ability to handle our particular situation is the connecting link.

FELLOWSHIP WITH CHRIST

"Abide in Me, and I in you."
John 15:4

Fellowship with Jesus is the true purpose of life and the only foundation for eternity. It is real, this daily fellowship He offers us.

HOPE

... I will wait for the LORD ...
I will even look eagerly for Him.
Isaiah 8:17

For each of us — no matter
what our situation or how we feel
we have failed — there is hope.

APRIL 4

EXHIBITIONISM

*There will be silence before Thee,
and praise in Zion, O God ...*
Psalm 65:1

Scripture makes it clear that the Holy Spirit is not fond of exhibitionism. After all, no trumpets herald the pinky-gray opalescent dawn. No bugles announce the opening of a rosebud. God speaks not in the thunder or the roaring wind, rather in a "still, small voice."

SOVEREIGNTY

" ... do you think that I cannot appeal to My Father, and He will at once put at My disposal more than twelve legions of angels?"
Matthew 26:53

It would seem to us that if ever the free will of wicked men was in control, it was at the execution of Jesus Christ by crucifixion. "Not so," was Jesus' assertion. Never for an instant during the acting out of that drama did God abdicate as sovereign ruler.

PLEASING GOD

*Whatever you do, do your work heartily,
as for the Lord rather than for men.*
Colossians 3:23

We are told that in our daily tasks –
whatever our vocation or profession
or daily round – we are to seek to
please God more than man.

MATERIAL NEEDS

*"... your heavenly Father knows
that you need all these things."*
Matthew 6:32

As for whether God means for
us to include material needs in our
petitions, certainly Christ was inter-ested
in men's bodies as well as
their souls. He was concerned about
their diseases, their physical hunger.
Christianity, almost alone among
world religions, acknowledges
material things as real and important.

OBEDIENCE

"Thy will be done, on earth as it is in heaven."
Matthew 6:10

God does not want our obedience out
of fear. Our obedience to Him is the
fruit of lives growing in the rich soil of
love and trust. Our obedience is to be
at once both the result of our loving
God and also the proof of our love.

OBEDIENCE

> *"I did not come to abolish
> [the Law], but to fulfill [it]."*
> Matthew 5:17

But what exactly are we to obey? Since Jesus often mentioned His commandments, I found it helpful to read the Gospels through, setting down in a notebook the commandments that Christ Himself gave us. There are a remarkable number of them and many are surprisingly precise.

OBEDIENCE

*And when they saw Him,
they worshiped Him ...*
Matthew 28:17

Not a one of us is going to drop his fishing nets, leave all and go after Jesus – unless he feels he can trust Him. One memorable sentence quoted by Quakeress Hannah Smith sums it up: "Perfect obedience would be perfect happiness if only we had perfect confidence in the power we were obeying.

OBEDIENCE

"Incline your ear and come to Me."
Isaiah 55:3

Always and always the understanding comes after the obedience.

OBEDIENCE

*For by it [faith] the men
of old gained approval.*
Hebrews 11:2

So Abraham obeyed. "He went out,
not knowing whither he went." He did
not need to know because God knew.

THE LEADING OF THE SPIRIT

" *... when He, the Spirit of truth, comes,
He will guide you into all the truth ...*"
John 16:13

Sometimes even as I would open my
mouth to speak, there would be a
sharp check on the inside. I soon learned that the Holy Spirit sought to prevent careless words or critical words or
even too many words. Nor would
He tolerate even a trace of sarcasm,
or faithless words of doubt or fear.

JUDGING OTHERS

*"For in the way you judge,
you will be judged ..."*
Matthew 7:2

Jesus was simply stating a law of life
when He told us, "Judge and you will be
judged." Put this way, judging others
constantly cultivates more soil for the
thistles of fear-of-man to grow in.

CONCENTRATION

*And their eyes were opened
and they recognized Him ...*
Luke 24:31

God asks that we worship Him
with concentrated minds as well as
allowing the Spirit to direct our wills
and emotions. A divided and scattered
mind is not at its most receptive.

LOVE

"And you shall love the LORD your God with all your heart and with all your soul and with all your might."
Deuteronomy 6:5

We are going to be capable of loving only to the extent that we abandon ourselves to another with no reservations.

PRAYER

*"Listen to me, you who ... seek the LORD:
Look to the rock from which you were hewn ..."*
Isaiah 51:1

Praying requires patience. God's perfect timing oftener than not seems slow – slow – slow to us.

LISTENING

"And I will make all My mountains a road,
And My highways will be raised up."
Isaiah 49:11

I found that in the everydayness of
life when the inner guidance did not
obviously violate any of God's loving
laws or hurt another, it was important
to obey and thus experiment with
obedience. That was how I learned
to recognize the Holy Spirit's voice.

THE NEXT LIFE

*... then I shall know fully just as
I also have been fully known.*
1 Corinthians 13:12

Scripture piles reassurance upon reassurance that at the death of the physical body, the real person inside lives on without interruption. The Bible tells us that the next life is not only a fully conscious one with every intellectual and spiritual faculty intact but that these faculties are heightened.

INNER HEALING

*May Thy compassion come
to me that I may live ...*
Psalm 119:77

When we become aware of damaged
areas in the unconscious, we can call on
the power of the Holy Spirit. He can
walk back with us into the past, drain
out all the poison, then create a highway
for our God to come marching trium-
phantly into the present with His long-
forgotten, oft-delayed plan for our lives.

JESUS' VOICE

*"My sheep hear My voice, and I
know them, and they follow Me."*
John 10:27

It is when we try to hear Christ's
Voice for the daily decisions that we
begin to know Jesus personally. Most
people are astonished at His interest in
the details of this relationship: how well
He knows us, all the little things we
thought we had successfully hidden.

PROTECTION

God is to us a God of deliverances ...
Psalm 68:20

If we were willing to accept the Spirit's help and to listen to His voice, many of the evils, difficulties and accidents that befall us would be avoided. I believe this to be an important answer to the question so often asked, "How could a loving God allow such-and-such a dreadful calamity to happen?"

TRUSTING GOD

*Blessed be the Lord, who
daily bears our burden ...*
Psalm 68:19

So if your every human plan and calculation has miscarried, if, one by one, human props have been knocked out, and doors have shut in your face, take heart. God is trying to get a message through to you, and the message is: "Stop depending on inadequate human resources. Let Me handle the matter."

FAITH

*"And all things you ask in prayer,
believing, you shall receive."*
Matthew 21:22

In one of the greatest blank-check
promises Jesus left us, He pinned
everything to faith.

FAITH

*Now faith is the assurance
of things hoped for ...*
Hebrews 11:1

*F*aith always has to be in the
present (denoting completed
action), as contrasted with hope,
which is always in the future.

FAITH

Commit your way to the LORD,
Trust also in Him, and He will do it.
Psalm 37:5

There is much in Scripture stressing
our need to have faith in God.
Psalm 37:5 takes us a step further.
It not only admonishes us to trust,
it promises that when we do, God
will act in a supernatural way to
answer our need. Dwell on that for
a moment. We trust, God acts.

FAITH

For with Thee is the fountain of life;
In Thy light we see light.
Psalm 36:9

Clearly it was Jesus' desire that we
be rid of disease. What was His plan
for achieving this? He said that faith
in His Father's willingness and ability
to give His children all good gifts is
the key. In His eyes there was no
evil that faith could not vanquish,
no need that faith could not supply.

SUPERSPIRITUALITY

*And he was teaching them
many things in parables ...*
Mark 4:2

Substituting a type of superspirituality
for Jesus' homespun practicality can be
one subtle way many of us try to keep a
safe distance between Him and us.

HUMAN NEED

*And in the same way the Spirit also
helps our weakness; for we do not
know how to pray as we should ...*
Romans 8:26

Actually, when we human beings
feel most capable of handling life
on our own, invariably that is when
we are most in need of Jesus' help
mediated to us by the Spirit.

APRIL 30

ABIDING

> " ... *he who abides in Me, and I
> in him, he bears much fruit ...*"
> John 15:5

Our human hang-up is thinking that
spirituality is something we do. "Not
so," says Jesus. "Rather it is My life in
you." The branch's part is simply to
remain connected to the Vine, to abide
there so that the life-giving sap can flow.

MAY

DREAMS

*Then the mystery was revealed
to Daniel in a night vision.*
Daniel 2:19

The unconscious mind does not
think analytically, but symbolically
or pictorially. Dream symbols are
provocative in their wide variety
and above all in their originality.

DREAMS

*" ... this mystery has ... been revealed
to me ... that you may understand
the thoughts of your mind."*
Daniel 2:30

Our dreams are often intensely
personal and self-reflective. Something deep within seeks to give us a
message. Different characters in our
dreams are usually parts of our own
being. Aspects of our personality that we
have ignored or even cast out of our
consciousness now seek to be heard.

ALL-OUT TRUST

> *... Though the yield of
> the olive should fail,
> And the fields produce no food ...
> Yet I will exult in the LORD.*
> Habakkuk 3:17-18

*T*here are periods when God's face is shrouded, when His dealings with us will appear as if He does not care, when He seems not to be acting like a true Father. Can we then hang onto the fact of His love and His faithfulness and that He *is* a prayer-answering God?

ALL-OUT TRUST

When my anxious thoughts multiply within me,
Thy consolations delight my soul.
Psalm 94:19

Can we, *at the moment* when
His face is hidden, exult in
the God of our salvation?

MAY 5

THE FAMILY

Today, if you would hear His voice,
Do not harden your hearts.
Psalm 95:7-8

Consider Jesus' admonition that
we forgive seventy times seven.
Perhaps Christ was not thinking
specifically of the family unit when
He spoke those words, or I think
He might have trebled the figure.

THE FAMILY

*... fathers, do not provoke your children
to anger; but bring them up in the
discipline and instruction of the Lord.*
Ephesians 6:4

The family is meant to be the training
ground for life, a true microcosm for
the world outside the home where
person has to get along with person,
pupils with each other and with teach-
ers, employees with bosses, management with labor, nation with nation.

THE FAMILY

*... as many as received Him, to them He
gave the right to become children of God ...*
John 1:12

The master design for us to
advance toward our heavenly
home via the nitty-gritty of
family life would be just like Him.

CLEANSING

*And He [Jesus] stretched out His
hand and touched him, saying,
"I am willing; be cleansed."*
Matthew 8:3

Jesus healed because the love of
God flowing irresistibly through Him
in a torrent of good will simply swept
evil away as the debris that it is.

THE CROSS

" *... not what I will, but what Thou wilt.*"
Mark 14:36

In the Garden of Gethsemane Jesus
deliberately set Himself to make
His will and God's will the same.
God has given you and me free will
too. And the voluntary giving up of our
self-will has a cross at the center of it.

THE CROSS

*[Let us fix] ... our eyes on Jesus, the author
and perfecter of faith, who for the joy set
before Him endured the cross, despising
the shame, and has sat down at the
right hand of the throne of God.*
Hebrews 12:2

The crucifixion and resurrection
are history's watershed.

THE CROSS

... *"Repent, and let each of you be
baptized in the name of Jesus Christ
for the forgiveness of your sins ..."*
Acts 2:38

With the cross, God wiped out the
old creation that was flawed in Eden.
The Gospel's momentous news is
not only that Jesus died on that
cross, but that you and I and our
flawed natures also died with Him.

THE CROSS

*(E)ven when we were dead in our trans-
gressions, [God] made us alive together
with Christ ... and raised us up with Him ...*
Ephesians 2:5-6

Not only that, even as I was "in"
Christ on His Cross, so I also rose
with Him, have been set in the
heavenlies with Him, and I am
now complete only in Him.

THE CROSS

*[God] ... seated us with Him ... in order
that in the ages to come He might show
the surpassing riches of His grace in
kindness toward us in Christ Jesus.*
Ephesians 2:6-7

*E*ver afterward there would be men
and women who would glory in that
cross "towering o'er the wrecks of
time" – the wrecks that we always
manage to make in every century. They
would glory because the cross stands as
the final symbol that no evil exists that
God cannot turn into a blessing.

THE HEART'S DESIRE

*... Neither has the eye seen
a God besides Thee,
Who acts in behalf of
the one who waits for Him.*
Isaiah 64:4

God has a "fullness of time" for
the answer to each of our prayers.
It follows then, that He alone knows
the magnitude of the changes that
have to be wrought in us before we
can receive our heart's desires.

THE HEART'S DESIRE

... let us not lose heart in doing good, for in due time we shall reap if we do not grow weary.
Galatians 6:9

God alone knows the changes
and interplay of external events
that must take place before our
prayers can be answered.

MADE PERFECT

*[The body] ... is raised in glory
... it is raised in power.*
1 Corinthians 15:43

The Scriptures say that we shall have a spiritual body after death. This spiritual body will give us much the same appearance that we have had on earth, except that if imperfect or deformed or diseased, all will be made perfect.

THE RESURRECTION

*"See My hands and My feet, that
it is I Myself; touch Me and see ..."*
Luke 24:39

Those who speak of some sort of "spiritual resurrection" are missing the point.
Nothing short of the resurrection of the
flesh would have been any victory at all.
Satan would not have been deceived;
Jesus' surprised, incredulous disciples
would not, and neither would we.

FAITH VS. FEAR

"In the world you have tribulation, but take courage; I have overcome the world."
John 16:33

Faith is always right; fear and despair are always wrong.

VICTORY

*"All things have been handed
over to Me by My Father ..."*
Luke 10:22

When Christ's apostles returned, after
having healed successfully, He rejoiced
with them, "I watched Satan falling
from heaven like a flash of lightning."
As restrained as the narrative usually is,
a lilting, triumphant quality breaks
through here. Luke says that Jesus
"rejoiced greatly" at that hour.

VICTORY

*"Take My yoke upon you,
and learn from Me ..."*
Matthew 11:29

We can allow an apparent defeat to turn into victory through trusting in the principle of resurrection. As Easter was not a passive event, neither is this kind of waiting. Here, too, something must be put to death, usually worry or trying to do it yourself.

GRIEF

He has sent me to bind up the brokenhearted ...
Isaiah 61:1

The Bible does not ignore sorrow
as a fact of human experience.
Some of the loveliest words of
Scripture are for the sore of heart.

ABSTRACTIONS

" ... *if God so arrays the grass of the field ... will He not much more do so for you, O men of little faith?*"
Matthew 6:30

Most of us are not as realistic as our God. We like to deal with high-flown theological abstractions. He deals with the lilies of the field, the yeast in the housewife's bread, patches on garments.

DECISION

"No one can serve two masters ..."
Matthew 6:24

It is as if nothing had changed since that moment eons ago when man was presented with his stark choice: Would he believe God or Satan? Time is still holding its breath for our answer. Which way will each man, each woman, decide now?

HEALING

... He said, "It is not those who are healthy who need a physician, but those who are sick."
Matthew 9:12

Jesus came to earth to show us the Father's will. He who created the incredible human body still heals today, but not as a divine magician. We need to seek His way, His timing and the lessons He wants us to learn along the way.

HEALING

*[Jesus] ... healed all who were ill in
order that what was spoken through
Isaiah the prophet might be fulfilled,
saying, "He Himself took our infirmities,
and carried away our diseases."*

Matthew 8:16-17

Healing is not an end in itself;
it is a dividend of the Gospel.

HEALING

And when the Lord saw her,
He felt compassion for her ...
Luke 7:13

Jesus' chief motive in healing seems to
have been nothing more or less than
pure compassion. The word *compassion*
is used over and over to describe His
attitude toward the sick. That was why
He often went out of His way to heal
when the sufferer had neither asked
for nor thought of His doing so.

HEALING

... she was saying to herself, "If I only touch His garment, I shall get well."
Matthew 9:21

Practically speaking, we shall have taken our greatest step forward in the realm of spiritual healing when the average Christian becomes as sure of God's will for health as he is of his doctor's. Only those who have settled this in their own minds, can press forward in the adventure of spiritual research.

HEALING

*And all the multitude were trying
to touch Him, for power was coming
from Him and healing them all.*
Luke 6:19

He [Jesus] did not once say in
regard to health, "If it is God's will."

HEALING

And He touched her hand,
and the fever left her ...
Matthew 8:15

There is no beatitude for the sick
as there is for others like the bereaved
of those who suffer persecution. Nor
did there ever fall from Jesus' lips
any statements that ill health would
further our spiritual growth or benefit
the Kingdom. Rather, He not only
wants to heal our diseases, He also
wants us to stay healthy.

HEALING

*Jesus said to him, "Arise, take
up your pallet, and walk."*
John 5:8

Jesus healed out of pure compassion
because He was ever "The Father's
Restorer." True, after Jesus healed the
man at the Pool of Bethesda, He told
him that now he would be wise to
repent and change lest something
even worse happen. But the healing
came before the man's change and
in no way seemed dependent on it.

THE GIVER

*The man believed the word
that Jesus spoke to him ...*
John 4:50

I've learned that our Lord waits
patiently until we stop playing
games with Him. The instant we
leave off our childish fooling around,
He knows it and responds. It had
taken me eighteen months of trying
everything else, but at last I wanted
the Giver more than His gifts.

JUNE

FULFILLMENT

And we know that God causes all things to work together for good to those who love God ...
Romans 8:28

True praise grows out of the recognition and acknowledgment that in His time God will bring good out of bad. There is the intolerable situation on the one hand and the fulfillment of Romans 8:28 on the other hand.

SEPARATION

*For I am convinced that neither death,
nor life ... nor any other created thing,
shall be able to separate us from the love
of God, which is in Christ Jesus our Lord.*
Romans 8:38-39

Nothing can separate us from
His love except our own blind
unwillingness to receive.

JUNE 3

REVELATION

*For if we died with Him, we
shall also live with Him.*
2 Timothy 2:11

Surely there is no joy like that first
rush of discovery in experiencing for
oneself that the Lord is alive in one's
life. And I had stumbled into that
revelation in the last way I would
have thought logical – through the
relinquishment of myself to Him.

PRAYER LOG

*... a book of remembrance
was written before Him.*
Malachi 3:16

If we hadn't been recording both
the prayer requests and the answers
with dates, we might have assumed
these to be "coincidences." With those
written notations marking the answers
to prayer, we found our gratitude to
God mounting. The prayer log was a
marvelous stimulus to faith.

ANSWERS TO PRAYER

*And He did not do many miracles
there because of their unbelief.*
Matthew 13:58

Gradually I saw that a demanding spirit,
with self-will as its rudder, blocks prayer.
I understood that the reason for this is
that God absolutely refuses to violate
our free will; that, therefore, unless self-
will is voluntarily given up, even God
cannot move to answer prayer.

FOLLOWING HIS LEAD

... He leads me beside quiet waters.
Psalm 23:2

My problem was that often I was not content to have the Good Shepherd lead me into truth. Like a rambunctious sheep, I kept running on ahead, nosing around the pastureland, always thinking that the truth I sought must surely lie immediately on the other side of the nearest hill.

JESUS' WILL

" ... now I am going to Him who sent Me ..."
John 16:5

Since Jesus' perfect humanity was as real as His divinity, His would have been a strong human will, stronger than any of ours. Over and over He reiterated that he had handed over that will.

JESUS' WILL

... and a voice came out of heaven, "Thou art My beloved Son, in Thee I am well-pleased."
Luke 3:22

*R*eading between the lines of the Gospel records, I believe that Jesus relinquished His will each time He desired to heal a sufferer, then immediately looked to the Father for what to do.

JUNE 9

JESUS' WILL

*And he began teaching in their
synagogues and was praised by all.*
Luke 4:15

So persuaded was Jesus of His
Father's complete love, trustworthi-
ness and omnipotent power over all
evil that He could relinquish His own
will quickly. And just as quickly there
flowed back from the Father the particular Word to give the sufferer along
with the necessary faith. Thus occurred
the resultant miracle healings.

JUNE 10

SELF-WILL

Seek the Lord while He may be found ...
Isaiah 55:6

*T*he words "Thou shalt have no other gods before Me" had to apply to my personal desire-world. There was nothing for it but to "put away" that most beloved of all idols inscribed "What I want." The scrapping of a treasure is always painful.

JUNE 11

SELF-WILL

He who separates himself seeks his own desire ...
Proverbs 18:1

*T*he temptation to hang onto self-will is
tagged "man's autonomy" and the bait
is our covetousness for understanding. It
is a temptation to which I, for one, have
succumbed as often as most people by
always wanting to know "Why?"

JUNE 12

SELF-WILL

*The heart of the righteous
ponders how to answer ...*
Proverbs 15:28

We need to be careful not to confuse
what the old egocentric self wants – to
succeed, to get well, to be loved – with
that positive, trusting, obedient attitude
that wants only God's will for us.

TRUE DESIRE

... *"Do you wish to get well?"*
John 5:6

How much the story of the man at the Pool of Bethesda says to me every time I read it! I thought that I yearned for healing, but in fact I was not ready to shoulder the full responsibilities of vigorous health. True prayer is dominant desire. If a person is divided he will experience emptiness and frustration.

TRUE DESIRE

[The man] ... had been
thirty-eight years in his sickness.
John 5:5

*T*here is something we can do about
contradictions inside us. First, we can
present our long-standing prayers to
God for analysis. If there is any division
of will, He will put His finger on it.
Second, we can acknowledge this inner
inconsistency and present it to God for
healing. At this point He will almost
always issue us a directive.

TRUE DESIRE

And immediately the man became well ...
John 5:9

The moment that we rise to obey Him, we discover a great fact: His words *are* life – with power to restore the atrophied will, to quicken pallid desire, to resurrect us from the graveclothes of a half-dead existence.

OUR PATTERN

*And they came to a place named
Gethsemane; and He said to His
disciples, "Sit here until I have prayed."*
Mark 14:32

Jesus' prayer in the Garden of
Gethsemane, I came to see, is the pattern for us. Christ used His free will to
turn the decision over to His Father.

WISDOM

> " ... *from the tree of the knowledge of*
> *good and evil you shall not eat ...*"
> Genesis 2:17

*W*isdom ... understanding – tempting bait. Except for the thoughts God chooses to share with us, it's still forbidden fruit. So long as we wear the garment of flesh, we can never understand the mind of our Creator.

JUNE 18

CHILDREN

From the mouth of infants and nursing babes Thou hast established strength ...
Psalm 8:2

God uses children and grandchildren to keep older people flexible.

CHILDREN

" *... I say to you, that their angels in
heaven continually behold the face
of My Father who is in heaven.*"
Matthew 18:10

We are not to clutch our children to
ourselves. What we hold too tightly
we can drive away or break. When
we give our children up to God, He
will eventually give them back to us.

CHILDREN

"Whoever then humbles himself as this child, he is the greatest in the kingdom of heaven."
Matthew 18:4

In the Kingdom of God the heart is tender. We grown-ups have only to watch little children to realize how calloused we have become.

PRESUMPTION

... Revive me according to Thy word.
Psalm 119:154

*H*ow can we tell the difference
between presumption and faith?
Presumption assumes something to
be true in the absence of God's proof
to the contrary. Faith hears and re-
ceives God's word first-hand via the
Spirit speaking to our spirit, and
moves forward only on that word.

BAPTISM

"As for me, I baptize you in water for repentance, but He who is coming after me ... will baptize you with the Holy Spirit ..."
Matthew 3:11

It is as *sinners* that we receive Christ for salvation and are baptized in water. It is then as *sons and daughters* that we receive the baptism of the Spirit.

THE FATHER'S WILL

" ... the Son can do nothing of Himself, unless it is something He sees the Father doing ..."
John 5:19

Jesus meant it when He said that the Son does only what He sees the Father doing. That's altogether different from doing something because God hasn't said not to do it.

FELLOWSHIP WITH GOD

... the life that He lives, He lives to God.
Romans 6:10

Even at the moment when Christ was bowing to the possibility of an awful death by crucifixion, He never forgot either the presence or the power of God.

OBEDIENCE

A tranquil heart is life to the body ...
Proverbs 14:30

When we run out ahead of God, an element of daring God and of boldness bordering on impertinence, even unbelief, enters the situation. But then when we have gotten His directives and obeyed them, we no longer have to carry the responsibility for the results.

OBEDIENCE

All of us like sheep have gone astray ...
Isaiah 53:6

It's good to remember that not even the Master Shepherd can lead if the sheep do not follow Him but insist on running ahead of Him or taking side paths.

OBEDIENCE

"But as for me, I would seek God ..."
Job 5:8

Obey ... obedience ... trust ... is
all over the Gospels. The pliability
of an obedient heart must be complete from the set of our wills
right on through to our actions.

OBEDIENCE

... that you may obey Jesus Christ ...
1 Peter 1:2

When we come right down to it,
how can we make obedience real
except as we give over our self-will in
reference to each of life's episodes as
it unfolds — whether we understand it
or not, and even if evil appears to
have initiated the episode in question?

JUNE 29

OBEDIENCE

*As obedient children, do not be
conformed to the former lusts ... but like
the Holy One who called you, be holy ...*
1 Peter 1:14-15

It should not surprise us that at the
heart of the secret of answered prayer
lies the law of relinquishment.

DIVISION

*(Y)ou also, as living stones, are being built up
as a spiritual house for a holy priesthood ...*
1 Peter 2:5

The God I know does not want us to
divide life up into compartments – "This
part is spiritual, so this is God's province, but that part over there is physical,
so I'll have to handle that myself."

JULY

BEING BORN AGAIN

... walk in newness of life.
Romans 6:4

Our "born again" life is never our own natural life raised to its highest development. Rather, it is that life scrapped, dead, "crucified with Christ." Then to take the place of that old natural life, the Divine life condescends to its lowliest home – your heart and mine.

JULY 2

GOD'S CARE

The LORD reigns; let the earth rejoice ...
Psalm 97:1

If we are to believe Jesus, His Father and our Father is the God of all life and His caring and provision include a sheep-herder's lost lamb, a falling sparrow, a sick child, the hunger pangs of a crowd of thousands. These vignettes say to us, "No creaturely need is outside the scope or range of prayer."

GOD'S SUPPLY

For the LORD is a great God,
And a great King above all gods.
Psalm 95:3

As long as we have a low threshold of
expectation, we probably won't turn to
God for help; our own efforts will handle
it. But when we decide to be totally His
person at His disposal and take on some
enormous task He requires of us, then
we are going to find ourselves thrown
upon His unlimited supply.

JULY 4

THE INVISIBLE HAND

(I)n all things show yourself to be an example of good deeds ...
Titus 2:7

It was George Washington's habit to begin and close each day with a time of prayer, alone in his room. How important this was to him is reflected in his public speeches: "No people can be bound to knowledge and adore the Invisible Hand which conducts the affairs of men more than those of the United States."

GOD'S POWER

The sea is His, for it was He who made it;
And His hands formed the dry land.
Psalm 95:5

One of Christ's fundamental premises was that God the Father controls all of earth's material resources. Simple words, but what a tremendous assertion! Most of us do not really believe this at all. Yet the Bible emphatically declares it.

GOD'S CREATION

*The earth is the LORD's,
and all it contains ...*
Psalm 24:1

The magnificence of His handiwork is seen in the tumbling seas, in a sunset slashing the Grand Canyon. Ride to the top of the mountain at St. Moritz, gasp with awe at the snow-covered panorama of rugged peaks spread out at one's feet. Or see the turquoises and blues in the waters around Moorea and Bora-Bora in the South Seas.

GOD'S PRACTICALITY

"Declare and set forth your case ..."
Isaiah 45:21

Jesus would not allow those who came running after Him wailing, "Lord, have mercy," to stop there; He was forever forcing them out of this "general blessing" area by asking questions like "What do you want Me to do for you?" In other words, "Use your mind, My son. Make up your heart. God is not the Father of sloppy thinking."

SELF-SUFFICIENCY

*[Be] ... imitators of those who through
faith and patience inherit the promises.*
Hebrews 6:12

Since God does exist, then the
cult of self-sufficiency is mistaken —
tragically so in some cases,
misleading in all. In my case, the
most spectacular answers to prayer
have come following a period when I
could do nothing for myself at all.

THE SUPREME REALITY

> *(I)n [Christ] ... are hidden all the
> treasures of wisdom and knowledge.*
> Colossians 2:3

So we take the first hard steps of obedience. And lo, as we stop hiding our eyes, force ourselves to walk up to the fear and look it full in the face – never forgetting that God is still the supreme reality – the fear evaporates. Drastic? Yes. But it is one sure way of releasing prayer power into human affairs.

GUIDANCE

... the prayer of the upright is His delight.
Proverbs 15:8

*T*he more extensive our need, the more important it is to get God's guidance on pinpointing where and how He wants His supply to come to us. It's as if once we find the first right thread to pull, the whole of our tangled problem begins to unravel.

FATHERHOOD

*"[The Lord] ... will be with you. He
will not fail you or forsake you."*
Deuteronomy 31:8

We can trust the character and love
of the Father in heaven to surpass
that of the best earthly father we
have ever known or can imagine.

COMFORT

> ... *strengthen the hands that are*
> *weak and the knees that are feeble.*
> Hebrews 12:12

God comforts us with strength by
adding resources. His way is not
to whittle down the problem but to
build up the resources. I opened my
New Testament and found there
exactly that concept of comfort.

GIVING

Cast your bread on the surface of the waters,
for you will find it after many days.
Ecclesiastes 11:1

Here is an exciting principle for all those in life's holes. Of what do we have a shortage? Money? Ideas? Friends? Love? Prayer-power? Creativity? Strength? Health? Whatever it is, when we, under God's direction, give away out of our shortage, like the tide returning we get back abundance.

DISCIPLINE

For those whom the Lord loves He disciplines ...
Hebrews 12:6

God's sternness in dealing with
me did not seem quite like love. Yet
I thought of the many times when it
had taken far more love for me to
hold my son to what I knew was right
than to indulge him. This is the kind
of firmness that is even a proof of love.

GOD'S LOVE

... "HOLY, HOLY, HOLY, IS THE LORD GOD, THE ALMIGHTY ..."
Revelation 4:8

God's love is not dependent on our earning it. God is "for us" first, last and always. By every word and action, by all the force of His personality, Christ sought to tell us that the Father is always nearer, mightier, freer to help us than we can imagine.

GOD'S LOVE

... *"When you pray, say: 'Father, hallowed
be Thy name. Thy kingdom come."*
Luke 11:2

The Gospels make it clear that to
Jesus the Father is all-loving, is of the
essence of love, cannot help loving.

KNOWING GOD

*At that very time He rejoiced greatly in
the Holy Spirit, and said, "I praise Thee,
O Father, Lord of heaven and earth ..."*
Luke 10:21

What builds trust in the Creator? Only
knowing Him so well – His motives, His
complete good will – being certain that
no pressures will make Him change,
knowing Him for a long enough time to
be sure of these things.

DISCIPLINE

It is for discipline that you endure ...
Hebrews 12:7

Truth may be painful, but it makes
us free. God is not interested in
coddling us, but in liberating us
for further creativity, for the new
life that we are forced to make.

CREATIVITY

For by Him all things were created ...
Colossians 1:16

*T*he essence of creativity is to seek Him first. We begin with a seed idea of a seed talent and create something that other people need or enjoy. That plunges us directly into the stream of the Creator's unending creativity and generosity.

NEGATIVISM

*I would have despaired unless
I had believed that I would see
the goodness of the LORD
In the land of the living.*
Psalm 27:13

All encounters in life, every personality, every institution, every relationship, is a mixture of the good and the bad. When we habitually focus on the bad, we are training ourselves in negativism.

NEGATIVISM

*O Lord, Thou hast brought
up my soul from Sheol ...*
Psalm 30:3

*I*n my case, I woke up twenty years into adulthood to find myself deeply schooled in serious negativism. That, in turn, can bathe all of life in emotional gloom. When the habit continues into midlife or later, the dark glasses of criticalness can lead to long periods of melancholy and even to serious depression.

JULY 22

HABITS

*For all who are being led by the
Spirit of God, these are sons of God.*
Romans 8:14

The Holy Spirit can indeed change
our desires and our tastes and our
habit patterns. But He can't do
this until we trust Him enough
to put ourselves in His hands.

GOD'S PLANS

*[God] ... is able to do exceeding abundantly
beyond all that we ask or think ...*
Ephesians 3:20

God's plans for His children are
always so much more bountiful than
our best-laid plans for ourselves.

RICHES

And my God shall supply all your needs according to His riches in glory in Christ Jesus.
Philippians 4:19

God still controls all the riches of earth and heaven. As children of the King, we are not to think poverty. His promise to each of us: *If you give of yourself, your time, your material resources to others, I will open the windows of heaven and pour down My blessing upon you.*

TRIALS

*... faith, if it has no works,
is dead, being by itself.*
James 2:17

We should not shrink from tests
of our faith. Only when we are
depending on God alone are we in
a position to see God's help and
deliverance, and thus have our faith
strengthened for the next time.

THE FATHER'S REALM

And God saw all that He had made,
and behold, it was very good.
Genesis 1:31

To call our Father in heaven a King, in my opinion, is to understate the truth. Consider the prodigality of the Father's world. He did not create a single kind of fern, but some 10,000 kinds; not one type of palm tree, but 1500 different palms.

GRIEF

*Then Job answered the Lord, and said ... "I
will ask Thee, and do Thou instruct me."*
Job 42:1, 4

Trying to force oneself to be brave
will not heal the heart. It is forever
true that when the storms of life
are savage, it is the tree that
bends with the wind that survives.

GRIEF

... Martha, the sister of the deceased, said to Him, "Lord ... he has been dead four days." Jesus said to her, "Did I not say to you, if you believe, you will see the glory of God?"
John 11:39-40

Self-pity – that special illness
at the heart of all grief.

JULY 29

UNDER THE LAW

> ... *"I will put My law within them,
> and on their heart I will write it ..."*
> Jeremiah 31:33

In His changing of our desire-world
the Holy Spirit will deal with each of
us differently. Given that, any church
or religious group that seeks to place
us back "under law" with lists of
"Thou shalt nots" is denying the
Spirit's work and interfering with it.

MOTIVATION

*"For what will a man be profited, if he gains
the whole world, and forfeits his soul?"*
Matthew 16:26

When we go forth to stamp out
sin, disease, poverty, oppression –
as He did – do we keep uppermost in
our minds the heart-stirring vision of
the world as God intended it to be?
Or does hatred of the enemy we are
opposing gradually fill our horizon?

LOVING OUR ENEMIES

"But I say to you, love your enemies ..."
Matthew 5:44

"Love your enemies. Do good to those who hate you ..." Here Christ was making a clear distinction between the iniquity, which He hated, and the sinner who, even though his own will was responsible for his sin, was nevertheless now the victim of it, bound by it.

LOVING OUR ENEMIES

" *... and pray for those who persecute
you in order that you may be sons
of your Father who is in heaven ...*"
Matthew 5:44-45

Indeed, this command to love our
enemies is often not possible for us
worldlings; it is a miracle God Himself
has to work in the human heart.

FINANCES

> *"The LORD will open for you*
> *His good storehouse, the heavens ..."*
> Deuteronomy 28:12

I learned that money is really only ideas that have been converted into a form usable in the exchange markets of earth. The corollary is that these ideas must be of a kind that will be of some help to other people.

FINANCES

*Then he made two sculptured
cherubim in the room of the holy of
holies and overlaid them with gold.*
2 Chronicles 3:10

The way to pray for economic
resources is to ask God for new
and creative ideas that will make a
contribution – no matter how small –
to lighten the tasks or illumine
the lives of one's contemporaries.

AUGUST 4

THE WILL

The Lord knows the thoughts of man ...
Psalm 94:11

*T*he motivating force at the center of our physical being is our will. It is the governing power in us, the spring of all our actions. Before God we are responsible only for the set of that will – whether we decide for God's will or insist on self-will.

THE WILL

Be glad in the LORD, you righteous ones ...
Psalm 97:12

Our Maker knows that our
feelings are unruly, unreliable
gauges. So if we see to it that
our intentions (our motives)
are right, we can trust God
to see to the results.

UNBELIEF

*[The Holy Spirit] " ... will convict
the world concerning sin ...
because they do not believe in Me."*
John 16:8-9

Why does Scripture not only
call unbelief a sin, but declare it
to be the fountainhead of all sin,
the sin that encompasses all other
sins? Because by our unbelief we reject
Jesus Christ, who He is, all He stands
for, what He came to earth to do.

AUGUST 7

GRUMBLING

*And the LORD spoke to Moses,
saying, "I have heard the
grumblings of the sons of Israel ..."*
Exodus 16:11-12

God regards even the lowest rung of
protest – complaining and grumbling –
not as a petty personality flaw, or even
as an offense against another person,
but as serious sin against Him directly.

TRUTH

And He said to them, "Follow Me ..."
Matthew 4:19

God wants us to use all our mind, along with our emotions and will, to love and serve Him. Therefore, we need have no fear about where Truth will lead us. He is still out ahead of the greatest scholars or scientists or theologians.

AUGUST 9

JESUS' ABILITY

For as many as may be the promises
of God, in Him they are yes ...
2 Corinthians 1:20

Every time I reject Jesus'
ability to handle any problem
or problem area of my life, I am
rejecting Him as the Lord of life.

NEEDS MET

*Therefore, since we receive a kingdom which
cannot be shaken, let us show gratitude ...*
Hebrews 12:28

I realized that I need never meet
any future difficulty alone, that
help from a loving God would ever
be available for the asking, that resources beyond imagining are always
at our disposal – provided only that
we are willing to put ourselves in
the stream of God's purposes.

TESTING GUIDANCE

Thy word is a lamp to my feet ...
Psalm 119:105

*T*he inspiration that reaches us via the unconscious should be subjected to certain tests. The writers of Scripture insist that that we are open to influences not only from the Holy Spirit but also from perverse and evil spirits. Anyone who means business about God's leading will need to turn again to the Bible as a textbook.

TESTING GUIDANCE

All Thy commandments are faithful ...
Psalm 119:86

God's voice will never contradict itself. That is, He will not give us a direction through the inner Voice that will ever contradict His voice in the Scriptures.

FREED FROM SIN

> *The Spirit of the Lord*
> *GOD is upon me,*
> *Because the LORD has anointed me ...*
> *To proclaim liberty to captives ...*
> Isaiah 61:1

Jesus claimed to be the Savior, to be able to save us from any sin, any bondage, any problem. By disclaiming that with regard to any one of my problems, I am calling Jesus a liar and a charlatan — a fake prophet.

FREED FROM SIN

"For God did not send the Son into the world to judge the world, but that the world should be saved through Him."
John 3:17

We think of sin as the breaking of laws, whereas Jesus thinks of sin as being bound. And Jesus came to earth, He announced at the beginning of His public ministry, for the express purpose not of condemning us, but of releasing all of us sin-captives.

FREED FROM SIN

*If we say that we have no sin, we are deceiving
ourselves, and the truth is not in us.*
1 John 1:8

Until we see ourselves as bound in
many specific areas and in need of
freeing and saving, obviously we will
have no need of the Savior. Our danger
then will be that of approaching Jesus
not as a Savior but as a Santa Claus
for the good gifts He can give us.

AUGUST 16

PERSUASION

*Therefore if any man is in
Christ, he is a new creature ...*
2 Corinthians 5:17

As the printed page is increasingly
peppered with four-letter words,
we can't help wondering: Isn't the
obscenity really our frustration at
the poverty of language that no longer
really communicates to people's minds
and hearts? Perhaps then, the subcon-
scious reaction goes, people can be
shocked into paying attention.

PERSONAL GROWTH

*"He who overcomes, I will grant to him
to sit down with Me on My throne ..."*
Revelation 3:21

My experience has been that it is only
out of a state of tension that growth
can come. It is a strange paradox that
we have to be willing to suffer the
tension for a time, knowing that it is
the bridge to the next step in our lives.

JESUS' WAY

*Then He poured water into the basin,
and began to wash the disciples' feet ...*
John 13:5

The way of the cross, Jesus' way. The
way that puts others ahead of self.

PEACE OF MIND

*" ... where I am, there
shall My servant also be."*
John 12:26

Peace of mind, happiness, contentment,
and all their first and second cousins
come to us only as by-products. The
paradox is that he who tries basket
weaving, not because he is fascinated
by weaving, but in order to avoid his
emotional problem, will end up a still-
frustrated person, loathing his baskets.

RULERSHIP

*For by one Spirit we were
all baptized into one body ...*
1 Corinthians 12:13

Many people are afraid of the Holy
Spirit. Often unspoken is the fear,
"If I assent to the Spirit, won't He
then just take over and make me do
all sorts of kooky things?" But from
a great pool of Christian experience
comes the answer. No, the Helper
never violates anyone's free will.

RULERSHIP

... Everlasting joy will be theirs.
Isaiah 61:7

The Holy Spirit, like each Person of the Trinity, has supreme respect for our personhood. He will never trample upon that or take us any further than we are willing to go.

THE LIGHT OF THE WORLD

> *... Jesus spoke to them, saying,*
> *"I am the light of the world ..."*
> John 8:12

I wonder if Christ means for us to take His "I am the light of the world" more literally than we do. Of course, the statement also points to a theological truth. But He who created the atom and the sun remains the power center, the dynamo of the physical universe.

WRITING

He who neglects discipline despises himself ...
Proverbs 15:32

A person writing a book cannot
wait for times of inspiration. Usually
the spurts of inspired writing come
as dividends from hours upon hours
of grinding labor every day.

WRITING

*... Get wisdom and instruction
and understanding.*
Proverbs 23:23

I discovered what many writers
know, that it was well to end a day's
work in the middle of a paragraph,
even in the middle of a sentence.
Then one's mind is forced to carry the
unfinished work until the next work
period, and the picking up is easier.

WRITING

Do you see a man skilled in his work? He will stand before kings ...
Proverbs 22:29

Clear communication in writing depends, at least in part, on discipline. Trying to avoid both sentimentality and diffuseness was as exhausting as reining in a pair of runaway horses.

PROTECTION

"Blessed is the man who trusts in the Lord ...
For he will be like a tree
planted by the water ...
And will not fear when the heat comes ..."
Jeremiah 17:7-8

In promise after promise, the
Bible seeks to teach us that in
God and in His resources there is
physical protection surer than any
weapon or defense known to man.

ROMANCE

*"He has brought me to his banquet hall,
And his banner over me is love."*
Song of Songs 2:4

It was God who thought up romance in the first place. He alone, at the center of the man-woman relationship, can give to physical attraction the lustre, the idealism, the romance, the durability of which we dream.

LOVE

*"Comfort, O comfort My
people," says your God.*
Isaiah 40:1

Every human being needs love.
Most of our troubles spring from
the lack of it. Like thirsty men
in a desert, we perish without it.

JESUS' NAME

*"But for you who fear My name
the sun of righteousness will rise
with healing in its wings ..."*
Malachi 4:2

When we pray "in Jesus' name," we are not simply verbalizing a word or a phrase; rather, our petition is to the complete character of the Lord and all of the power implicit in His name.

JESUS' NAME

" *... and you will go forth and skip
about like calves from the stall.*"
Malachi 4:2

*T*he Scripture abounds in "holy mysteries" and the full meaning of praying in
the name of Jesus is one of those mysteries. In heaven, the mystery is understood; on earth, we shall probably never
know it fully. Yet as we step out in faith
using that name, we do learn bit by bit.

COMMUNICATION

I thank my God in all my remembrance of you.
Philippians 1:3

*F*riendship and love can follow
only in the wake of the heart's
articulation. Mind must speak
to mind; spirit to spirit.

SEPTEMBER

RELIGION

[God] ... reconciled us to Himself through Christ, and gave us the ministry of reconciliation.
2 Corinthians 5:18

To some people religion is an isolated compartment, so narrow as to be stifling. Perhaps that is why so many flee it.

HARDNESS OF HEART

... encourage one another day after day ... lest any one of you be hardened by the deceitfulness of sin.
Hebrews 3:13

We are warned that toying with sin or deliberately harboring even small sins in our lives results in an accretion of the hardening process in us.

FEAR

*"Therefore do not be anxious for tomorrow;
for tomorrow will care for itself."*
Matthew 6:34

"*F*ear not" is one of the most
reiterated exhortations in Scripture.

FEAR

The LORD is the defense of my life;
Whom shall I dread?
Psalm 27:1

When we see fear through Jesus' eyes, it is the acting out of our disbelief in the loving Fatherliness of God. By our worrying and fretting, we are really saying, "I don't believe in any God who can help me." Thereby we are sinning against God by impugning His character and calling Him a liar.

SEPTEMBER 5

FEAR

For He Himself is our peace ...
Ephesians 2:14

Behind Jesus' sharp reaction
to our faithless fears lay His
consistent viewpoint that this is our
Father's world still in His control.

FEAR

> " ... *as the Father gave Me*
> *commandment, even so I do.*"
> John 14:31

It may seem to us at first thought that any dependence is the opposite of strength or a mature personality. But when we look closely at Jesus, we see that this is not so. Always the Master gave the impression of a moment-by-moment companionship and dialogue with the Father, yet here was a Man afraid of nothing.

CREATIVITY

*In the beginning God created
the heavens and the earth.*
Genesis 1:1

God, always the Creator, helps us with
our creative tasks when we ask Him to.
It shouldn't have surprised me to find
that this meant very practical aid — in
my case, help with sentence structure
and transitions. All too many people
still think of God as interested only in
their morals and church attendance.

BELIEVERS

*... He Himself bore our sins in His
body on the cross, that we might
die to sin and live to righteousness ...*
1 Peter 2:24

During the Last Supper conversation
Jesus made it clear that the promises He
was making that night were not meant
just for the eleven men within the sound
of His voice, but for future believers as
well. And what He promised for the
future could scarcely be more exciting.

PROBLEMS

*Here is the perseverance and
the faith of the saints.*
Revelation 13:10

When life caves in, we are to
seek God in our problem. God
has a plan for every life by which
He will bring good out of evil.

COMFORT

*"As one whom his mother
comforts, so will I comfort you ..."*
Isaiah 66:13

If His comfort were limited to pity
or commiserating with us (as much
human sympathy is), it would lead us
to self-pity and that's no help at all.
Rather, the Spirit's comfort puts
courage into us, empowers us to cope
with the strains and exigencies of life.

KNOWING GOD

This hope we have as an anchor of the soul ...
Hebrews 6:19

The need of all of us — whether we realize it or not — is to know whether there really is a God and, if so, to know Him in a direct and personal way through Christ. When we know Him and understand something of His love for us, then we can trust and follow Him. Only then shall we lose the pang of our heart hunger.

REVELATIONS OF JESUS

... because He abides forever ...
Hebrews 7:24

Because the Holy Spirit is a living, always-contemporary Personality, down all the centuries there must be an ever-unfolding manifestation of Jesus, His personality, His ways of dealing with us, along with new, fresh disclosures of the mind of the Father.

SEPTEMBER 13

HEAVEN

*After these things I looked, and behold,
a door standing open in heaven ...*
Revelation 4:1

Sometimes a person crossing the threshold between life and death gives those watching a glimpse of what lies beyond. The universal testimony in these instances is that death is nothing to be feared; that there is beauty — often rapturous music, reunion with those who have gone before, recognition, warmth and love — on the other side.

CREATIVE WRITING

*And all the sons of Israel, seeing the fire
come down and the glory of the LORD upon the
house, bowed down on the pavement with their
faces to the ground, and they worshiped ...*
2 Chronicles 7:3

"No creative work," the Lord told me,
"has final impact unless it touches the
reader at the level of the emotions."

DREAMS COME TRUE

*Blessed be the God and Father of our
Lord Jesus Christ, who has blessed us ...*
Ephesians 1:3

There is no limit to what the combination of dreams and prayer can achieve. I have seen amazing results in many areas — like finding the right mate or the right job, or locating the ideal house, or rearing children, or building a business.

DREAMS COME TRUE

*But as for me, my prayer
is to Thee, O LORD ...*
Psalm 69:13

Before handing your dream over
to God, ask yourself these questions:
Will my dream fulfill my needs and
talents? Does my dream take anything or any person belonging to
someone else? Am I willing to
make all my relationships right?
Do I want this dream with my
whole heart? Am I willing to wait
patiently for God's timing?

DREAMS COME TRUE

Seek the LORD while He may be found ...
Isaiah 55:6

As for the danger that our dreams may spring from our selfish human will rather than God's will, there are tests for this. Only when a dream has passed such a series of tests – so that we are certain that our heart's desire is also God's dream *before* we pray – can we pray with faith and thus with power.

DREAMS COME TRUE

Now may the God of hope fill you
with all joy and peace in believing ...
Romans 15:13

There seem to be periods when the heart's desire is like a seed planted in the dark earth and left there to germinate. This is not a time of passiveness on our part. There are things we can and must do — fertilizing, watering, weeding — hard work and self-discipline. But the growth of that seed is God's part of the process.

DREAMS COME TRUE

*... being fully assured that what He had
promised, He was able also to perform.*
Romans 4:21

Long before we see the fruition of
our hopes, in fact the very moment
a God-given dream is planted in our
hearts, a strange happiness flows into
us. I have come to think that at that
moment all the resources of the universe
are released to help us. Our praying is
then at one with the will of God.

A SPECIAL WORK

Bless the LORD, you His angels,
Mighty in strength, who perform His word ...
Psalm 103:20

We should never hesitate to try the impossible. God does have a special work for us to do in the world. Should this involve a big dream, we must believe that the bigger the dream, and the more loving and unselfish it is, the greater will be God's blessing on it.

THE PERFECT BALANCE

*(F)or the kingdom of God is ... righteousness
and peace and joy in the Holy Spirit.*
Romans 14:17

In the Holy Spirit we have the
perfect balance of God's love —
infinite tenderness on the one side,
infinite strength on the other.

INTELLECT VS. FAITH

... whatever a man sows, this he will also reap.
Galatians 6:7

Our virtual deification of human
intellect goes straight back to
Thoman Aquinas (1227-1274)
who taught that while man's will fell
from grace, his intellect did not.
Whenever anyone sets up his reasoning
against God's, he is going the Aquinas
way of humanistic autonomy, even
though he may piously call it faith.

IMMORTALITY

" ... everyone who lives and believes in Me shall never die. Do you believe this?"
John 11:26

Not only did Jesus tell us about immortality, but to prove it He rose from the dead and over a period of forty days appeared and reappeared to more than five hundred witnesses.

TRUE WISDOM

*" ... unless a grain of wheat falls into the earth
and dies, it remains by itself alone ..."*
John 12:24

*T*he only true wisdom is facing
up to what we actually are – creatures – and then yielding ourselves
to the wisdom of our Creator. This
yielding is relinquishment. And as we
relinquish our own defective human
judgment, it feels like death because
it *is* death – the beginning of the
end of the old Adam in us.

SEPTEMBER 25

WAITING

*The LORD is good to those
who wait for Him ...*
Lamentations 3:25

The Lord seems constantly to
use waiting as a tool for bringing
us the very best of His gifts.

WAITING

"For you will go out with joy ...
Instead of the thorn bush the
cypress will come up ..."
Isaiah 55:12-13

Waiting itself, if practiced according to biblical patterns, seems to be a strange but dynamic kind of communication between man and God. It is God's oft-repeated way of teaching us that His power is real and that He can answer our prayers without interference and manipulation from us.

WAITING

*... And in the shadow of
Thy wings I sing for joy.*
Psalm 63:7

When we leave our prayers with the Father, we find for ourselves what the saints and mystics affirm, that during the dark waiting period when self-effort ceases, a spurt of astonishing spiritual growth takes place in us. Afterward we have qualities like more patience, more ability to hear His voice, greater willingness to obey.

WAITING

Wait for the LORD;
Be strong, and let your heart take courage ...
Psalm 27:14

Waiting seems to be a kind of acted-out prayer that is required more often and honored more often than I could understand until I saw what remarkable faith-muscles this act develops.

WAITING

... Weeping may last for the night,
But a shout of joy comes in the morning.
Psalm 30:5

The Bible extols waiting, partly because it requires qualities that the Lord wants to encourage in us, like patience. But there is another reason too. Waiting works. It is a joining of man and God to achieve an end, and the end is always a form of the Easter story.

WAITING

> *... those who wait for the Lord,*
> *they will inherit the land.*
> Psalm 37:9

Jesus had a great deal to say about His Father's timing, the principle that there is a God-given sequence and rate of growth for everything in His Creation — "First the blade, and then the ear."

OCTOBER

ROUGH TIMES

> *When he falls, he shall*
> *not be hurled headlong;*
> *Because the LORD is the*
> *One who holds his hand.*
> Psalm 37:24

You and I are living in rough times.
We must make our way through
minefields of evil, booby traps of
deception, brush fires of sickness,
wastelands of economic disaster, burning
deserts of disappointment. "I won't
take you out of this world," Jesus told
us. "But don't be afraid, because I've
overcome that world of dangers."

OCTOBER 2

PRAYER

*... one of His disciples said to
Him, "Lord, teach us to pray ..."*
Luke 11:1

God has dared to arrange it so
that He is actually dependent upon
us in the sense of our prayers being
necessary and all important to the
carrying out of His will on earth.

PRAYER

Delight yourself in the LORD;
And He will give you the desires of your heart.
Psalm 37:4

As we recognize our ignorance about praying aright and our helplessness, and actively seek the Spirit's help, our prayer life becomes the anteroom to amazing adventures.

GOD'S TIMING

The steps of a man are
established by the LORD;
And He delights in his way.
Psalm 37:23

I remember once being in a situation where the Lord told me to stand silently by, saying nothing, even though I thought I knew the answer to a problem. Even within this smaller scope I was to wait on His timing, His invisible action in another human heart. It was an astounding experience in poised expectancy.

OCTOBER 5

SELF-SUFFICIENCY

Bless the LORD, O my soul,
And forget none of His benefits.
Psalm 103:2

We are helpless without the God who made us and whose Spirit animates us. Yet the cult of self-sufficiency is not yet dead. It beats daily at our eardrums. It encourages selfishness. It devaluates working for the joy of working instead of for the reward of money; it scorns living to serve other people.

OCTOBER 6

SELF-SUFFICIENCY

*Remember His wonders
which He has done,
His marvels, and the judgments
uttered by His mouth.*
Psalm 105:5

Happiness flees when self
takes the center of the stage.

PRAYER

*How precious also are
Thy thoughts to me, O God!
How vast is the sum of them!*
Psalm 139:17

Mysteries about prayer are always
ahead of knowledge – luring, beckoning
on to further experimentation.

IDOLATRY

... do not be idolaters ...
1 Corinthians 10:7

Idealizing can soon become idolizing, and no human being should idolize another. We open ourselves to inevitable disillusionment when we do. And we do the object of our idolizing an injustice, for pedestal-sitting can be a lonely business.

OCTOBER 9

UNDERSTANDING

... *"I have loved you with
an everlasting love ..."*
Jeremiah 31:3

Was Jesus teaching us how to use
the law of relinquishment when He
said, "Resist not evil"? Stop fleeing
from and denying this terrible prospect.
Look squarely at the possibility of what
you fear most. "Obey Me," He says.
"Then – after that – you will know
and begin to understand."

THE NEED FOR PRAYER

*[May] ... the Father of glory ... give
to you a spirit of wisdom and of
revelation in the knowledge of Him.*
Ephesians 1:17

All around us are those caught
in bondages, imprisoned in fears,
hampered by disease to whom Jesus
longs to bring His release and His
joy. But He waits on *our* prayers.
It's a solemn thought.

OCTOBER 11

VISUALIZING

*I pray that the eyes of your
heart may be enlightened ...*
Ephesians 1:18

It's because everything starts with an
idea that dreaming, visualizing, is
important. In fact it can be a way
of prayer – a very effective way.

OCTOBER 12

LONELINESS

*... walk by the Spirit, and you will
not carry out the desire of the flesh.*
Galatians 5:16

Since God made us for companionship,
loneliness is not His plan for us. But
there is a price to be paid in seeking
God's remedy. This includes a decision
to give up self-pity, the determination
not to compromise honor, and the
willingness to let Him fill our heart
with His love, which can then spill
out into loving concern for others.

KNOWING

*[Give]... thanks to the Father, who
has qualified us to share in the
inheritance of the saints in light.*
Colossians 1:12

*I*n some situations the Good
Shepherd leads us from relinquishment on into *knowing*. Such knowing
is different from trying to think positively or making affirmations. It is not
our doing at all; it is the gift of God.

OCTOBER 14

GOD'S DESIRES

> " ... *your Father knows what you
> need, before you ask Him.*"
> Matthew 6:8

God's dreams are usually more
wonderful than ours. The problem for
most of us is how to stretch ourselves
enough to accept His munificence.

OCTOBER 15

RELINQUISHMENT

*Humble yourselves, therefore, under
the mighty hand of God, that He
may exalt you at the proper time ...*
1 Peter 5:6

*E*ven while it hopes, our relinquishment
must be the real thing — and this giving
up of self-will is the hardest thing we
human beings are ever called on to do.

RELINQUISHMENT

For by these He has granted to us
His precious and magnificent promises ...
2 Peter 1:4

Whenever a loving Father grants our
wish, the Word appears in exterior
circumstances and the miracle happens –
we understand that relinquishment
and faith are not contradictory.

GOD'S IDENTITY

"Father, glorify Thy name."
John 12:28

I realized how often we attribute emotions and deeds to God that we would ascribe only to the most depraved of human minds. Probably no personality in the universe is so maligned as that of the Creator.

GOD'S IDENTITY

*Jesus said to him, "... He who has
seen Me has seen the Father ..."*
John 14:9

When we persist in mistaken and
tragic ideas of the Creator, how can
God show us what He is really like? He
solved this problem in the Incarnation.

OCTOBER 19

JOY

You also became imitators of us and of the Lord, having received the word in much tribulation with the joy of the Holy Spirit.
1 Thessalonians 1:6

The promise is not that the Christian will have only joyous circumstances, but that the Holy Spirit will give us the supernatural gift of joy in whatever circumstances we have.

JOY

... about midnight Paul and Silas were praying and singing hymns of praise to God, and the prisoners were listening to them.
Acts 16:25

*T*hose other prisoners must have been listening with incredulity to Paul and Silas, for there is nothing natural about singing and praising while one's feet are chained in stocks. Obviously, genuine joy in such circumstances is impossible for us humans; it is clearly supernatural.

TRUSTING JESUS

"... lo, I am with you always ..."
Matthew 28:20

As we pray in faith, our hands are still in His. Our hearts are still obedient. But now he has led us out of the frightening darkness, with only the pressure of His hand to reassure us, into the sunlight. All along our hearts told us so. Relinquishment? Faith? Just daring to trust Jesus.

PRAYING IN SECRET

*But He Himself would often slip
away to the wilderness and pray.*
Luke 5:16

How Jesus loved to pray in secret
Himself! He had a habit of rising up
a great while before day and going
outdoors — to a mountainside or some
other deserted place — to pray. Perhaps
because of the small, crowded Palestin-
ian houses, that was the only way He
could find privacy and solitude.

PRAYING IN SECRET

*[Jesus] ... went off to the mountain to pray, and
He spent the whole night in prayer to God.*
Luke 6:12

Before major decisions – such as
His choosing of the twelve apostles –
Jesus would pray alone an entire night.
And going back to the beginning of
His public ministry, we find Jesus
going off into the desert for forty
days and nights of seclusion and concentrated prayer. He knew that power was
needed; in secret He would find it.

PRAYING IN SECRET

*"God is spirit; and those who worship Him
must worship in spirit and truth."*
John 4:24

There are other reasons why Jesus
instructs us to pray in secret. Real
power in prayer flows only when
man's spirit touches God's Spirit.
As in worship, so in prayer.

PRAYING IN SECRET

... I meditate on Thee in the night watches.
Psalm 63:6

Transparent honesty before Him
is easier for us in isolation.

THE HOME

Ascribe to the LORD, O families of the peoples,
Ascribe to the LORD glory and strength.
Psalm 96:7

Husbands and wives are basically incompatible. Parents are incompatible with their children. God made us all different. That's why the home is His classroom for molding and shaping us into mature people.

RELEASE FROM BONDAGE

*"These things I have spoken to you,
that My joy may be in you ..."*
John 15:11

Jesus spent His days going about looking into pain-filled eyes and in summary fashion – with delight – releasing men and women from the enemy's bondages. These were joyous tasks because the Lord of life loathed sickness and disease and broken relationships and insanity and death. So day by day He left behind a string of victories.

GOD'S CHARACTER

" ... how much more shall your Father
who is in heaven give what is good
to those who ask Him!"
Matthew 7:11

Jesus acted as if there was never
any question of the Father's willingness to supply all needs. Divine love
delighted in dispelling pain, in restoring
sanity, in straightening crooked limbs
and opening blind eyes, even in
banishing premature death.

THE INNER RESERVOIR

*"When therefore you give alms,
do not sound a trumpet before you ..."*
Matthew 6:2

Jesus told us that if we want to become fulfilled and productive persons, we must reverse the usual process. That is, we are to divest ourselves of weaknesses, faults and sins by confessing them openly, while kindnesses and good deeds are to be kept secret. The result is an inner reservoir of power.

CONFESSION

*If we confess our sins, He is faithful
and righteous to forgive us our sins and
to cleanse us from all unrighteousness.*
1 John 1:9

Facing up to ourselves in confession
is therapeutic, provided we move
on to forgiveness and do not wallow
in our wrongdoing.

JOY IN TRIALS

" ... I have overcome the world."
John 16:33

Certainly Jesus was aware of life's problems and disappointments: "In the world you have tribulation," He promised His disciples. "But," he added, "take courage; I have overcome the world." Or in other words, "Cheer up! The worst that the world can do is no match for Me."

NOVEMBER

JESUS' JOY

[God] ... has anointed Thee
With the oil of joy above Thy fellows.
Psalm 45:7

"Thou hast loved righteousness, and hated wickedness; therefore God, Thy God, has anointed Thee with the oil of joy above Thy fellows." He who knew no sin and *is* righteousness had a personality sparkling and overflowing with a degree of gladness that none of us can match. How could it be otherwise!

NOVEMBER 2

FORGIVENESS

*" ... if you do not forgive men, then your Father
will not forgive your transgressions."*
Matthew 6:15

I became aware of a compartment in my
being in which I had locked certain
persons whom I disliked. They could go
their way; I would go mine. But now
Christ seemed to be standing by the
locked door saying, "That isn't forgiveness. It won't do. No closed doors are
allowed. The Kingdom of God is the
kingdom of right relationships."

TRUST

Surely our griefs He Himself bore ...
Isaiah 53:4

When anyone of us has a painful experience that the mind cannot equate with a loving God, there is this remedy: "I want You and Your presence, Lord, even more than I want understanding. I choose You." When we ask this, He then gives peace and illumination as His gift.

NOVEMBER 6

JOY

Serve the LORD with gladness;
Come before Him with joyful singing.
Psalm 100:2

Joy is a sure sign of the King's approval.

TRUST

Surely our griefs He Himself bore ...
Isaiah 53:4

When anyone of us has a painful experience that the mind cannot equate with a loving God, there is this remedy: "I want You and Your presence, Lord, even more than I want understanding. I choose You." When we ask this, He then gives peace and illumination as His gift.

NOVEMBER 4

IN RESIDENCE

… In Thy presence is fulness of joy …
Psalm 16:11

Queen Elizabeth's standard flying over
Buckingham Palace in London is the
sign that the queen is in residence. Joy
looking out of the Christian's eyes is the
sign that the King is in residence within.

NOVEMBER 5

MANAGEMENT

*As for me, I shall behold
Thy face in righteousness ...*
Psalm 17:15

The keys and the management of my "house" had to be turned over to Christ. For how could I ask Him to heal me until He was completely in charge?

JOY

Serve the LORD with gladness;
Come before Him with joyful singing.
Psalm 100:2

Joy is a sure sign of the King's approval.

HEARING GOD

*He made known to us the mystery of
His will ... with a view to an administration
suitable to the fulness of the times ...*
Ephesians 1:9-10

Seeking the substantiating of divine
facts to my natural mind means that
I go to Jesus and ask, "Lord, speak to
me about this. What do You want to
tell me about it? Let me see this situation through Your eyes."

DIFFICULT PEOPLE

"(B)less those who curse you ..."
Luke 6:28

As soon as we begin to obey Him, we find that blessing those with whom we are having difficulties and the *answer* to these difficulties go hand in hand.

NOVEMBER 9

DIFFICULT PEOPLE

" ... for He causes His sun to rise
on the evil and the good ..."
Matthew 5:45

*I*f you and I were running the
world, probably we would not allow
the wicked to prosper. But the simple
truth is that Jesus was and always is
the Realist. He simply took it for
granted that because God is all love,
the wicked *will* often prosper.

NOVEMBER 10

DIFFICULT PEOPLE

*"For if you love those who love
you, what reward have you?"*
Matthew 5:46

"If you are going to be true children
of your Father in heaven," said Jesus,
"then pray for the very best to happen
to everyone you know — no matter how
they may have hurt you." Is He saying
that wickedness is of no consequence
to God? Not at all! The point is that
accusing prayers do not change people.
Only joyous love redeems.

NOVEMBER 11

DIFFICULT PEOPLE

" ... the joy of the Lord is your strength."
Nehemiah 8:10

*W*e can love our "enemy" enough
to ask gladness for him, only if
He who was anointed with so
much gladness does it for us.

DIFFICULT PEOPLE

(K)eep yourselves in the love of God ...
Jude 21

Now obviously we cannot bless
and pray for people who despitefully
use others or with whom we are at
odds unless we recognize that no self-
effort can manage this and let Christ –
living in us – love others for us.

DIFFICULT PEOPLE

> " ... he who believes in Him
> shall not be disappointed."
> 1 Peter 2:6

Praying blessings on an "enemy" is not a risky way to pray, once we see that God's way is to make "His sun to rise on the just and on the unjust," and that His sun of joy is the only power in the universe capable of transforming hearts — no matter what their problems.

ENTERING IN

> " *... ask, and you will receive,*
> *that your joy may be made full.*"
> John 16:24

*G*rowing up in a believing family is not to be undervalued. It is still the ideal beginning, because it is the foundation of the happiest possible childhood. Yet I know now that something more is needed: Each human being must enter into Life for himself. There is no such thing as inheriting Christianity.

ENTERING IN

... clothe yourselves with humility ...
1 Peter 5:5

*L*et's not mistake it: Entering into a direct Father-child relationship does take childlikeness. The door through which we enter into Life is a low door. And sometimes it is the humble and the needy who can show the rest of us the way.

NOVEMBER 16

REVELATION

*... by revelation there was made
known to me the mystery ...*
Ephesians 3:3

When we realize the range of
important questions that will always
elude the net of final intellectual or
scientific proof, then we begin to
appreciate the significance of revelation.
Surely here is a most important gift
we should ask for more often.

NOVEMBER 17

JESUS' LOVE

... the love of God has been poured out within our hearts through the Holy Spirit ...
Romans 5:5

Perhaps the greatest distance any of us ever has to travel is that long trek between the head and the heart. Just so, the love of Jesus is something that I must *experience*, and only the Holy Spirit can make me feel that great, tender love.

NOVEMBER 18

INTERVENTION

"[God] ... does great and
unsearchable things,
Wonders without number."
Job 5:9

I think it a mistake to think of God's
intervention only in terms of great
events and dramatic circumstances – a
sudden healing, or the saving of a life in
jeopardy. After all, most of our days are
full of ordinary events and common
experiences. Are we to believe that
God has no interest in these?

CLAIMING HIS RICHES

You do not have because you do not ask.
James 4:2

The riches of grace must be claimed. The process goes like this: God has made a promise. If there are conditions attached to it, we do our best to meet them. We make an act of claiming this promise at a specific time and place. God fulfills the promise in His own time and His own way.

THE BIBLE

With Thy counsel Thou wilt guide me ...
Psalm 73:24

We have to study the Bible intelligently, not as if the Scriptures were a sort of holy rabbit's foot, but for its wisdom in the broad sweep of its teaching about the nature of God and of man.

HEALING PRAYER

My times are in Thy hand ...
Psalm 31:15

Many authentic healings through prayer are a gradual process rather than a one-time miracle. The complete healing thus takes time and persistently repeated prayer work. And this slower timing, by the way, is consistent with all normal processes of the body, as well as of everything in nature.

HEALING PRAYER

*"And I say to you, ask, and
it shall be given to you ..."*
Luke 11:9

*T*he joyous news is that we do not need
to wait for the special mission of the
healing evangelist. God wants all His
people to believe in His good will of
health and to step out and experiment
in prayer. He wants to use all of us.

HEALING PRAYER

" ... *because of his persistence he will get
up and give him as much as he needs.*"
Luke 11:8

I wonder now why I ever expected
five or ten minutes of prayer to cure
everything. Or why any of us has accepted the principle often taught that
to pray more than once for a healing
betrays a lack of faith. The Lord taught
the opposite. And in two separate
parable-stories on prayer He com-
mends dogged perseverance.

PRAYER

*(F)or God is not a God of
confusion but of peace ...*
1 Corinthians 14:33

*T*he purpose of all prayer is to find God's will and to make that will our prayer, so that as Jesus bade us pray in the Lord's Prayer, the Father's will may be done as perfectly on earth as it is in heaven.

PRAYER

*... if we ask anything according
to His will, He hears us.*
1 John 5:14

If there are any conditions attached to a promise we receive from God, we do our best to meet them, for He who will not let us down also will not let us off. To illustrate: The condition of having our sins cleansed is our forgiveness of others; the condition of material blessing is that we give priority to the Kingdom of God.

INNER JUDGMENT

In all your ways acknowledge Him,
And He will make your paths straight.
Proverbs 3:6

In relation to the matter of inner judgment, the Quakers were fond of saying, "Mind the checks." They meant that when we feel a strong doubt that a particular course is right, then wait. Don't move on it. Or to put it positively, we should always move forward in faith – never out of fear.

IN A STORM

*... as they were sailing
along [Jesus] ... fell asleep;
and a fierce gale of wind
descended upon the
lake, and they began
to be swamped ...
And they ... woke Him up ....*
Luke 8:23-24

*T*he peace that Jesus gives us
through the Comforter is not dependent on any outside circumstances. It
is given right in the midst of great
activity or stress or trouble or grief
while the storm rages all around us.

IN A STORM

[Jesus] ... rebuked the wind and the surging waves, and they stopped, and it became calm.
Luke 8:24

I was also, minute by minute, learning something else – that our God can handle even the worst that can happen to us as finite human beings. Since Christ is beside us, no troubles that life can bring need cast us adrift. This is a knowledge that can release us from lifelong bondage to fear.

HEARING GOD

*... Martha was distracted
with all her preparations ...*
Luke 10:40

I wonder whether God does not try more often than we know to save His children from the accidents and disasters of our lives on this earth. But many of us do not practice the art of listening to the inner Voice with regard to small everyday matters. Because we are not tuned in, He cannot get His message through to us even in emergencies.

NOVEMBER 30

HEARING GOD

*[God] ... gives perseverance
and encouragement ...*
Romans 15:5

If a strong inner suggestion is from
God, it will strengthen with the
passing of time. If it is not from
Him, in a few days or weeks it
will fade or disappear entirely.

DECEMBER

THE NEXT WORLD

And ... the living creatures give glory and honor and thanks to Him who sits on the throne, to Him who lives forever and ever.
Revelation 4:9

Our world is connected with joy and hope to another; we who refuse to explore its spiritual and physical boundaries with zest and a sense of adventure, who will not lift our eyes to its far horizons, cheat only ourselves.

DECEMBER 2

MIRACLES

... power belongs to God.
Psalm 62:11

"*P*ower belongs to God." Jesus
believed this so totally that over
and over He moved out to stake
His life and His entire reputation
on the validity of this fact.

DECEMBER 3

MIRACLES

> ... *"All authority has been given
> to Me in heaven and on earth."*
> Matthew 28:18

*J*esus knew perfectly well about natural law — seedtime and harvest, disease and death. All this made not one whit of difference to Him. Very simply, Jesus' faith was that His Father was over and above all natural law; He was omnipotent over anything in earth or in heaven.

MIRACLES

He who did not spare His own Son, but delivered Him up for us all, how will He not also with Him freely give us all things?
Romans 8:32

*T*he disciples' acceptance of Jesus' bodily resurrection changed their viewpoint about everything. In the face of this stupendous miracle-fact, any other miracle was possible and probable. Then God could do *anything*. Believing that, they were prepared to let the Spirit use them to stand the Roman world on its head.

GOOD AND EVIL

> *... in all these things we overwhelmingly
> conquer through Him who loved us.*
> Romans 8:37

A good, hard look at evil as it is presented in the Bible and an obedient
following through of the whole story left
me with one overwhelming impression —
a great feeling of confidence and victory.

GOOD AND EVIL

*And the seventy returned with
joy, saying, "Lord, even the demons
are subject to us in Your name."*
Luke 10:17

The Bible story of the conflict between good and evil is not downbeat
at all, but upbeat; it is the story of
the total defeat of evil because of
the absolute power of Christ.

DECEMBER 7

GOOD AND EVIL

... do not give the devil an opportunity.
Ephesians 4:27

I remember our quoting at one
another one of Hannah Smith's favorite
maxims: "All discouragement is of the
devil." Of course the remedy is to realize
the source to the depression and to
remind oneself that spiritual reality
can never be gauged by feelings.

DECEMBER 8

STEPS OF FAITH

... the testing of your faith produces endurance.
James 1:3

*T*hose saints who have had the most experience here tell us that God uses our most stumbling, faltering faith-step as the open door to His doing for us "more than we ask or think."

DECEMBER 9

INTERCESSION

*" ... if two of you agree on earth about
anything that they may ask, it shall
be done for them by My Father ..."*
Matthew 18:19

The Bible insists that we have to ask for
God's help in order to get it. That is the
point of petitionary prayer. And the
asking seems to have more power when
many join their petitions in agreement.

DECEMBER 10

FAULTS

Never take your own revenge ...
Romans 12:19

Continually, we need to beware of
our incorrigible human blindness to
our own faults as contrasted with the
way we see other people's faults as
if under a giant magnifying glass.

DECEMBER 11

FORGIVENESS

But Jesus was saying, "Father, forgive them ..."
Luke 23:34

At the heart of the Christian Gospel lies forgiveness, the greatest miracle of all.

DECEMBER 12

FORGIVENESS

"And forgive us ... as we also have forgiven ..."
Matthew 6:12

Forgiveness has two sides that are inseparably joined: the forgiveness each of us needs from God, and the forgiveness we owe to other human beings. Most of us prefer not to face up to the fact that God's forgiveness and man's are forever linked.

FORGIVENESS

... be kind to one another ...
Ephesians 4:32

Every one of us is guilty before God. There are sins of the mind and the spirit as well as of the body. Yet God is willing freely to forgive us, no matter what we have done, *provided* we are willing to "be kind one to another, tenderhearted, forgiving each other."

FAITH FIRST

... Jesus, the author and perfecter of faith ...
Hebrews 12:2

Until science can finally prove life
after death beyond evidential experiences, we are backed up against faith.
For anything relating to the spirit,
the irreversible order is faith first, then
knowledge. That is because faith has
a way of slicing through prejudicial
and intellectual barriers and opening
the eyes of the spirit.

DECEMBER 15

FAITH FIRST

... he who comes to God must believe ... that He is a rewarder of those who seek Him.
Hebrews 11:6

In Jesus' ministry of healing the spirit, the mind and the body, faith seems to have been necessary before the divine act, not (as logic would have it) afterward.

TRIALS

> *[God] ... delivered us from the domain of darkness, and transferred us to the kingdom of His beloved Son.*
> Colossians 1:13

Paul learned that God allows us to have disappointments because He wants us to see that our joy is not in worldly pleasures. Our joy is in the fact that we have a relationship with God. Few of us ever understand that message until circumstances have divested us of any possibility of help except by God Himself.

UNBELIEF

Now the Lord is the Spirit; and where the Spirit of the Lord is, there is liberty.
2 Corinthians 3:17

The truth is that none of us can go anywhere in the Christian life so long as we are chained with unbelief. For until we believe that Jesus is the Savior of our life, for whatever our problem is, there is nothing He can do for us.

DECEMBER 18

UNITY

*And the congregation of those who
believed were of one heart and soul ...*
Acts 4:32

The passion of Jesus' heart for oneness
will be fulfilled – but only by the
Helper's work in our world. After
all, this oneness is of man's inner spirit,
and only the Spirit can melt our hard
hearts and our stubborn insistence that
we are right and everyone else wrong.

DECEMBER 19

UNITY

*... we, who are many, are one body in Christ,
and individually members one of another.*
Romans 12:5

Scripture continually insists
on the principle of our connec-
tedness as a fact of human life:
"We [are] members one of another."

DECEMBER 20

LISTENING

*"Take My yoke upon you,
and learn from Me ..."*
Matthew 11:29

*I*s it possible for an opinionated woman
in her autumn years to become like a
child and sit at the feet of Jesus with one
idea – to hear what He will say?

FEAR

"Do not be afraid, little flock ..."
Luke 12:32

Knowing that all people struggle with fear, Jesus often prefaced what He was about to say to His fellow humans with the words "Fear not." Therefore my prayer is, "Lord, I hand my fears over to You, fears of all kinds."

HABITS

... *"I will put My law within them,*
... and I will be their God ..."
Jeremiah 31:33

I see now how God helps us change long-standing habits. What happens is that our tastes begin to change. Something that we liked a lot suddenly is not so appealing. When we understand that it is the Lord Himself working, then we can stop resisting our own changing tastes, thank Him and flow with the new direction of the tide.

SURRENDERED

*... He laid down His life for us; and we ought
to lay down our lives for the brethren.*
1 John 3:16

No wonder we can do no mighty
works until the surrender to Jesus is
complete. Until He has been allowed
to come and make His home in me –
letting all self go – I will be praying for
others, doing His work, in my name
and in my nature rather than in His.

DECEMBER 24

THE DOOR TO HOPE

... blessed is he who trusts in the Lord.
Proverbs 16:20

*T*here is a crucial difference between acceptance and resignation. Resignation lies down in the dust of a godless universe and steels itself for the worst. Acceptance says, "I'll look unblinkingly at my situation. But I'll also open my hands to accept willingly whatever a loving Father sends." Acceptance never slams the door on hope.

GREATER WORKS

*(F)or the gifts and the calling
of God are irrevocable.*
Romans 11:29

Was Jesus seriously promising that
we — you and I — would not only do
these same works, but even *greater*
works? Could He be serious? We find
that His early apostles did take this
preposterous promise at face value
and proceeded to act upon it.

DEPENDING ON GOD

*"Now they have come to know that everything
Thou hast given Me is from Thee."*
John 17:7

Jesus' helplessness meant a
total dependence upon His
Father for everything.

THE HOLY SPIRIT

*"... I will ask the Father, and He
will give you another Helper ..."*
John 14:16

The Holy Spirit is a Person – one of
the three Persons of the Godhead. As
such, He possesses all the attributes
of personality. He has a mind; He
has knowledge; He has a will.

THE HOLY SPIRIT

" ... He abides with you, and will be in you."
John 14:17

The Spirit, being a Person, is a Friend whom we can come to know and to love. One of His most lovable characteristics is that He deliberately submerges Himself in Jesus; He works at being inconspicuous.

THE HOLY SPIRIT

> *... the Lord GOD will cause*
> *righteousness and praise*
> *To spring up before all the nations.*
> Isaiah 61:11

As our willingness and receptivity increase, we will also experience repeated fillings of the Holy Spirit. These will come as we step out in ministry. Special filling and special outpouring will be given for situations we alone could never handle. This has been the experience of many individuals across the centuries.

DECEMBER 30

THE HOLY SPIRIT

*And your ears will hear a word behind
you, "This is the way, walk in it ..."*
Isaiah 30:21

Jesus' promise to you and me is that the
Helper will be with us always, day and
night, standing by for any protection we
need and for every emergency. Our only
part is to recognize His presence and to
call upon Him in joyous faith.

THE HOLY SPIRIT

> " *... it is to your advantage that I go away; for if I do not go away, the Helper shall not come to you ...*"
> John 16:7

We wonder how anything could be more wonderful than the physical presence of our Lord. Yet Jesus never spoke lightly or thoughtlessly. And here we have His solemn word in His Last Supper talk with His apostles that there *is* something better – His presence in the form of the Holy Spirit.

W9-AVY-785

BEST OF

Beijing

Eilís Quinn

Colour-Coding & Maps

Each chapter has a colour code along the banner at the top of the page which is also used for text and symbols on maps (eg all venues reviewed in the Highlights chapter are orange on the maps). The fold-out maps inside the front and back covers are numbered from 1 to 8. All sights and venues in the text have map references; eg, (2, C2) means Map 2, grid reference C2. See p128 for map symbols.

Prices

Multiple prices listed with reviews (eg Y10/5) usually indicate adult/concession admission to a venue. Concession prices can include senior, student, member or coupon discounts. Meal cost and room rate categories are listed at the start of the Eating and Sleeping chapters, respectively.

Text Symbols

- ☎ telephone
- ✉ address
- 🖳 email/website address
- $ admission
- ☽ opening hours
- ⓘ information
- Ⓜ metro (subway)
- 🚌 bus
- ♿ wheelchair access
- ✕ on-site/nearby eatery
- 🧒 child-friendly venue
- Ⓥ good vegetarian selection

Best of Beijing
2nd edition – March 2006
First published – March 2004

Published by Lonely Planet Publications Pty Ltd
ABN 36 005 607 983

Australia Head Office, Locked Bag 1, Footscray, Vic 3011
☎ 03 8379 8000, fax 03 8379 8111
🖳 talk2us@lonelyplanet.com.au

USA 150 Linden St, Oakland, CA 94607
☎ 510 893 8555, toll free 800 275 8555
fax 510 893 8572
🖳 info@lonelyplanet.com

UK 72–82 Rosebery Ave, Clerkenwell, London EC1R 4RW
☎ 020 7841 9000, fax 020 7841 9001
🖳 go@lonelyplanet.co.uk

This title was commissioned in Lonely Planet's Melbourne office and produced by: **Commissioning Editor** Rebecca Chau **Manuscript Assessment** Alan Murphy **Coordinating Editor** Andrea Dobbin **Coordinating Cartographer** Owen Eszeki **Layout Designer** Steven Cann **Editor** Nigel Chin **Cartographer** Sarah Sloane **Managing Cartographer** Corinne Waddell **Cover Designer** Jim Hsu **Project Manager** Eoin Dunlevy **Mapping Development** Paul Piaia **Desktop Publishing Support** Mark Germanchis **Thanks to** Adriana Mammarella, Sally Darmody, Carol Chandler, Bruce Evans, Rebecca Lalor, Quentin Frayne, Celia Wood

Photographs by Lonely Planet Images and Ray Laskowitz except for the following: p6, p14, p19, p20, p21, p22, p23, p24, p25, p26, p29, p30, p31, p32, p37, p39, p40, p41, p42, p43, p45, p47, p51, p54, p55, p57, p58, p59, p63, p65, p68, p70, p72, p73, p75, p77, p78, p80, p82, p84, p86, p87, p89, p90, p93, p95, p97, p98, p99, p100, p103 Phil Weymouth, p12 Manfred Gottschalk, p49 Keren Su, p50 John Hay, p85, p92 Hilary Smith. Photo on p18 courtesy Factory 798.
Cover photograph Traditional Beijing Opera performer/singer on stage at the Liyuan Theatre. Beijing, China, Dennis Cox/Photolibrary. All images are copyright of the photographers unless otherwise indicated. Many of the images in this guide are available for licensing from Lonely Planet Images: www.lonelyplanetimages.com.

ISBN 1 74059 841 5

Printed by Markono Print Media Pte Ltd, Singapore

Contents

From the Publisher

THE AUTHOR
Eilís Quinn

Eilís grew up in Vancouver, Canada, where visits to the city's mammoth Chinatown sowed a fascination with China and foreign languages. A degree in East Asian Studies finally took her to the Middle Kingdom for real, where she fell for Beijing's manic energy the moment she got off the plane. Back in Canada, with degrees in Chinese, Russian and German, she resisted the pull of yet another language BA and opted for journalism instead. She went on to toil in the newsrooms of the Canadian Press news wire service, the New York Daily News, the Toronto Star and the Montreal Gazette.

Heartfelt thanks to my fellow travellers for the tips, time and emails. And to Wu Min, Enoch Cheng and each and every Beijinger who turned me the right way when I was lost or otherwise took me under their wing: thank you so, so much.

The first edition of this book was written by Korina Miller.

LONELY PLANET AUTHORS

Why is our travel information the best in the world? It's simple: our authors are independent, dedicated travellers. They don't research using just the Internet or phone, and they don't take freebies in exchange for positive coverage. They travel widely, to all the popular spots and off the beaten track. They personally visit thousands of hotels, restaurants, cafés, bars, galleries, palaces, museums and more – and they take pride in getting all the details right, and telling it how it is. For more, see the authors section on **www.lonelyplanet.com**.

PHOTOGRAPHER
Ray Laskowitz

Ray Laskowitz has spent the better part of 30 years photographing, editing and designing for various newspapers, photographic agencies and publishers. He has spent the last 13 years splitting his time between the US and parts of China and Southeast Asia. The former New Orleans resident is now relocating his base to New Mexico where he hopes to expand his coverage of the Southwest and West while continuing photographing in Asia. Beijing is Ray's seventh commissioned shoot for Lonely Planet, having previously shot in New Orleans, Los Angeles, San Francisco, Montreal, Las Vegas and Chicago.

SEND US YOUR FEEDBACK

We love to hear from travellers – your comments keep us on our toes and help make our books better. Our well-travelled team reads every word on what you loved or loathed about this book. Although we cannot reply individually to postal submissions, we always guarantee that your feedback goes straight to the appropriate authors, in time for the next edition – and the most useful submissions are rewarded with a free book. To send us your updates – and find out about Lonely Planet events, newsletters and travel news – visit our award-winning website: **www.lonelyplanet.com/feedback**.

Note: We may edit, reproduce and incorporate your comments in Lonely Planet products such as guidebooks, websites and digital products, so let us know if you don't want your comments reproduced or your name acknowledged. For a copy of our privacy policy visit **www.lonelyplanet.com/privacy**.

Introducing Beijing

Frantic, feverish and ready to bubble over at the top, there's a special kind of buzz in Beijing and you'll feel it as soon as you hit the street.

Cars, pedicabs and rickshaws kick up dust as they race in fits and starts for control of the streets. *Hútòngs* (alleyways) belch out cyclists, playing children and the earthy-sweet smell of Chinese food, while armies of cloth-shoed, yellow-helmeted construction workers change the city's skyline in the background.

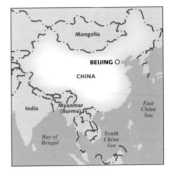

In the midst of it all are the city's gob-smacking sights, where thousands of travellers surrender to the mystery of places like the Forbidden City and pivot unbelievably at the vastness of Tiananmen Square.

Best of all, as the city gets ready to host the 2008 Olympic Games, it's getting a facelift you wouldn't believe. Thickets of dinosaur-like cranes sway on the horizon as skyscrapers, gleaming shopping malls and subway lines sprout up below. Old sights are being spruced up, modern attractions are being added and the nightlife and restaurants have never been better.

And these days the people are as much a reason to visit Beijing as the sights. The Olympics is the capital's coming-out party to the world, Beijingers are getting ready to show their best face and people are descending on the city from all over China, injecting new energy into everything from the arts to business. It all makes the city more thrilling and chaotic, more manic and fascinating than ever before.

You've picked the perfect time to come throw yourself into the mix.

Life in the fast lane

Neighbourhoods

It's hard to find a dull neighbourhood in Beijing. The Forbidden City sits in the middle of it all like a bull's-eye on the map. Spreading north and northeast is where many of Beijing's less-flashy folk live. Here you'll find many temples and small museums devoted to Beijing notables. The Lama Temple marks the northern boundary of the **Dongcheng District** (4, F3). Qianhai Lake is where locals go for a dip in the summer or for a drink in the cafés that line its shores. The ultra-modern Wangfujing Dajie slices through the east of this district, with fashionable shops and hotels.

To the east, **Chaoyang** (4, J4) caters to Beijing's foreign residents, with the Russian quarter clinging to the north side of Ritan Park. Chaoyang is where you more often come to shop and dine than to sightsee. Within this area and to the northeast of the Workers' Stadium, **Sanlitun Embassy Area** (5) is crowded with trendy bars and restaurants, while **Jianguomenwai Embassy Area** (4, H4) to the south is lined with prominent shops and malls.

Chongwen (4, E6), to the south of the Forbidden City, has come under the wrath of bulldozers,

OFF THE BEATEN TRACK
Nothing beats watching Beijing wake up in the morning. Walk the empty city to Tiananmen Square for the dawn flag-raising ceremony. Then grab a Beijing breakfast of soy milk and fried dough sticks while store fronts slide open, vendors unpack and people flood the streets with energy.

with new apartment complexes replacing older courtyard houses. The draws here are the Temple of Heaven and Panjiayuan Market. West of here, **Xuanwu** (4, B6) includes the chaotic Qianmen neighbourhoods of Dazhalan Market and Liulichang, with Niujie Mosque in the south and the China Millennium Monument to the north. Northwest of the Forbidden City is the suburban **Haidian District** (8, D3), home to the zoo, aquarium and university, and stretching all the way to the Summer Palace and Fragrant Hills Park.

Though mountainous along the north and west the city is otherwise flat. Ringed by four major roads and crisscrossed by wide boulevards, navigating downtown is relatively simple – until you enter the maze of *hútòngs* (alleyways) between the thoroughfares.

Marching to the beat of a different drum: morning exercise classes on Wangfujing Dajie

Itineraries

ONE DAY

Mingle in Tiananmen Square, taking in the views from Qianmen and Tiananmen Gate. Take in the mystery of the Forbidden City before wandering up through Jingshan Park for a sunset view of the City's golden rooftops. Dine at the Courtyard, where you can visit its gallery and linger in the cigar lounge. Top the evening off with a stroll around the Forbidden City's moat.

TWO DAYS

As for one day, but also take in the Summer Palace. Hop in a rickshaw near Prince Gong's for a tour of Beijing's *hútòngs* (alleyways). Dine at Baguo Buyi while taking in a *biàn liǎn* (Sichuan face-change performance). Head west to Lotus Lanes, where umpteen bars and restaurants hug the banks of Qianhai Lake. Wind down the evening at Rive Gauche or, if you feel the night is just beginning, take your pick of the discos dotting the lake's west bank.

THREE DAYS

As for two days, then visit the Lama Temple. Spend the afternoon treasure hunting along Dazhalan Jie and Liulichang Jie. Later, amble south to the ornate Huguang Guild Hall to take in the exhibit on traditional Beijing opera before settling down to the real thing in the atmospheric performance hall.

BEIJING ART TRAIL

Take in a temporary exhibit at the Beijing Art Gallery of Imperial City for insights into Ming and

WORST OF BEIJING

- Over-aggressive street vendors thwacking you in the arms and ribs with their merchandise
- Hordes of tourists with sharpened elbows pushing their way to the front of queues
- Witnessing spitting like you've never seen or heard before
- Store clerks that either ignore you completely or cling so close you feel their breath on your neck

Qing design tastes. Then head across the street to the Wan Fung Art Gallery for a glimpse into contemporary Chinese art. Jump on a bus or in a taxi and head to Factory 798. Have lunch at one of the many bistros and spend the afternoon exploring the galleries and craft shops. Finish the day with a glass of wine at one of the bars while you watch the artists pack up and head home for the day.

Highlights

TIANANMEN SQUARE 天安门广场 (4, D5)

You may have seen it a hundred times on TV but you will still find yourself catching your breath when you first glimpse this massive history-laden square. In imperial days it was the site of government offices, off-limits to everyday Beijingers. Even looking at the square was considered a crime. Then on 1 October 1949 it was those same ordinary people that clogged the square to hear Mao declare the founding of the People's Republic of China. Wanting to project the stature of the Communist Party, Mao later ordered the square enlarged. He succeeded in creating a vessel of over 400,000 sq metres where he could review Red Guard parades with a million of his closest friends. When Mao died in 1976 people from all over the country jammed into the square to pay their respects.

INFORMATION
- ☎ 6524 3322
- ✉ Tiananmen Dong or Tiananmen Xi
- 💲 Y15, compulsory bag check Y3-5
- ⏲ 8.30am-4.30pm
- Ⓜ Tiananmen Dong, Tiananmen Xi
- ♿ excellent
- 🍴 Wangfujing Snack Street (p74)

Standing guard, Tiananmen Square

In 1989 student pro-democracy demonstrators set up on Tiananmen before they were forced out by army tanks and soldiers and the bloody aftermath was beamed around the globe. Leaving the world with no doubt that the Communist Party had every intention of staying in power despite market reforms, the government made sure it didn't let demonstrators set up shop again. Ever since, the square has been closely monitored by security cameras and People's Liberation Army (PLA) soldiers, ready to pounce at the first sign of trouble. Despite kite flyers, children and tourists snapping photos, the atmosphere at the square is so reverent, it may be the only place in Beijing where you see people respect the 'no spitting' signs.

You'll get to know Tiananmen well as you traverse it back and forth to the many sights nearby.

Mao rests in his **mausoleum** (p41), with the regal **Qianmen** (p34) beyond. To the west is the **National Museum of China** (p30) and to the east lurks the **Great Hall of the People** (p33).

CALLING ALL EARLY BIRDS

Whatever you do, don't miss Tiananmen Square's sunrise flag-raising ceremony or the flag lowering at sunset. Get there early for both as the crowds can be huge. In the evening it's elbow to elbow as people circle the flag pole and crane their necks to see the soldiers pour over Tiananmen Gate's centre bridge. The soldiers are drilled to march at 108 paces per minute, 75cm per pace, and the ceremony is timed so the flag disappears underneath Tiananmen Gate at the same second that the sun goes down. The same happens in reverse at sunrise except with a scratchy recording of the Chinese national anthem playing in the background. The crowd is usually exclusively Chinese and they start belting out the words as soon as the music starts. Traffic along Dongchang'an Jie and Xichang'an Jie is stopped for both ceremonies.

While the cement plain of Tiananmen Square is the people's stage, the gate of the powerful is **Tiananmen (Gate of Heavenly Peace)** to the north of the square. Built in the 15th century and restored in the 17th, imperial royalty and communist leaders alike have used Tiananmen as a rostrum for viewing troops and for proclaiming the law of the land to assembled crowds.

Seven parallel bridges lead over a stream to the gate's five doors. In imperial days the centre bridge and door could only be used by the emperor. Since the arrival of the Communist Party, this door has been crowned with an enormous portrait of Mao. To the helmsman's left is written 'Long Live the People's Republic of China' and to his right, 'Long Live the Unity of the Peoples of the World'.

A visit to Tiananmen is your chance to see the gate from the inside and to savour the vista of the world's largest square directly ahead of you.

Stone lion guarding Tiananmen Square

FORBIDDEN CITY 紫禁城 (7)

For 500 years the walls of the Forbidden City drew an impenetrable line between the imperial household and the general population. Exceptionally well preserved, the palace was first opened to the public in 1949, allowing visitors to step into a world of emperors, eunuchs, ceremony and splendour.

INFORMATION

- ☎ 6513 2255
- ✉ Tiananmen Dong, through Tiananmen Gate
- 💲 Apr–Oct Y60/20, Nov–Mar Y40/20, kids under 1.2m free
- 🕐 8.30am-5pm Apr–mid-Oct, 8.30am-4.30pm mid-Oct–Mar
- ℹ audio tour by Roger Moore Y40, plus cash deposit; guided tours at the entrance
- Ⓜ Tiananmen Dong or Tiananmen Xi
- ✖ Purple Vine Teahouse (p69), the Courtyard (p71)

The palace was originally established by Emperor Yongle (via a million labourers) between 1406 and 1420. In order to show his power and wealth and yet 'humbly' accept his natural inferiority to the gods, the palace has a mere 9999.5 rooms, half a room less than the Jade Emperor's heavenly palace. With 800 buildings covering 720,000 sq metres, the palace is so large that a full-time restoration squad is continuously repainting and repairing. It's estimated to take 10 years to do a full renovation.

The buildings you see today are mainly post-18th century. Fire has always been a threat to the wooden palace, with six major and countless minor blazes sending buildings up in smoke. Many fires were the result of fireworks displays gone awry or wayward lanterns. Invading Manchus burned the palace to the ground in 1644 and eunuchs torched a number of buildings in 1923 in an attempt to cover up their looting of palace treasures. Imperial guards fought the blazes with water stored in huge vats, many of which still dot the palace grounds.

Fourteen Ming emperors and 10 Qing emperors called the Forbidden City home. Many became absorbed in the splendour of life inside the palace, to the detriment of their rule and the living conditions outside.

The Palace of Heavenly Purity in the Forbidden City

The vast interior of the Forbidden City

Often emperors would hand over the dull task of ruling to the court eunuchs in order to take up the more interesting hobbies of collecting concubines or writing poetry.

The **Hall of Supreme Harmony** is the largest structure in the palace grounds, used for occasions such as the emperor's birthday, and coronations. The hall is decorated with 13,844 dragons.

In front of the hall is a sundial and standard measuring container, alluding to the emperor's mastery of both time and space. Also in front of the hall is a bronze turtle, symbolising longevity and stability. Inside the hall, the throne is guarded by two *luduān* (mythical beasts believed to understand all languages and able to cover 9000 leagues of distance in a day).

The **Palace of Heavenly Purity** was the living quarters of the emperors. This building contained nine bedrooms, each with three beds. To safeguard against attack while he slept, the emperor would retire to a different bed each night. Further north, the elaborate **Palace of Earthly Tranquillity** was the sleeping quarters of the Ming empresses; during the Qing dynasty it was used for only three days of each reign as the nuptial chamber.

Do not confuse Tiananmen (Gate of Heavenly Peace) with the entrance to the Forbidden City. To reach the City's ticket office, follow the crowds past Tiananmen until you can't go any further without paying. There's a snazzy new audioguide (Y40) on offer in addition to the famous Roger Moore–narrated version. Flashing red lights illuminate several walking routes on its front panel, and the narrations start spontaneously as you near 'reception distance' of the City's various sights. However, if a fellow traveller should interrupt you to, say, ask for directions or the time just as a palace intrigue is unfolding on tape, you're out of luck. With no stop, pause or rewind options, by the time you wave them off it will be too late. You'll spend the rest of your day wondering whodunnit. Better to stick with the folksier, more entertaining 007 version.

SUMMER PALACE 颐和园 (2)

The playground of the royal court, these enormous grounds were where the imperial family and entourage came to escape the interminable heat of the

INFORMATION

- ☎ 6288 1144
- 🖳 www.summerpalace-china.com in Chinese
- ✉ Yiheyuan Lu, Haidian District
- $ Y30/15, incl all sights Y50
- 🕙 tickets sold 6.30am-6pm, grounds close 8pm Apr-Oct, tickets sold 7am-5pm, grounds close 7pm Nov-Mar
- ⓘ audioguides Y30
- Ⓜ Wudaokou, then bus 375 or 15min taxi ride
- 🚍 303, 346 or 808 from Qianmen area (1-2hr depending on traffic)

The Tower of Fragrant Buddha

city. A day can easily be spent here taking in the sights, strolling along tree-lined paths and floating in a paddleboat on Kunming Lake.

Long a royal garden, the grounds were embellished and expanded by Emperor Qianlong in the 18th century. In 1860 many of the buildings were severely damaged during the Second Opium War. Eighteen years later, Empress Dowager Cixi began a refit. She used money earmarked for a modern navy and, perhaps in honour of this, spent a large chunk of it on a huge, tasteless **marble boat**. You'll find it in the northeast of Kunming Lake. The Summer Palace was razed and neglected a few more times, prompting a string of further restorations.

The main entrance to the Palace is in the east of the grounds. Just inside this gate is the **Hall of Benevolence and Longevity**, the chief palace structure where the emperor handled state affairs and received envoys. Among the bronze animals in front of the hall is the mythical *qílín* (Chinese unicorn). Nearby is the **Garden of Virtue and Harmony** (Y5), where you can see traditional costumes and props.

To the north, the artificial **Longevity Hill** contains the majority of the park's interesting buildings. **Cloud Dispensing Hall** was one of the few structures to escape the attention of Anglo-French forces, and the impressive **Tower of Fragrant Buddha** (Y10) offers fabulous views across the lake. The **Long Corridor**, which runs for over 700m along the northern shore of Kunming Lake, is painted with countless mythical scenes.

In the west of the grounds, an excellent walk spans the lake across **Jade Belt Bridge**, **Mirror Bridge**, **Chain Bridge** and **Willow Bridge**. Three-quarters

Part of the exquisitely decorated Long Corridor in the Summer Palace

of the palace grounds are consumed by Kunming Lake. You can take a **ferry** (Y8; ☯9am-4pm) across it, cruise on a **pleasure boat** (Y6; ☯9am-4pm) around it or **paddle** (per hr 'new'/'old' boats Y40/20, deposit Y200; ☯8am-4.30pm) on it.

In the very north of the complex is **Suzhou Street** (Y10). Originally exclusive to the emperor and his entourage, the shopping street has been rebuilt in classic Ming style, and its stalls are once again open for business. All purchases must be made with antique Ming coins; exchange your Renminbi at the top of the street.

DRAGON WOMEN

Like many other Qing-dynasty teenagers, at the age of 15 Cixi gave up her true love to become one of Emperor Xianfeng's concubines. Her cunningness and intelligence soon made her a favourite of the emperor, particularly after she gave birth to his only son in 1856. Cixi's subsequent rise to power was largely due to the convenient deaths of her adversaries. Xianfeng died at the age of 30 and his empress followed suit a few years later. This made Cixi's five-year-old son, Tongzhi, the new emperor, and Cixi herself the ruling Dowager Empress.

Cixi held the government reins for over 40 years in total, galloping over anyone who got in her way – including her own son. Other opponents were slowly starved, thrown down wells or locked away. She spent her reign focusing on her own position rather than the country's; at the end of her life she left nine storerooms of personal treasures, a refurbished Summer Palace, and the Qing dynasty in an irreparable state of decline.

Though Cixi's actions are the most notorious, they are by no means exceptional in the annals of imperial China. Acceptance into the imperial court was one of the few ways girls had access to education, learning calligraphy, painting and music, as they tried to stay in the emperor's favour. Once there, survival often meant getting rid of your rival before they got rid of you. Empress Wu (625–705) of the Tang dynasty came to court just like Cixi did and rose rapidly through the imperial harem. It was said she even killed her own daughter in order to cast blame on Emperor Taizong's wife. It worked. His wife was demoted and Wu became reigning empress, wreaking havoc on her predecessor and every court official that had criticized her climb to power. *Flowers in the Mirror* is a historical novel inspired by her life and written by Qing writer Li Ju-chen.

TEMPLE OF HEAVEN 天坛公园 (6)

More park than temple and fairly overrun with tour groups, the Temple of Heaven (Tiantan) is well worth a visit for its exceptional and unique Ming buildings. This sight has become a symbol of Beijing, decorating tourist literature and loaning its name to products ranging from tiger balm to plumbing fixtures.

INFORMATION

- ☎ 6702 8866
- ✉ Tiantan Donglu
- 💲 low/high season park Y10/15, incl all sights Y30/35
- 🕑 8am-5.30pm Apr-Oct, 8am-5pm Nov-March
- ⓘ audioguide (from south entrance) Y20
- Ⓜ Qianmen, then bus 120 or taxi
- ✖ Gongdelin Vegetarian Restaurant (p69)

Danbi stone carved stairway, Hall of Prayer for Good Harvests

The temple was built in 1420 as a vast stage for the solemn rites performed by the Son of Heaven (aka the emperor), who came here to pray for good harvests, to seek divine approval and to atone for the sins of the people. Similar ceremonies were performed as early as 2600 BC and remained an important part of imperial life through to the early 20th century.

The most significant ceremony took place just before the winter solstice, when the emperor and his enormous entourage of elephant chariots, horses, lancers, musicians and 2000 ministers made their way, in total silence, from the Forbidden City to the temple.

The emperor was purified in the **Hall of Abstinence** by fasting from meat, alcohol, women, music and work. He then made sacrifices to the gods and reported to them on the events of the previous years. He would return a month later to beseech the heavens for good luck, especially with the coming year's harvest. As this ceremony was believed to decide the nation's future, any hitch in the proceedings was regarded as a bad omen.

The temple complex is built for the view of the gods. Seen from above, the temples themselves are round and their bases square, a pattern deriving from the ancient Chinese belief that heaven is round and earth is square. The shape of the 267-hectare park also reflects this, with the northern end a semicircle and the southern end a square.

Beginning in the south, the architecture of the **Round Altar** is based on the imperial number nine and multiples of nine.

Just northeast of here, **Echo Wall** is a perfect half-circle, so a whisper at one end is carried around to the other side. Your chances of experiencing this are slight, however, given the hundreds of tourists attempting to have their 'whispers' heard.

Also in this courtyard are the **Triple-Sounds Stones**: clap your hands while standing on them and listen for the echo, once from the first stone, twice from the second and thrice from the third. The octagonal **Imperial Vault of Heaven** at the back of the courtyard is a mini-version of the Hall of Prayer for Good Harvests. It once held the tablets of the emperors' ancestors, used in the winter solstice ceremony.

> **DON'T MISS**
> • Ringing the giant bell near the Hall of Abstinence
> • The sacrificial stove, east of the Gate of Prayer for Good Harvests
> • The annex to the west of the Hall of Prayer for Good Harvests

The newly opened **Divine Music Administration** sits in the west of the park. The building, formerly a bacterial laboratory built by the Japanese after they invaded Beijing during WWII, now houses an impressive collection of traditional Chinese instruments and pictures of how they were used during imperial ceremonies.

In the north of the grounds, the round **Hall of Prayer for Good Harvests** is mounted on a three-tiered marble terrace and decorated in blue, yellow and green glazed tiles, representing heaven, earth and the mortal world. Inside, immense pillars symbolise the four seasons and 12 months of the year. The intricately decorated ceiling is all the more impressive for its lack of nails or cement support. The hall was struck by lightning and burnt to the ground in 1889; it was rebuilt the following year using Oregon fir. The hall was closed for renovations at the time of writing but was set to reopen in May 2006.

Water calligraphy in the Temple of Heaven

LAMA TEMPLE 雍和宫 (4, F1)

Beijing's most colourful temple is overflowing with tapestries, frescoes, statuary, plumes of incense smoke and prostrate worshippers. The immaculately maintained buildings are an architectural feat and it is easy to understand why this is one of Beijing's most popular sights.

INFORMATION

- ☎ 6404 4499
- ✉ 12 Yonghegong Dajie
- $ Y25
- ⏱ 9am-4pm
- ℹ English/Chinese audioguide Y20/10; guided tours at front gate
- Ⓜ Yonghegong-Lama Temple
- ✖ Xu Xiang Zhai Vegetarian Restaurant (p74)

Seated Buddha at Lama Temple

Fancy living in a place like this? Count Yin Zhen did – until he became Emperor Yongzheng and packed his bags for the Forbidden City. His former residence became Yonghe Palace until 1744 when it was converted into Lama Temple, a lamasery for legions of Mongolian and Tibetan monks. Today it remains one of the most renowned Tibetan Buddhist temples outside of Tibet.

When Yongzheng's successor, Emperor Qianlong, came to power, Lama Temple took on new significance. A Buddhist, Qianlong claimed to be sympathetic to followers of the religion but, in actuality, directed his energies into pacifying the discontented Mongolians and Tibetans by 'training' (and controlling) their Lamas at Lama Temple.

Nevertheless, the temple had a ghoulish reputation for supposedly harbouring the more sinister aspects of Tibetan Buddhism, such as human sacrifice. When photographer James Ricalton visited in the late 19th century, he noted: '…it is one of the most dirty, dingy, smoky, ramshackle establishments in the whole world and filled with one thousand five hundred Mongolian and Tibetan ignorant fanatics, called priests.'

In 1792 Qianlong further extended his minority control by instituting a new system for choosing Buddhist leaders that was not unlike a rigged lottery. Possible names were chosen in consultation with Qianlong and placed in two golden vases. One was taken to Lhasa to draw the Dalai Lama's name and the other remained at Lama Temple to draw the Panchen Lama.

The lamasery has five halls, each one taller and more impressive than the previous. They are designed and decorated in a mosaic of styles – Mongolian, Tibetan and Han – and are surrounded by courtyards and galleries. The lamasery's erotic statuary of intertwining gods and humans were once used to educate emperors' sons in the more pleasurable facts of life. Today they are draped in yellow cloth so as not to corrupt your gaze.

> **DON'T MISS**
> • The intricate mandala sand painting in Falun Dian Hall, made entirely of natural colouring
> • The altar of the 6th Panchen Lama, kept in the western exhibition hall
> • The pair of regal lions guarding the lamasery

The most Tibetan-styled building is **Falun Dian**, the fourth hall, which is used for study and prayer. Here you'll find a large bronze statue of Tsong Khapa (1357–1419), founder of the Gelukpa (Yellow Hat sect), and frescoes depicting his life.

In the last hall, **Wanfu Ge**, you have to crick your neck to take in the astounding 26m-high Maitreya Buddha. Believe it or not (and the *Guinness Book of World Records* did, as certified on a plaque outside), the statue is carved from a single block of sandalwood. The pungent smoke curling up from the yak-butter lamps reminds you that the wood originates in Tibet.

At the rear of the lamasery are two exhibition halls. Inside the western one are relics from the Tibet-China relationship and in the eastern hall is an introduction to the genealogy of the Dalai Lama and photos depicting the activities of today's lamas. While both halls are intriguing, the eastern one is lacking in English explanations and the information displayed in both halls should definitely be taken with a bucket of salt.

Praying at Lama Temple

FACTORY 798 艺术新区 (8, J1)

This is one of the freshest new spaces in Beijing and every day it draws the city's most creative artists and impassioned art collectors. Whether you love photography or sculpture, painting or video installations, you'll find a gallery here devoted to it.

INFORMATION

☎ 6438 4862

✉ cnr Jiuxianqiao Lu & Jiuxianqiao Beilu

$ free

⏱ varies; most stores 10am-6pm, bars & bistros stay open longer

🚌 403

Beijing's newest creative space: Factory 798

The factory halls were built in the 1950s with the Soviet Union's money and East Germany's architectural and industrial know-how. It went on to churn out electronics for decades before being shut down as Beijing urbanised and its industrial sector moved further and further away from the exponentially expanding city centre.

In 2002 the city's artistic community started to take an interest in this giant industrial carcass. They left it as is on the outside but went to work on the insides, divvying it up amongst themselves.

These days you can come and see the results for yourself. One moment you are walking along a dark musty hall. Then, turn a corner, and you might find yourself in the middle of an art opening at the **White Space gallery** (p32) or among the installations at **Beijing Tokyo Art Projects** (p31).

Later, you may wander into the studio of someone like controversial designer **Feng Ling** (p57), her 4m-long dresses, emblazed with the revolutionary red star, hanging from soaring staircases.

You can easily spend a day at Factory 798. Small but classy cafés and bars serving Western-style food are easy to find here, so there is plenty of choice for lunch or an early supper. This is also one of the few places in Beijing you can come to really escape from traffic and crowds. Though the occasional motorcycle may zoom by, there are next to no cars on the factory grounds. All you'll see are clusters of relaxed art lovers ambling from one warehouse to another.

VICTIM OF ITS OWN SUCCESS?

Rumours are rampant in the artistic community that the city Mandarins are so impressed with how popular Factory 798 has become they'd kind of like to have a piece of the pie themselves. Some artists and 798 devotees fear that as soon as the Olympics are over and the tourists have gone home, the city will sweep in and turn the factory complex into office space and luxury condos. Other artists say that the Olympics will increase 798's profile, guaranteeing it will be left alone. Only time will tell.

PRINCE GONG'S RESIDENCE 恭王府 (4, C2)

Rockeries, pools of water, elaborately carved gateways, plants, pavilions and corridors are all seamlessly pieced together into one of Beijing's largest private residences. Believed to be the setting of Cao Zueqin's 18th-century classic *Dream of the Red Mansion*, the palace was bestowed upon Prince Gong by his half-brother, Emperor Xianfeng, in the mid-19th century.

Gong is famous for negotiating with the British during the Second Opium War. With the Summer Palace burned to a crisp, the Forbidden City under threat of a match, and Emperor Xianfeng hiding in Chengde, Gong agreed to all of the Tianjin Treaty terms, including handing over large sums of silver and part of Kowloon to British Hong Kong. In exchange, much of Beijing was left standing and the British supported the Qing against the Taiping Rebellion.

Traditional Chinese gardens are a fusion of nature and architecture, designed to ease, move and aid the mind. The key elements are rocks and water, with every item carefully and purposefully placed. Windows, corridors and rockeries are positioned to enhance or shape your view. For example, as you first enter into this complex, your vision is slightly obscured by a tall rockery; the intention is to break up your view over the entire garden, creating a number of smaller scenes.

INFORMATION

- ☎ 6618 5005
- ✉ 14 Liuyin Jie
- $ Y20/10, incl opera performance & tea ceremony Y60
- ⏱ 8.30am-4.30pm
- ℹ guided tours at the entrance
- Ⓜ Gulou, then taxi southwest
- ✕ Sichuan Fandian (p73)

Lanterns hanging at Prince Gong's Residence

Situated in the east of the grounds, the **Grand Opera House** dates back to the Qing dynasty. Unfortunately, unless you're attending an opera (p92), it's rarely open to the public.

This sight is lacking in English translations and those that do exist are cryptic. If you're really keen to know what you're looking at, join a guided tour at the front gate.

DON'T MISS

- The thousands of brightly coloured carp in Square Pond
- Finding 'happiness' inside the rockery of Terrace for Inviting the Moon
- The more tranquil courtyards in the east of the complex

DONGYUE TEMPLE 东岳庙 (4, H3)

Surrounded by shopping centres and high-rises, Taoist monks busily attend to the business of the spirit world. With its roots somewhere in the Yuan dynasty, Dongyue Temple is a calm and intriguing retreat.

INFORMATION

- ☎ 6553 2184
- ✉ Chaoyangmenwai Dajie
- 💲 Y10/5
- 🕒 8am-4.30pm
- Ⓜ Chaoyangmen, then bus 110
- ✕ Xiheyaju Restaurant (p75)

A prayer for any occasion

DON'T MISS

- Bronze Wonder Donkey, the riding animal of God Wen Chang
- The temple's elaborate archway to the south; split from the Dongyue complex by Chaoyangmenwai Dajie, the orphan arch sits on its own amidst modernity and skyscrapers
- Trying your luck at bouncing a coin off a bell in the main courtyard

In the main courtyard of the temple, thousands of small red wooden prayer cards have been tied to anything that'll stand still – trees, fences, the front of the temple – and the effect is staggering. Written on each card is a prayer for good fortune, wealth, longevity or bouncing babies. Also in this courtyard is a forest of steles recording the history, beliefs and renovations of the temple over the ages.

Daiyuedian Hall at the back of the temple was first built in 1322 and houses a shrine to the God of Mount Taishan, who is master of 76 departments of heaven, 18 layers of hell and all of the mortal world. You can deposit a coin or two for healthy finances at the **Department for Bestowing Material Happiness**, or pay your respects to feathered friends at the **Department for Flying Birds**. Many of the characters within these departments (particularly those at the **Department for Wandering Souls**) are straight out of a Hollywood horror film.

At the very back of the complex (beginning on the western side) is a fascinating museum. The captions are in Chinese but the photographs and objects tell their own stories of life in old Beijing. If it rains while you're visiting the temple, you're in luck – the **Little Golden Beam** to the west of **Daiyue Palace** will shine with copper specks. Many believe they are gold and that by striding over this slab your wishes will be granted.

BEIHAI PARK 北海公园 (4, C2)

The origins of Beihai Park are somewhat mysterious. It was once frequented by emperors looking for a breath of fresh air, but its history tumbles further back to the days of Kublai Khan, who established Beijing as a capital in 1279. Today, all that remains of Khan's palace is a giant jade wine urn in the Round City near the southern entrance to the park.

At first glance the park appears to be little more than a lake, however, there is a wealth of sights to take in. Dominating **Jade Islet**, the 36m **White Dagoba** was originally built in 1651 for a visit by the Dalai Lama. The dagoba has since been knocked down twice by earthquakes. The small **Hall of Beneficent Causation**, south of the dagoba, is graced with beautiful glazed Buddha tiles.

The north shore of the park is dotted with temples. The most popular temple complex, **Xitian Fanjing**, houses **Daizhe Hall**, home to three enormous bronze Buddha statues, each with a shock of blue hair. **Jingxinzhai** is worth a visit for its rockeries, painted corridors, restored imperial rooms and the occasional turtle in its ponds.

North West Paradise is the park's most stunning temple. Built by Emperor Qianlong as an offering for his mother's eternal happiness, it is the largest square pavilion in China. Its interior is a carving of the western heavens inhabited by countless Bodhisattvas.

INFORMATION

- ☎ 6403 1102
- ✉ Wenjin Jie (south gate); Di'anmenxi Dajie (north gate)
- $ park & temples Y10, Jade Islet Y12
- ☽ park 6am-8pm, sights 9am-4.45pm
- Ⓜ Tiananmen Xi, then bus 5
- ✖ Fangshan Restaurant (p71)

DON'T MISS

- Riding the ferry on North Sea Lake
- Visiting the park in the evening to see older residents playing traditional music, and singing and dancing
- Wang Da Guan's paintings in Kuaixue Hall (p31)

Take a twirl around Beihai Park

LIULICHANG 琉璃厂 (4, C6)

With gracefully curved tiled roofs, brightly painted doors and cobbled streets, picturesque Liulichang exudes an old-world atmosphere. The shops lining the streets were once the stomping grounds of the upper-crust Ming and Qing societies; today they are treasure-troves of old coins, lanterns, paper-cuttings, furniture, pottery, swords, books, jade and other objects from days of yore. Visiting them is like stepping back in time.

INFORMATION

- ✉ Liulichang Xijie & Liulichang Dongjie
- 💲 free
- 🕙 10am-6pm
- Ⓜ Hepingmen
- 🍴 Tianhai Canting (p70)

Jade shop, Liulichang Xijie

West off Nanxinhua Jie, **Rong-baozhai** (19 Liulichang Xijie) has a vast collection of scroll paints, woodblock prints, paper, ink and brushes. Continuing west, the road narrows and takes on a more market-like appearance, with small stalls and tables. This is where you can practise some traditional Chinese bartering.

Heading east from Nanxinhua, you can watch chops being carved in **Xie Xian Shun** (107b Liulichang Dongjie). Carry on to **Yidege** (67 Liulichang Dongjie), where Indian inks have been sold since 1865, and **Daiyuexuan Brush Shop** (73 Liulichang Dongjie), which has provided local artists with top-quality paint brushes since 1916. In the doorways around **Xinghai Yuehaixuan Musical Instruments** (97 Liulichang Dongjie) you will often hear melodies being plucked on traditional *yuèqín* (guitars) or *gǔzhēng* (zithers). At the far eastern end of Liulichang, **Beijing Songtangzhai Museum** (p28) is worth a visit.

WHITE CLOUD TEMPLE 白云观 (8, D5)

Long-haired, bearded monks rest in the courtyard while incense sticks as big as bratwurst send clouds of smoke spiralling into the air. You get the distinct impression that little has changed at White Cloud Temple since it was first established in AD 739. This was once northern China's centre of Taoism and its huge complex contains countless shrines and courtyards.

Each of the halls is dedicated to a different Taoist official or marshal, from the God protecting Taoism (Wanglingguan) to the God of Wealth. The hall honouring Founder Qi is worth a look for its interior clay walls depicting scenes from the book of Qi.

Southeast of the complex is the **Temple of the God of Thunder**, which houses interesting bronze statues depicting four heavenly generals and the Thunder God himself, in charge of natural disasters, blessings, life and death.

As you enter the temple complex, you pass over a bridge. Beneath it hang two bells; for luck, you can attempt to strike them with old gold coins (you can get some at a nearby stall; Y10 for 50 coins). In the alley outside the temple, vendors sell incense sticks, prayer cards and lots of other Taoist gear.

White Cloud Temple is particularly worth visiting if you're in Beijing over the Spring Festival. During this time the temple fair brings together thousands of worshippers, artisans and street performers.

INFORMATION

☎ 6346 3531
✉ Baiyun Lu
$ Y10
☼ 8.30am-4.30pm May-Sep,
   8.30am-4pm Oct-Apr
Ⓜ Nanlishilu, then walk or taxi 1km

The White Cloud Temple lives up to its name

FRAGRANT HILLS PARK & BEIJING BOTANICAL GARDENS
香山公园, 北京植物园 (8, A2 & 8, B1)

Both in the same part of the Western Hills, you can take your pick from either of these nature retreats for a change of pace from the city.

FRAGRANT HILLS PARK INFORMATION

☎ 6259 1283
✉ northwest Beijing
$ Y10/5
⏱ 8am-6pm
Ⓜ Wudaokou, then 30min taxi ride

The park is set in a forest and has beautiful gardens, teahouses and paths. You can reach **Incense Burner Peak** by **cable car** (one way/return adult Y30/50, child Y10/15; ⏱ 8.30am-5pm). Follow the excellently maintained forest-lined trail down (1½ hours).

Near the north gate, **Azure Clouds Temple** (Y10; ⏱ 8.30am-4.30pm) was built in 1331 as a nunnery. At the back of the temple complex, climb the steps up to **Vayra Throne Pagoda**. Originally built in 1748, it now contains Sun Yatsen's 'Dress Tomb' (ie his hat and clothes). The ex-leader's body was kept here for a couple of years while his mausoleum was being constructed in Nanjing.

A couple of kilometres down the road is the Botanical Gardens, with 200 hectares of flora and fauna from the north, northeast and northwest of China.

The stained walls of the Zhao Monastery, Fragrant Hills Park

The **Beijing Botanical Gardens Conservatory** (Y50/40; ☺ 8.30am-4pm) is home to over 3000 types of plants from every corner of the globe, including a carnivorous house with Venus flytraps and pitcher plants, a rainforest, desert plants and orchids. In the east of the grounds is a model of **Yellow Leaf Village**, taken from Cao Zueqin's *Dream of the Red Mansion*. Apparently Cao got much of his inspiration for this Qing family saga from this area.

Inside **Wofu Temple** (Y5; ☺ 8am-5pm) is an enormous reclining effigy of Sakyamuni that is well worth the 15-minute walk from the entrance gate. The Buddha weighs 54 tonnes, is 5.3m from elbow to toe and apparently enslaved 7000 people in its casting during 1321. Above Buddha are the characters *zìzài dàdé,* meaning 'great accomplishment comes from being at ease'. He seems to be taking it literally but, just in case, emperors have given him a number of pairs of gargantuan shoes should he decide to take a stroll. With lotus ponds and the Western Hills in the backdrop, the temple setting is stunning.

BEIJING BOTANICAL GARDENS INFORMATION

- ✉ northwest Beijing
- 💲 Y5/2.5
- ☺ 6am-7pm high season, 7am-5pm low season
- Ⓜ Wudaokou, then 30min taxi ride
- ♿ good

Sculpture in the Botanical Gardens

Stroll through Fragrant Hills Park

RED GATE GALLERY 红门画廊 (4, G6)

Beneath the giant wooden rafters of the ancient Dongbianmen Watchtower, in a room cooled by vast slate floors, hangs an array of avant-garde art. Established by an Australian art historian, Red Gate Gallery displays Beijing's most innovative and electric modern art. After years of prohibitive restrictions that pushed contemporary work into the corner, the gallery's 15 resident artists are once again stretching their paintbrushes, views and ideas in addressing modern-day issues.

INFORMATION

- ☎ 6525 1005
- ▯ www.redgategallery.com
- ✉ levels 1 & 4, Dongbianmen
- $ free
- ☺ 10am-5pm
- ⓘ information sheets at the door
- Ⓜ Beijingzhan-Beijing Railway Station

With painting, sculpture, papercutting, photography, performance art, lithographs, silkscreen printing and mixed media, the contrast of the modern work in an ancient setting is dramatic, to say the least. With around eight different shows each year, you might also find travelling exhibitions from other parts of China and abroad.

See the work of China's leading young artists at the Red Gate Gallery

DID YOU SEE *THAT*?

It's probably not the first thing you'll think about if you are coming to Beijing, but performance art is taking off here in a big way. Besides locals, artists from all over China home in on Beijing when it's time to launch their thought-provoking spectacles. You could encounter it anywhere and should be prepared. Recently, poet Ye Fu spent a month living in a giant bird's nest looking over the city so he could feel the 'real' Beijing. Broadcast live on the Web, thousands watched Ye's every twitch and wink. Beijinger Xiao Yu caused international headlines when he exhibited a foetus's head grafted on to a seagull's body at the Bern Museum of Art, prompting an investigation by the Bern district attorney's office. But not all are so outrageous. Some dial it back a bit, like artist Han Bing who, in homage to his native village, can be seen in the streets of Beijing walking a head of leafy green cabbage on a leash.

Sights & Activities

MUSEUMS

Ancient Coin Museum
古代钱币展览馆 (4, C1)

The silver and gold coins and intricate paper money displayed are absolutely gorgeous, but the museum suffers for lack of English captions. However, you can also go upstairs for views across the city, as well as to the Beijing East Gallery (p31). Outside you can browse through the ancient-coin market.

☎ 6201 8073 ✉ Deshengmen Watchtower (at junction where Deshengmenwai Dajie turns into Deshengmennei Dajie) 💲 Y10 🕑 9am-4pm Tue-Sun 🚌 5 or 44

Ancient Observatory
古观象台 (4, G5)

Ming and Qing emperors relied heavily on the predictions of astrologers to plan their military moves. This observatory was built in 1437 and laden with cutting-edge instruments to facilitate their work. These dragon-festooned instruments are now on the rooftop, set against a modern skyline of cranes, high-rises and satellite dishes. Exhibition

Ancient Observatory

halls in the courtyard introduce different Chinese astrologers.

☎ 6512 8923 ✉ Jianguomen Beidajie, near Jianguomennei Dajie 💲 Y10/5 🕑 9-11.30am & 1-4pm Tue-Sun Ⓜ Jianguomen

Beijing Art Gallery of Imperial City
皇城艺术馆 (7, B5)

This recently opened museum is bright, modern, spacious and the place to come for a peek into the architecture and design tastes of old Beijing. Keep an eye out for their wonderful temporary exhibits.

Subjects can range from Qing carvings to imperial furniture.

☎ 8511 5114 ✉ 9 Changpu Heyan 💲 Y20/10 🕑 9am-4.30pm Ⓜ Tiananmen Dong 🦽 good

Beijing Art Museum
北京艺术博物馆 (8, D3)

It's got an impressive collection of lacquers, porcelain and embroidery but the standout exhibit is a vast collection of Buddhist figures, including some exotic Tantric pieces. Travellers frustrated with the often mystifying

THE UGLY SIDE OF PROGRESS

Go to the halls of any mainstream museum in Beijing and you'll see the wildlife and flowers of Chinese masters like Qi Baishi. But step into any of the city's modern art galleries and you'll see a whole generation of emboldened artists tackling themes like social change and the Cultural Revolution. Su Xin Ping's work is inspired by socialist realism, but, rather than glorifying the selfless worker, he depicts lonely, alienated, bewildered figures. Sculptor Liang Shuo's work focuses on the migrant workers who stream into the city looking for a better life only to fall between the cracks. Painter Cui Guotai's canvases are devoid of people, but choked with gutted factories, abandoned construction sites and speeding trains.

As one of the city's art lovers was overheard saying at a recent gallery opening: not always easy to look at, but always stimulating.

English labels at many of the city's museums will welcome the clear, thoughtful English captions. The museum is scattered amongst the halls of Wanshou Temple (p36).
☎ 6841 3380 ⊠ cnr Suzhou Jie & Xisanhuan Beilu $ Y30 (incl admission to Wanshou Temple) ☺ 9am-4.30pm Tue-Sun Ⓜ Gongzhufen, then bus 944

Beijing Songtangzhai Museum
北京松堂斋民间雕刻博物馆 (4, C6)
This cluttered, intimate museum is filled with 1000 wood and stone folk carvings from across China. The doorways, screens, panels and objects on display are carvings with traditional images depicting ancient legends. Some of the pieces are over 2000 years old. If you understand Chinese, the guides are top-notch and will show you around for free.
☎ 8316 4662 ⊠ 14 Liulichang Dongjie $ donation on your way out ☺ 9am-6pm Tue-Sun Ⓜ Hepingmen

China Cultural Heritage Bookstore
文化遗产书店 (4, C6)
This wonderful museum tells the story of Chinese writing, printing and book binding through photos, text and exhibits. It's also got what may be the best English captions in the whole city. Even non-bookworms will love this place. There's a Cathay Bookstore branch upstairs which sells Chinese-only books.
☎ 6303 1602 ⊠ 57 Liulichang Xijie $ free ☺ 9am-6pm Ⓜ Hepingmen

Imperial College
国子监 (4, E1)
Built by the grandson of Kublai Khan in 1306, this is where the emperor annually expounded the Confucian classics to an audience of thousands of kneeling students, professors and court officials. It's a lovely place to wander and there's a square temple in the middle of the grounds surrounded by a moat.
☎ 6406 2418 ⊠ 15 Guozijian Jie $ Y6 ☺ 9am-6pm Ⓜ Yonghegong-Lama Temple

Lu Xun Museum
鲁迅博物馆 (4, A3)
Lu Xun (1881–1936) is often regarded as the father of modern Chinese literature. He wrote in everyday language instead of the complex classical Chinese used by most writers of the day. Aligned with the communists, his novels examine the sometimes very painful realities of everyday people as they struggle through modern Chinese society. He is best known for *The True Story of Ah Q* and *Diary of a Madman*. You'll need to pick up the informative but slightly tedious audioguide (Y20, Y200 deposit) to make sense of the Chinese-only exhibits.
☎ 6615 6548 ⊠ 19 Gongmenkou Ertiao $ Y5/3 ☺ 9am-3.30pm Tue-Sun Ⓜ Fuchengmen

Military Museum
军事博物馆 (8, D4)
This mammoth museum displays 5000 years' worth of Middle Kingdom military might. Missiles, tanks and fighter planes are eyed up by statues of Mao and his buddies on the ground floor. There's some great exhibits on the upper levels, like 'Ancient Wars', which explains the development of Chinese military strategy. Other halls breathlessly glorify conflicts such as the Opium War. Each exhibit has bilingual English-Chinese explanations, except for those in the Hall of Resisting US Aggression and Aiding Korea, where they are conspicuously absent.
☎ 6686 6135 ⊠ 9 Fuxing Lu $ Y20/10 ☺ 8am-5.30pm Apr-Oct, 8am-5pm Nov-Mar Ⓜ Junshibowuguan-Military Museum

National Art Museum of China
中国美术馆 (4, E3)
Recently reopened after extensive renovations, this museum has a thrilling mix of contemporary Chinese and European paintings with frequent exhibitions of abstract art from abroad. You'll also find Chinese folk art and calligraphy. English explanations and literature are next to nonexistent in the exhibits but English audioguides are sometimes available for temporary shows.
☎ 6401 7076 ⊠ 1 Wusi Dajie $ adult/senior & student/child Y20/10/5 ☺ 9am-5pm Tue-Sun ☒ 103 or 111 ♿ good

National Aviation Museum
中国航空博物 (1, B2)
Dozens of planes are on display inside this gargantuan hillside museum. Still more aircraft are perched outside on the 'secret' runway, where

HÚTÒNGS

Squeezed between wide boulevards, high-rises and shopping centres lies the labyrinth of Beijing's vibrant *hútòngs* (alleyways). Each one is home to a mini-community with an ancient and often colourful past.

Hútòngs were generally given utilitarian names such as Jianchang (Arrow Factory) and Zaoshu (Date Tree), offering not-too-subtle hints as to the landmarks or trades you could find along them. Other *hútòngs* were named after their shape or size, such as Koudai (Pocket), referring to a dead-end *hútòng*, or Biandan (Bamboo Pole), referring to a long, narrow *hútòng*. The resulting difficulty was (and is) distinguishing between the many *hútòngs* with identical names – for example, there are 11 *hútòngs* named Biandan.

During the Cultural Revolution, many communities changed the names of their *hútòngs* to something with a more revolutionary ring to it, such as Miezi Hutong (Destroy the Capitalist Lane) or Hongxiaobing Hutong (Little Red Guard Lane).

Hútòngs are traditionally lined with *sìhéyuàn* (four-sided courtyard homes). Originally, the height of the *sìhéyuàn* walls, the size of the door and the shape of the door stones all told of the type of merchant, official or family that lived inside. Until recently, a *sìhéyuàn* could only be one storey; anything greater was considered presumptuous, as inhabitants would be able to look down on the emperor, should he happen by. Other rules have also relaxed over time, such as the required *hútòng* width (some have measured in at just 50cm wide) and direction (they once all ran east-west in accordance with feng shui).

As department stores and faceless high-rises clamour into town behind bulldozers and wrecking crews, it's difficult not to sigh with regret at the steady disappearance of Beijing's *hútòngs*. Families rooted here for countless generations are being packed up and moved to apartment compounds far from the centre. And yet, while we lament the loss of the unique charm of these old quarters, these families may welcome the chance to escape the dangerous coal heating, inadequate or nonexistent plumbing, and precarious wiring that remain prevalent in many *hútòngs*.

But the demise of the alleys are affecting more than their former residents. The amount of traffic and pollution that results from tearing down even a small *hútòng* community is just now being appreciated. But it's unlikely the clock will turn back: walk anywhere in the city these days and you won't have to go very far before seeing a courtyard home with a big, red-painted *chāi* (the character for demolish) on its wall.

Despite this woeful situation, there are still some *hútòngs* for you to wander around (see p38); in fact, if anything is going to save *hútòngs* from oblivion, it's the keen interest tourists have taken in them. On warm evenings, when families escape the heat of their *sìhéyuàn* and take to the *hútòng*, it is worth renting a bike and exploring old Beijing.

The mighty Military Museum (p28)

you can also climb aboard Mao's private plane (Y5). English captions (albeit some quite primitive ones) label most exhibits. The museum is a distant 60km north of downtown.

☎ 6178 4882 ✉ Xiaotangshan, Changping District $ Y40/20 ⏱ 8am-5pm 🚌 912 from Andingmen directly to museum (about 2hr)

National Museum of China
中国国家博物馆 (7, C6)

If your dream museum includes porcelain exhibits, orotund tributes to little-known Party members, and some truly frightening Hollywood wax celebrities, you'll find nirvana here. For everybody else, this museum is nonetheless worth a gander. The visiting exhibitions are varied and professional

and can range from modern Korean art to Aboriginal culture. The positively alarming Marilyn Monroe figure on the wax floor should be avoided at all costs.

☎ 6512 8901 ✉ Tiananmen Square (east side) $ Y30/15 ⏱ 8.30am-4.30pm Ⓜ Tiananmen Dong

Natural History Museum
自然博物馆 (6, A2)

This huge building is filled with fossils, stuffed animals and computer-animated dinosaurs that kids will love. For adults, there is a riveting human anatomy display on the top floor where you can see human cadavers and spliced genitalia. The tanks and jars are getting a bit murky but you can probably guess what you're looking at.

☎ 6702 4431 ✉ 126 Tianqiao Nandajie

$ Y30/15 ⏱ 8.30am-5pm Ⓜ Qianmen, then bus 20

Poly Art Museum
保利艺术博物馆 (4, G2)

This must-see museum is a feast for the senses. Ancient bronzes are showered with delicate white light as bells chime softly in the background. Indian music plays in the next room, where Buddha and Bodhisattva statues are illuminated by a single light each and appear to float in the dark. Many of the objects were originally looted by the West and only recently returned to China, bought up at international auctions by the state-owned conglomerate that established the museum.

☎ 6500 8117 ✉ 14 Dongzhimen Nandajie, inside Poly Plaza $ Y50/25 ⏱ 9.30am-4.30pm Tue, Thu & Sat, groups by appointment only Mon, Wed & Fri Ⓜ Dongsishitiao

Wangfujing Palaeolithic Museum
王府井古人类文化遗址博物馆 (4, E5)

This archaeological site displays artefacts, bone tools and fossils discovered during the construction of the Oriental Plaza. There are also skull casts of Peking Man and two frighteningly well-preserved 200-year-old bodies from a site in eastern Beijing. No English captions.

☎ 8518 6306 ✉ Basement, Oriental Plaza, 1 Dongchang'an Jie $ Y10/5 ⏱ 10am-4.30pm Mon-Fri, 10am-6.30pm Sat & Sun Ⓜ Wangfujing, exit A ♿ good

GALLERIES

Art Gallery of the China Millennium Monument
千年时间画廊 (8, D4)
In addition to a permanent collection of Oriental and Occidental art, the Gallery of Modern Art and the Multimedia Digital Art Gallery host touring exhibitions from around the globe.
☎ 6857 3281 ⌨ www .bj2000.org.cn ✉ north of 9a Fuxing Lu on Yuyuantan Nanlu ⑤ Y30/20 ⊙ 8.30am-6pm Ⓜ Junshibowuguan-Military Museum

Beijing East Gallery
艺森画廊 (4, C1)
Its exhibitions range from exciting modern Chinese art to abominably amateur Western-style paintings. Good or bad, this atmospheric, dimly lit space is set in an old watchtower and is worth a look. The Ancient Coin Museum (p27) is downstairs.
☎ 8201 4962 ✉ Deshengmen Watchtower (at junction where Deshengmenwai Dajie turns into Deshengmennei

Dajie) ⑤ free ⊙ 9am-5.30pm Tue-Sun Ⓜ 5 or 44

Beijing Tokyo Art Projects
北京东京艺术工程 (8, J1)
Set up in a former factory, this gallery specialises in showcasing Japanese, Chinese, Korean and other Asian artists. Count on there being one or two sprawling installations as well as challenging photography exhibits. This gallery is one of Factory 798's (p18) most stimulating spaces.
☎ 8457 3245 ⌨ www .tokyo-gallery.com ✉ Factory 798, cnr Jiuxianqiao Lu & Jiuxianqiao Beilu ⑤ free ⊙ 10am-6.30pm Tue-Sun 🚌 403

Courtyard Gallery
四合苑 (7, D3)
Avant-garde exhibitions from both home and abroad are nestled here next to the Forbidden City moat.
☎ 6526 8882 ⌨ www .courtyard-gallery.com ✉ 95 Donghuamen Dajie ⑤ free ⊙ 11am-7pm Tue-Sat, noon-7pm Sun

Ⓜ Tiananmen Dong, then bus 60

Creation Gallery
可创艺苑 (4, H4)
Opened and curated by the son of celebrated artist Li Keran, this gallery exhibits and sells paintings fresh off the easel. Exhibits change every two weeks so this is a good place to see what local painters are up to.
☎ 8561 7570 ⌨ www .creationgallery.com ✉ Ritan Donglu, northeast cnr of Ritan Park ⑤ free ⊙ 10am-7pm Ⓜ Yonganli, then bus 28 ♿ good

Kuaixue Hall
快雪堂 (4, C2)
Wang Da Guan's (1925–97) paintings reflected everyday life in early-20th-century Beijing and this gallery showcases some of his best work. The paintings are captivating for their detailed, sprawling scenes. One measures 14m and has a cast of thousands. You could stare at it for hours and keep seeing new things. However, here that's unlikely.

Photographic exhibition at the Courtyard Gallery

BARE-FOOT BELLE

According to the legend of the Bell Tower (p33), as the bell-maker cast the 42-tonne bell, his daughter plunged head first into the molten iron. He made a grab for her but only managed to hang onto her shoe as she slid into the furnace. Since then, the soft chime of the Ming-dynasty bell is said to sound like *xié*, the Chinese word for shoe.

Gift shop employees graft on to visitors the moment they walk in. You won't be able to contemplate anything for more than two seconds before being abruptly corralled with alarming verve towards the souvenirs.

✉ Beihai Park (north gate) $ free ⏲ 9am-4pm 🚌 118

Wan Fung Art Gallery
云峰画廊 (4, E5)

Set in a courtyard across from the Imperial Archives, this gallery exhibits contemporary art. Come in, have a cup of green tea and chat with the knowledgeable and enthusiastic staff.

☎ 6523 3320
🖳 www.wanfung.com.cn
✉ 136 Nanchizi Dajie

$ free ⏲ noon-6pm Mon, 10am-6pm Tue-Sun 🚇 Tiananmen Dong

Wenchang Gallery
文昌院 (2, C2)

If you've been exploring the Summer Palace and need a change of pace, slip into this tranquil gallery. There's an impressive collection of artefacts, many of which were looted during the Opium War and only recently returned from private European collections. Modelled on a Qing courtyard, the exhibits include carvings, bronze, intricate screens and pottery. Examples of Cixi's calligraphy are also prominently displayed.

☎ 6256 5886
✉ Kunminghu Lu, next to

Summer Palace east entrance $ Y20 ⏲ 8.30am-5pm 🚇 Wudaokou, then bus 331 or 726

White Space at 798
空白空间 (8, J1)

This stark, high-ceilinged space shows off some of the best modern Chinese art the capital has to offer.

☎ 8456 2054 🖳 www .alexanderochs-galleries .de ✉ Factory 798, cnr Jiuxianqiao Lu & Jiuxianqiao Beilu $ free ⏲ noon-6pm Tue-Sun 🚌 403

Xu Beihong Museum
徐悲鸿纪念馆 (4, B1)

Best remembered for his galloping horses, Xu Beihong (1895–1953) injected dynamism into Chinese painting and infused his work with Western techniques acquired on his extensive travels abroad. He's celebrated here in seven halls that display oils, gouache, pen and ink sketches and portraits.

☎ 6225 2042 ✉ 53 Xinjiekou Beidajie $ Y5/2 ⏲ 9am-4pm Tue-Sun 🚇 Jishuitan

The Wan Fung Art Gallery, in the courtyard of the Imperial Archives

HISTORICAL BUILDINGS & MONUMENTS

Beijing Exhibition Hall
北京展览馆 (8, E3)
Opened in 1954 to mark the fifth anniversary of the founding of the People's Republic of China, this hall is a monstrous cousin to Stalin's notorious 'seven sisters' buildings that dot the Moscow skyline. This one has Indian and Chinese flourishes that make it less drab than its Russian counterparts. It now hosts trade and professional conventions.
✉ Xizhimenwai Dajie
Ⓜ Xizhimen

Bell Tower
钟楼 (4, D1)
This tower was built in the late 1200s along the north-south axis of the imperial buildings. Scramble up the steep stone steps to see where bells once tolled on ceremonial occasions.
☎ 8403 6706 ✉ north end Dianmenwai Dajie, behind Drum Tower ⑤ Y15/8
⏰ 9am-5.30pm
Ⓜ Gulou, then bus 60

China Millennium Monument
中华世纪坛 (8, D4)
This gargantuan sundial is one of Beijing's most impressive modern structures. It supposedly turns once every 2.655 hours. There's a fantastic carved mural of 40 celebrated figures from China's cultural history inside. From the top of the dial are some great views across Beijing.
☎ 6852 7108
🖥 www.bj2000.org.cn

✉ 9a Fuxing Lu ⑤ adult/senior & student/child Y30/20/15 ⏰ 8am-6pm
Ⓜ Junshibowuguan-Military Museum

Dongbianmen
东南角楼 (4, G6)
This Ming-dynasty watchtower is punctured with 144 archers' windows and was once a part of the city wall. You can hunt down 'I was here' graffiti left by the international troops of the Allied Forces that overwhelmed the tower during the Boxer Rebellion. The impressive interior is home to a slightly less-impressive exhibition of the area's history.
☎ 6522 6008 ✉ 3rd fl, Dongbianmen, Jianguomen Beidajie ⑤ Y10/5
⏰ 9am-5pm Tue-Sun
Ⓜ Beijingzhan-Beijing Railway Station

Drum Tower
鼓楼 (4, D1)
Originally built in 1273 to mark the centre of the Mongol capital of Dadu, the tower has been repeatedly destroyed and rebuilt. The drums were once beaten to mark the hours of the day. Today, only one original instrument remains. The

drum-beating performances are worth the steep 69-step climb to the top.
☎ 8403 6706
✉ Gulou Dongdajie
⑤ Y20/10 ⏰ 9am-5.30pm, drum performances every half hr 9-11.30am & 1.30-5.30pm summer
Ⓜ Gulou, then bus 60

Great Hall of the People
人民大会堂 (7, A6)
Home of the National People's Congress, this intimidating colossus sprawls along the west flank of Tiananmen and is open to the public when the Congress is not sitting. Slip on the plastic booties provided and shuffle through the primly decorated halls and rooms named after Chinese provinces and regions.
☎ 6309 6668
✉ Tiananmen Square (western side) ⑤ Y30/15, compulsory bag check Y2-5
⏰ 8am-3pm
Ⓜ Tiananmen Xi

Imperial Archives
皇史宬 (4, E5)
This well-preserved courtyard building is the former repository for imperial records, decrees and encyclopaedic works. The Jade Book records the imperial

---

FOOT FETISH
It's said they stomped out of Sichuan, but now they're all the rage in Beijing. Foot massage parlours (p60) are as ubiquitous as fast-food joints and are replacing everything from tea breaks to business lunches. To respect yin and yang, men massage women's feet, and women massage men's. Those in the know say massaging the right place on the foot can cure you of whatever ails you in the rest of your body, from backaches to headaches. Whatever the truth, you'll walk out afterwards feeling like you're floating on a cloud.

family tree – not the easiest task considering the level of extramarital activity within the Forbidden City. The book weighs 150kg and is 1m thick. Look through the middle doors and you'll see the large gold boxes festooned with dragons where the documents were kept.

✉ 136 Nanchizi Dajie
$ free ☀ 9am-7pm
Ⓜ Tiananmen Dong

Monument to the People's Heroes
人民英雄纪念碑 (7, B6)

In the centre of Tiananmen Square, this monument stands on the site of the original Outer Palace Gate. Built in 1958, its 36m granite obelisk sports Mao Zedong and Zhou Enlai's calligraphy and is carved with scenes of key revolutionary events such as the Chinese destroying opium in the 19th century. Mao's contribution reads

'Eternal Glory to the People's Heroes'.

✉ Tiananmen Square
Ⓜ Tiananmen Dong
♿ excellent

Qianmen
前门 (6, A1)

Made up of what are now two separate structures (Zhengyang to the north, Arrow Tower to the south), this 15th-century gate once divided the ancient Inner City and the outer suburban zone. The city walls have long since disappeared, however, the majestic and unyielding Qianmen has become a compass point in Beijing. There's an incredible exhibit of old city photos in Zhengyang and the views from the top are fantastic.

☎ 6522 9384 ✉ junction of Qianmenxi Dajie & Qianmendong Dajie $ free to walk through; Zhengyang Gate Y10/5 ☀ 8.30am-4.30pm Ⓜ Qianmen

Silver Ingot Bridge
银锭桥 (4, D2)

Dividing Qianhai and Houhai Lakes is this picturesque, white marble bridge, although it has suffered a pounding from feet and carts over the past couple of centuries. It was last rebuilt in 1984.

✉ Houhai & Qianhai Lakes
🚌 5 or 118 ♿ good

Zhengyici Theatre
正乙祠剧场 (4, C6)

Ornate and colourful, this opera house was originally a Ming temple. It was reconstructed as a theatre during the Qing dynasty. It was undergoing a facelift at the time of writing but by early 2006 you should be able to look inside during the day and take in one of its flamboyant operas at night (p92).

☎ 8315 1649
✉ 220 Qianmen Xiheyan Jie
Ⓜ Hepingmen

Boat traffic floating under the Silver Ingot Bridge

PLACES OF WORSHIP

Confucius Temple
孔庙 (4, F1)

Following Qufu (the birthplace of the master), this is the second-largest Confucian temple in China. With ancient cypresses and a forest of steles (stretching 630,000 characters across 189 2.4m tablets) it's typically been a peaceful but sadly neglected site. Happily, it was undergoing staggered renovations at the time of writing and should be all spruced up by mid-2006.

☎ 8401 1977
✉ 13 Guozijian Jie ⑤ Y10/3
🕑 8.30am-5pm Ⓜ Yonghegong-Lama Temple

Fayuan Temple
法源寺 (8, E5)

Still a hive of activity, this temple was built in the 7th century and is now home to the China Buddhism College. Though still open to the public, this temple was undergoing some heavy-duty renovations at the time of writing. However, in spite of the odd sound of drills mixed with Buddhist chants, life here goes on as usual with the student monks in yellow robes playing table tennis and gossiping in the courtyards. Go to the back hall to see the unusual copper Buddha seated on a delicate 1000-petal lotus flower. The construction workers should be gone by summer 2006.

☎ 6353 3966 ✉ 7 Fayuansi Qianjie ⑤ Y5
🕑 8.30-11.30am & 1.30-3.30pm Thu-Tue Ⓜ Changchunjie, then bus 61

Great Bell Temple
大钟寺 (8, D2)

Weighing in at 46.5 tonnes, this is China's biggest bell. When cast in 1406, a special canal had to be built and allowed to freeze in order to transport the behemoth. The bell is decorated with more than 100 kinds of Buddhist sutras and Sanskrit incantations and over 230,000 Chinese characters. Climb the rickety steps and throw a coin through the top of the bell for good luck. There are also exhibitions here on bell casting, the history of bell making and visiting bell exhibitions from abroad.

☎ 6225 1843 ✉ 31a Beisanhuan Xilu ⑤ Y10/3
🕑 8.30am-4.30pm 🚌 361, 367 or 422

Guangji Temple
广济寺 (4, B3)

This simple temple has a history of over 800 years and is the current headquarters of the Chinese Buddhist Association. Incense and Buddhist chants waft through the shaded courtyard making this a lovely place to chill out in during the summer.

☎ 6616 0907 ✉ cnr Fuchengmennei Dajie & Xisi Beidajie ⑤ free 🕑 7.30am-

4.30pm Ⓜ Fuchengmen, then bus 102 or 103

Niujie Mosque
牛街礼拜寺 (8, E5)

Closed indefinitely for renovations at the time of writing, this ornate mosque dates back to the 10th century and is a fascinating blend of Muslim and Chinese styles. It's the largest of about 40 mosques around town.

☎ 6353 2564 ✉ 88 Niu Jie ⑤ Y10, Muslims free
🕑 8am-sunset Ⓜ Changchunjie, then bus 61

North Cathedral
北堂 (4, C3)

Built in 1887, this church suffered the brutalities of the Cultural Revolution and even had a stint as a factory warehouse. Outside, the entrance is guarded by two stone lions and flanked by two small Chinese pavilions. Latin and Chinese masses are held each morning.

☎ 6617 5198 ✉ Xishiku Dajie ⑤ free Ⓜ Fuchengmen, then bus 103; or Xidan, then bus 47

St Joseph's Church
东堂 (4, E4)

Having been burned and demolished umpteen times,

OLYMPIC MANIA

Beijing's Olympic machine is ripping up ground for new subway lines, building a giant complex in the north, repaving and widening roads… the list is endless. But besides coming across renovation crews at major tourist sites, the construction is unlikely to inconvenience the average subway-taking tourist. The city seems to be winning the race against the giant Olympic countdown clock beside Tiananmen Square. In fact, things are going so well, the Olympic committee has had to tell the city to slow down.

the 'East Cathedral' is fully repaired and open for business. The front courtyard is a favourite hangout for teenage skateboarders and exhausted shoppers.

✉ 74 Wangfujing Dajie 💲 free ⏰ 6.30-8am Mon-Sat, 9-10.30am Sun Ⓜ Wangfujing

St Michael's Catholic Church
东交民巷教堂 (4, E6)
There are daily masses held at this twin-spired, peaceful church. It's not much of a sight, but a pleasant place for worshippers to come together.
✉ Dongjiaomin Xiang 💲 free ⏰ Latin Mass 7am Sat & Sun Ⓜ Wangfujing, then bus 103 or 104

South Cathedral
南堂 (4, B6)
This church is the seat of the Catholic Diocese of Beijing. Rouse yourself for the early morning masses if you can. Watching dozens of elderly worshippers arrive and sing the whole mass in Latin as the priest blesses the sacraments is nothing short of stirring.
✉ northeast cnr Xuanwumen Dongdajie & Xuanwemennei Dajie 💲 free ⏰ Latin Mass 6am Sun-Fri, English Mass 10am Sun Ⓜ Xuanwumen

Wanshou Temple
万寿寺 (8, D3)
Originally consecrated for the storage of Buddhist texts, this is where the imperial gang would take a tea break en route to the Summer Palace. The Great Bell also originally hung here before being moved to the Great Bell Temple in the 18th century. Wanshou was destroyed by a fire in 1937 before being rebuilt in 1949 and reopened as a school. It did a stint as an army barracks in the '60s and '70s and was later renovated and opened to the public. Part of it now houses the Beijing Art Museum (p27).
☎ 6841 3380 ✉ cnr Suzhou Jie & Xisanhuan Beilu 💲 Y30 (incl admission to Beijing Art Museum) ⏰ 9am-4.30pm Tue-Sun Ⓜ Gongzhufen, then bus 944

JUMP RIGHT ON
You might not be used to seeing adults on jungle-gym equipment but in Beijing it's as common as kites. Get up close to the equipment and you'll see an unusual assortment of rotating wheels and moving panels. The goal is not to be the strongest or the fastest but to circulate the *qì* (energy). To try for yourself head to Longtan Park (opposite), where the machines have English instructions.

Wen Tianxiang Temple
文天祥祠 (4, E2)
This tiny, serene family shrine is dedicated to Southern Song poet Wen Tianxiang (1236–83), who was captured by the Mongols and incarcerated in Beijing. English captions explain his dramatic escape. In the grounds stands an ancient jujube tree, supposedly cultivated by Wen himself.
☎ 6401 4968 ✉ 63 Fuxue Hutong 💲 Y5/3 ⏰ 9am-5pm Tue-Sun Ⓜ Andingmen, then bus 108

Exterior of the Roman Catholic South Cathedral

PARKS & PUBLIC SPACES

Ditan Park (Temple of Earth)
地坛公园 (8, G3)

At the opposite end of the cosmos and the compass to the Temple of Heaven, Ditan Park was the site of imperial sacrifices to the Earth God. The altar is square shaped, symbolising the earth. It's not as spectacular as its southerly sister, except during the Chinese New Year temple fair and the sparkling Ice Festival in winter.

☎ 6421 4657 ✉ Andingmenwai Dajie 💲 Y1 ⏱ 9am-9pm Ⓜ Yonghegong-Lama Temple ♿ good

Grand View Garden
大观园公园 (8, E6)

Opened in 1988, this beautiful park was designed to look like the family gardens in the classic Chinese novel *Dream of the Red Mansion* by Cao Zueqin. They won't make much sense to you if you haven't read the book, but signs throughout the park mark the sites of key events in the sprawling love story/family drama. Cao fans will love it.

☎ 6354 4994 ✉ 12 Nancaiyuan Jie 💲 Y30/23 ⏱ 9am-4pm 🚌 59 ♿ good

Jingshan Park
景山公园 (4, D3)

Offering a gorgeous view over the golden rooftops of the Forbidden City and beyond, the hill in the centre of this park was created from the earth excavated to construct the palace moat. The hill protects the palace from the evil spirits (and dust storms) of the north. This beautiful and calm park is a great place to see Beijing's elderly exercising and stretching their legs up around their ears. In the east of the park is a locust tree where the last Ming emperor hanged himself as rebels swarmed at the city walls.

☎ 6403 3225 ✉ Jingshan Qianjie 💲 Y2 ⏱ 6am-10pm Ⓜ Tiananmen Xi, then bus 5 ♿ around the park but not up the hill

Longtan Park
龙潭公园 (8, G5)

Built in 1952, this park has activities tucked away in every corner. In the northeast there's outdoor gym equipment, ping-pong tables and a new, 500m track joggers will love. Elsewhere there's **rock climbing** (Y20; ⏱ 9am-5pm), **paddleboat rental** (double per hr Y50, deposit Y200) or the **kiddie's playground** (Y5; ⏱ 8am-8pm). Come in autumn to see the explosion of lotuses in the southeastern pond.

✉ Longtan Lu 💲 Y2 ⏱ 6am-10pm Ⓜ Beijingzhan-Beijing Railway Station, then bus 63 ♿ good

Old Summer Palace
圆明园 (8, C1)

In the 18th century Emperor Qianlong decided it might be nice to have a European palace, so he asked some Jesuits to design one for him. They went all out with elaborate fountains and baroque statuary. Unfortunately, during the Second Opium War it was pummelled to bits. All that remains is a melancholic array of broken columns and marble chunks. Photographs and models of the original buildings let you compare the before and after.

☎ 6262 8501 ✉ 28 Qinghua Xilu 💲 park Y10, palace ruins Y15 ⏱ 7am-7pm Ⓜ Wudaokou, then bus 375 or 726 ♿ park good, ruins OK

Stroll through peaceful Jingshan Park

WHERE DID YOU SAY THAT WAS?

The Beijing municipality covers an area of 16,800 sq km so it can be a real challenge to find where you are going. Many of Beijing's buildings are unnumbered, and addresses are usually given as directions such as 'down the alley across from the hotel'. On top of that, street names change at each major intersection, usually adding a direction or point of reference. Always try and have your destination written out in Chinese so you can show it to the locals and they can point you in the right direction.

Ritan Park

日坛公园 (4, H4)

Built in 1530 as an altar for ritual sacrifice to the sun, this lovely pine-filled park is a peaceful diversion. Head to the altar to watch the kite flyers. You're as likely to see businessmen struggling with big colourful kites as you are gaggles of laughing children.

☎ 6592 5576 ✉ Ritan Lu
$ Y1/0.50 ☼ 6am-9pm
Ⓜ Yonganli, then bus 28, then bus 29 ♿ good

Workers' Cultural Palace

劳动人民文化宫 (4, D5)

This park's name isn't much of a lure but the temple complex inside definitely is. Ming and Qing emperors once gathered here to worship ancestors and the buildings are striking. Unfortunately, the public can't enter the temples except during exhibitions.

☎ 6525 2189
✉ Dongchang'an Jie $ Y2
☼ 6am-9pm Ⓜ Tiananmen Dong

Yuyuantan Park

玉渊潭公园 (8, D4)

Shady trees, benches, wide paths and big lakes make this a very pretty park to get lost in. You can also rent paddleboats or pedal-/battery-powered boats (Y20/30 per hour). The deluxe Donald Duck model will set you back about Y40.

☎ 6256 5886 ✉ Xisanhuan Zhonglu $ Y2/1
☼ 6am-10pm Ⓜ Junshibowuguan-Military Museum
♿ good

Zhongshan Park

中山堂 (7, B5)

Sitting to the west of the Gate of Heavenly Peace and hedging up against the moat of the Forbidden City, this is a small oasis away from the crowds. An emperor once offered sacrifices to the God of Land and the God of Five Grains here. The square altar is symmetrical to the Altar of Ancestors in the Workers' Cultural Palace to the east. The park is a tribute to Sun Yatsen (1866–1925) and the hall behind the altar is dedicated to his life, with pictures, clothes and other personal effects (Y2).

☎ 6605 4594
✉ Xichang'an Jie $ Y3, incl private gardens Y5 ☼ 6am-10pm Ⓜ Tiananmen Xi
♿ OK

HÚTÒNGS

According to an old Beijing saying, there are 360 famous *hútòngs* (alleyways) in the city and as many nameless *hútòngs* as hairs on a cow. Well, the cow appears to have creeping alopecia as the *hútòngs* steadily disappear, replaced with boulevards and apartment blocks. See them while you can. For more on *hútòngs,* see p29.

Dajingchang Hutong

大经厂胡同 (4, E1)

Named after a printing factory that produced Buddhist scriptures, this narrow and twisting *hútòng* gives you a glimpse at some open courtyard gardens.

✉ north off Gulou Dongdajie Ⓜ Andingmen, then bus 104 ♿ good

Dongsi Batiao

东四八条 (4, F2)

Dating back to the Ming dynasty, this *hútòng* was once home to Mei Lanfang, a Beijing opera star, and later held the offices of Tian Han, composer of China's national anthem.

✉ south of Dongsishitiao Lu
🚍 113, 115 or 118 ♿ good

Mao'er Hutong

帽儿胡同 (4, D2)

This *hútòng* is usually flooded with rickshaw tours but is packed with history. No 45 was a military prefecture during the Qin dynasty, and Feng Guozhang, a northern warlord, once lived in No 13. Empress Wan Rong, the last emperor's wife, was born and raised along here. At the eastern end, Nanluogu Xiang

Xiaojiao Hutong: where the popular girls lived

is a lively *hútòng* filled with hole-in-the-wall craft shops and Western-style cafés.
✉ west off Nanluogu Xiang Ⓜ Andingmen, then bus 108 ♿ good

Qianliang Hutong
钱粮胡同 (4, E3)
This is where *qiánliáng* (coins) were stored during the Ming dynasty. There are still many old, tile-roofed buildings along this wide *hútòng*.
✉ btwn Meishuguan Houjie & Dongsi Nandajie Ⓜ Dongdan, then bus 101 ♿ good

Wudaoying Hutong
五道营胡同 (4, E1)
Wudaoying, or Five Soldiers' Way, refers to the five ways of martial arts. This residential *hútòng* was the home of Ming-dynasty martial-arts soldiers. Come on a summer evening and see residents out chatting, washing their hair and ogling newborns.

✉ south of Andingmen Dongdajie Ⓜ Yonghegong-Lama Temple ♿ good

Xiaojiao Hutong
晓教胡同 (4, E3)
This leafy *hútòng* is only about 100m long. As women with bound feet were once considered beautiful, Xiaojiao (little feet) refers to the young girls who lived here and were popular with the emperor. Just north, Dajiao (big feet) is where the less-popular girls lived.
✉ east off Dong-huangchenggen Beijie 🚌 58 or 108 ♿ good

Yuge Sixiang
玉阁四巷 (4, D1)
Named after a temple that was located around here, this *hútòng* is extremely narrow (keep your fingers crossed that you don't have to pass any cyclists).
✉ east of Jiugulou Dajie Ⓜ Gulou Dajie ♿ OK

FORMER RESIDENCES

Guo Moruo
郭沫若纪念馆 (4, C2)
A politically correct writer despite his elite roots, Guo Moruo (1892–1978) was awarded the Stalin Peace Prize in 1951 and survived the Cultural Revolution without a scratch. Guo's garden home contains his many books and manuscripts. Outside his home is a large Spirit Wall that was intended to keep out evil ghouls. (Chinese ghosts can only travel in straight lines.)
☎ 6612 5392 ✉ 18 Qianhai Xijie 💲 Y10/5 ⏱ 9am-4.30pm Tue-Sun, closed winter 🚌 13 or 118

Lao She
老舍纪念馆 (4, E4)
Author of *Rickshaw Boy* and *Tea House* and a lecturer at London's School of Oriental and African Studies, Lao She (1899–1966) was one of Beijing's most famous 20th-century writers. Severely persecuted during the Cultural Revolution, he committed suicide by drowning himself in a lake. On display in this little courtyard museum are first editions, personal belongings and photos, including a disturbing shot of his humiliation at the hands of the Red Guards on the eve of his death. Captions are in Chinese only but an English audioguide is available for Y5.
☎ 6559 9218 ✉ 19 Fengfu Hutong, off Dengshikou Xijie 💲 Y10/5 ⏱ 9am-4pm Tue-Sun Ⓜ Wangfujing, then bus 2 or 103

ONE-CHILD WONDER

The Communist Party instituted its One-Child Policy after 1979 statistics showed that soon there wouldn't be enough food to go around. Now it's struggling with a glitch. It seems some cagey couples have turned to fertility drugs to increase their chances of multiple births as having twins or triplets is not penalised by the government. It remains to be seen if doctors heed government directives to avoid treating such couples.

Mao Dun

茅盾故居 (4, E2)

Born in 1896, Mao Dun was alternately a journalist and writer and helped found the League of Left Wing Writers in 1930. When the Communists took power, he was Mao Zedong's secretary and culture minister until 1964 when he became another casualty of the Cultural Revolution. However, he was later rehabilitated and went on to work as an editor and writer until his death in 1981. There are no English captions but black-and-white photos and his personal effects are on display.

☎ 6404 0520 ✉ 13 Yuanensi Hutong $ Y5 🕙 9am-4pm Tue, Thu, Sat & Sun 🚌 104 or 118

Mei Lanfang

梅兰芳纪念馆 (4, C2)

An immensely popular actor of female roles, Mei Lanfang (1894–1961) popularised Beijing opera in the West and is even said to have influenced a certain Mr Chaplin. Mei Lanfang's courtyard home is stuffed to the gills with costumes, furniture and old opera programmes. Videos of his opera performances are shown in the east hall.

☎ 6618 0351 ✉ 9 Huguosi Jie $ Y10/5 🕙 9am-4pm Tue-Sun 🚌 55

Song Qingling

宋庆龄故居 (4, C1)

Venerated by the Chinese as the wife of Sun Yatsen, Madam Song remained in communist China while her wayward sister married Chiang Kai-shek and fled to Taiwan. From 1963 until her death in 1981, Madam lived in this mansion-like courtyard home with vast gardens. Captions say the house is evidence of her 'simple and thrifty life'. On display are personal items, clothing, books and pictures, all of which have good English captions.

☎ 6404 4205 ✉ 46 Beiheyan Lu $ Y20/5 🕙 9am-5.30pm May-Oct, 9am-4.30pm Nov-Apr, closed Mon Ⓜ Jishuitan

Courtyard of the Former Residence of Lao She (p39)

MARKETS

Dazhalan
大栅栏街 (6, A1)
Crammed full of silk outlets, tea shops, department stores and food, medicine and clothing specialists, this market is a happy kind of chaos. Many of Beijing's oldest shops can be found here. Have a look at Ruifuxiang (p64), with its green archway and columns. The eastern end of Dazhalan is for pedestrians only. Head north up the narrow alleys for market-stall mania.
✉ off Qianmen Dajie
$ free Ⓜ Qianmen ♿ OK

Donghuamen Night Market
东花门夜市 (4, E4)
Grasshoppers, kidneys, chicken hearts, smelly tofu, mystery meat on kebabs, yak butter and cheese – you may not want to buy lunch here but you'll definitely get an eyeful.
✉ Donghumen Dajie
$ free Ⓨ 5.30-10.30pm Ⓜ Wangfujing, then bus 101 ♿ OK

Panjiayuan Market
潘家园市场 (8, H6)
The 'Dirt' Market is a fantastic place to browse through Beijing's past, from antique furniture to Cultural Revolution memorabilia. Amongst its 50,000 daily visitors are some of China's best barterers, whose tactics can be a sight in themselves. The best time to come is the weekend when all 3000 vendors are out in full force. The earlier you come the better your chance to snatch up some spectacular finds.
☎ 6775 2403 ✉ Panjiayuan Lu, off Dongsanhuan Nanlu $ free Ⓨ sunrise-3pm Sat & Sun Ⓜ Guomao, then bus 28 ♿ OK

QUIRKY BEIJING

Beijing Aquarium
北京海洋馆 (8, D3)
How would you like to walk through a lush African rainforest and see piranhas? What about taking a tunnel escalator as giant turtles swim beside you? This is the biggest indoor aquarium in the world and it's home to every sort of marine life you can think of, from sharks and whales to coral reef habitats.
☎ 6833 8742 ✉ 18b Gaoliangqiao Xiejie, or through zoo on Xizhimenwai Dajie $ Y100/50 Ⓨ 9am-5.30pm mid-Apr–mid-Oct, 9am-5pm mid-Oct–mid-Apr Ⓜ Xizhimen, then bus 105

Beijing Gongti Bowling Centre
北京工体保龄球中心 (5, A1)
Something about bowling makes it phenomenally popular with Beijingers. On a Friday or Saturday night an invitation to bowling is just as likely as an invitation to a nightclub. This alley is one of the best, with 100 lanes and a young, friendly staff.
☎ 6552 1446 ✉ 2nd fl, Workers' Stadium (west entrance), Gongrentiyuchang Xilu $ Y100-150, shoes Y5 Ⓨ 8am-3am 🚌 118

Mao Zedong Mausoleum
毛主席纪念堂 (4, D6)
This historical giant has been kept pickled and on display since his death in 1976. Thousands of Chinese mourners gather every day, bowing to his statue and leaving flowers before going in to pay their respects. Join the queues to catch a glimpse.

A gastronomic adventure: Donghuamen Night Market

Pay your respects to Mao Zedong (p41)

☎ 6513 2277 ✉ Tiananmen Square $ free, compulsory bag check Y5, cameras Y5 ⏲ 8.30-11.30am Mon-Fri, 1.30-4.30pm Mon, Wed & Fri Ⓜ Qianmen ♿ good

Pedal Boats
(8, G5; 8, D4)
While most Westerners wouldn't consider a plastic boat to be a pretty pond ornament, they're all the rage in Beijing. In most parks around town you can pedal around the lake in one of these Flintstone-reminiscent vehicles. You can float in a giant duck, too.
✉ Longtan Park, Yuyuantan Park ⏲ 9.30am-4.30pm $ per hr Y20-40, deposit Y100-200

Underground City
地下城 (6, B1)
With a Soviet invasion looming and nuclear war on his mind, Mao decided in 1969 that the future of Beijing lay underground. Museum guides say 300,000 of Beijing's then five million residents began burrowing an underground city by hand.

A portion of this labyrinth is now open. Signposts to the Forbidden City and chambers labelled 'cinema' and 'hospital' give you an idea of the enormity of the project. Free 20-minute tours by surly fatigue-clad guides are in Chinese only.
✉ btwn 62 & 64 Xidamochang Jie, off Qianmen Dajie $ Y20/10 ⏲ 8.30am-5.30pm Ⓜ Qianmen

BEIJING FOR CHILDREN

Squeals of 'Another temple?' and 'Can we go yet?' are many a family's soundtrack as they shepherd their kids from Forbidden City to the Temple of Heaven. Not surprisingly, it's not the sights but everyday Beijing that seems to keep travelling kids here happy. The beasties hanging off skewers at the Donghuamen Night Market (p41) or the sky awash with kites in Tiananmen Square or one of the city's many parks can thrill kids in a way yet

another Bodhisattva can't. There are also pedal boats for rent at most lakes and *qì*-promoting jungle gyms (p36) all over the city. If that doesn't do the trick, the capital has plenty of child-oriented activities to keep kids occupied for hours.

Beijing Amusement Park
北京游乐园 (6, C3)
This vintage park is next door to family-friendly Longtan Park. If your kids were bored with the Temple of Heaven, send them for a thrill on the looping roller coaster or to enjoy the views from the Ferris wheel.
☎ 6711 1155 ✉ 1 Zuo'anmenwai Dajie $ Y90/60 ⏲ 8.30am-5.30pm Ⓜ Chongwenmen, then bus 8

Blue Zoo Beijing
富国海底世界 (5, A3)
Children rule at this always-packed aquarium. They run from tank to tank and whoop at ear-shattering decibels at the sight of eels, seahorses and glowing fish. The marine tunnel is Asia's longest and

the half-hour shark feedings (10am and 2.30pm) are always a favourite. There are detailed English captions on each tank explaining its inhabitants' behaviour, mating rituals and environment.
☎ 6591 3397, ext 1560 🖳 www.blue-zoo .com ✉ Workers' Stadium (south entrance), Gongrentiyuchang Nanlu 💲 Y75/50, over 80yr free ⏲ 8am-8pm (last ticket sold 6pm) Ⓜ Donsishitiao, then bus 118

China Puppet Theatre
中国木偶剧院 (8, F2)
This theatre regularly casts a spell over little (and not-so-little) ones with all kinds of colourful puppets. There are several performances every day that showcase everything from hand puppets to life-sized marionettes. Check listings or call for a schedule.
☎ 6425 4798 ✉ A1 Anhua Xili Ⓜ Gulou, then bus 380

ExploraScience
索尼探梦 (4, E5)
Perfect for inquisitive kids, this Sony-sponsored, interactive science exhibition

HONEY, I BROUGHT THE KIDS
With neighbours, grandparents and aunts to mind the little ones, babysitting agencies are rare in Beijing. Nevertheless, you shouldn't have too much trouble finding a sitter. Most large hotels have English-speaking babysitters available. Smaller hotels may not have an in-house service but should be able to offer you a personal recommendation. Or during the day, Fundazzle (below) can assign a personal child minder if you book in advance.

is full of gadgets, activities and camera-toting parents snapping photos of their little Einsteins.
☎ 8518 2255 🖳 www .explorascience.com.cn ✉ 1st fl, Oriental Plaza, 1 Dongchang'an Jie 💲 Y30/20 ⏲ 9.30am-5.30pm Mon-Fri, 10am-7pm Sat & Sun, closed 2nd Mon & Tue of every month Ⓜ Wangfujing ♿ good

Fundazzle
翻斗乐 (5, B3)
This indoor jungle gym will keep active tykes occupied on a rainy day. Kids need to bring socks but can leave their folks at home.
☎ 6501 6655 ✉ Workers' Stadium (south entrance),

Gongrentiyuchang Nanlu 💲 kids/parents per 2hr Y30/15, babysitting per hr Y30 (book in advance) ⏲ 9am-5.30pm Mon-Fri, 9am-7pm Sat, Sun & holidays Ⓜ Yonganli, then bus 28 🚌 118

Le Cool
国贸溜冰场 (4, J5)
Surrounded by shops that parents love, this popular ice rink is tops. It's got skating and hockey lessons for all levels. Gloves are obligatory so bring some along with you.
☎ 6505 5776 ✉ Basement 2, China World Trade Centre, 1 Jianguomenwai Dajie 💲 per 90min Y30-50 ⏲ 10am-10pm Ⓜ Guomao

Le Cool: for kids of all ages

Trips & Tours

WALKING TOURS
'Mazing Hútòngs

As long as you can negotiate one (very small) set of stairs, this tour is fantastic on a bike. Whether by foot or pedal, a compass will be handy in this labyrinth. Begin in the quietude of the **Imperial College** (**1**; p28) and **Confucius Temple** (**2**; p35). Head east, passing under the bright *páilou* (archway) at the end of Guozijian Jie (it's one of the few left in the

Prayer beads, Lama Temple

city). Follow the wafts of incense over the road to **Lama Temple** (**3**; p16). From here, head south and take a right down Fangjia Hutong. On the right, **No 13** (**4**) is a classic courtyard home. Cross over Andingmennei Dajie and continue west along **Xiejia Hutong** (**5**). Take the next right and then the second left. Follow this with another right, and a quick left onto **Guoxiang Hutong** (**6**), once a Mongolian emperor's address. Turn left at the end and head south. At the T-junction take a right; this is **Doufuchi Hutong** (**7**), home of Mao Zedong and his first wife. Take the first left south for the **Bell Tower** (**8**; p33) and **Drum Tower** (**9**; p33). Continue south and take the first right off Di'anmenwai Dajie, up a short flight of stone stairs. Another

right, followed by a left, will bring you to **Kaorouji Restaurant** (**10**; p72), where you can stuff yourself on lamb before continuing on to the **Silver Ingot Bridge** (**11**; p34) and taking in the street theatre around the lakes.

Distance 4.25km **Duration** 3½-4hr ▶ **Start** Ⓜ Yonghegong-Lama Temple ⦿ **End** 🚌 118 from Di'anmen Xidajie; or 5 from Di'anmennei Dajie

Lakeside Amble

Starting at Qianhai Xijie, head north past the knot of rickshaws and the Spirit Wall of **Guo Moruo's former residence** (**1**; p39). Turn left onto Qianhai Xiyan, then take the first right onto willow-lined **Liuyin Jie** (**2**) and the gardens of **Prince Gong's former residence** (**3**; p19). Continue north, then follow Houhai Nanyan east to **Hou Hai Café & Bar** (**4**; p84) for a drink. Cross over the **Silver Ingot Bridge** (**5**; p34) and follow the southeast trail along Qianhai Lake, past the fishermen and mah jong battlers. At the southern end of the lake, head west to the pedestrian underpass, where you can cross Di'anmen Xidajie to **Beihai Park** (**6**; p21). The path heading southwest will bring you to the ferry dock, where you can hop on a boat to **Jade Islet** (**7**). Dine at the imperial **Fangshan Restaurant** (**8**; p71), or at least poke your head in to gawk at the glittering gold décor. Climb up over the mountain, taking in the **White Dagoba** (**9**), and cross the bridge to **Round City** (**10**), from where you can take in the view of Zhonghai and Nanhai Lakes.

Distance 3.8km **Duration** 4hr
▶ Start 🚌 118 from Dongsishitiao; or 111 from Jishuitan ⬤ End 🚌 5 to Tiananmen Xi

Jade Islet, Beihai Park

Tiananmen March

If you're planning on spending a few hours in the Forbidden City (very easily done), start this tour in the early afternoon. That way, you'll

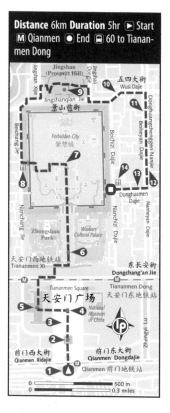

Distance 6km **Duration** 5hr ▶ **Start**
Ⓜ Qianmen ● **End** 🚌 60 to Tiananmen Dong

wind up at Jingshan Park for sunset, when the views across the city are best. The march begins at **Qianmen** (**1**; p34), before heading north to pay your respects at **Mao Zedong's Mausoleum** (**2**; p41). Cross **Tiananmen Square** (**3**; p8), dodging kite strings and tour groups, for a gander at the **Monument to the People's Heroes** (**4**; p34). For those interested in socialist design, stop in at the **Great Hall of the People** (**5**; p33) before scaling **Tiananmen** (**6**; p9). Enter into the splendour of the **Forbidden City** (**7**; p10), take in the highlights and re-emerge at the western exit. Stop in for refreshments at the **Purple Vine Teahouse** (**8**; p69) before heading north to **Jingshan Park** (**9**; p37). Follow the tree-lined trail to the top of the hill for views of the golden palace rooftops to the south and Beihai Park to the northwest. Take the east exit out of the park and walk south to the moat. Cross over **Wusi Dajie** (**10**) and follow it east to the pedestrian path between **Beiheyan Dajie** (**11**) and **Donghuangchenggen Nanjie** (**12**). As you head south, join families and exercising gran-

nies out for a twilight stroll. Take a right at **Donghuamen Dajie** (**13**) to the **Courtyard** (**14**; p71) for fine dining with a view over the moat.

Flying the flag: the Great Hall of the People

Shoppers' Shuffle

Wander up one side of **Liulichang Xijie** (**1**) and down the other before crossing Nanxinhua Jie to **Liulichang Dongjie** (**2**), a treasure-trove of history. Stop in at **Beijing Songtangzhai Museum** (**3**; p28) to see carving at its best, and then hang a left. Take the second right, just past the veggie market, to a pretty residential *hútòng*. Take the third right and head south along this busy street before turning left into the pedestrianised **Dazhalan Jie** (**4**). When you hit Qianmen Dajie, cross it for some classic *shāomài* dumplings directly across the street at **Duyichu** (**5**; p69). Retrace your steps across Qianmen Dajie and take the first right on to a manic, narrow market street. Shuffle north among the crowds until you reach a curved road with **Qianmen** (**6**; p34) looming on the other side. Head northwest and take the pedestrian underpass to the other side. You'll come out at Qianmen where you can walk through its enormous gate. Take the pedestrian underpass heading

Dinner-on-a-stick: Wangfujing Snack Street

east and then the one heading north and you'll find yourself on a shady sidewalk with views across **Tiananmen Square** (**7**; p8). Head north to the **National Museum of China** (**8**; p30). Continue north, take another underpass and enter the serene **Workers' Cultural Palace** (**9**; p38). Rest for a bit in the pavilions before taking the east exit and walking south to the beautiful courtyard of the **Imperial Archives** (p33) and **Wan Fung Art Gallery** (**10**; p32). Walk east along **Dongchang'an Jie** (**11**) and take a left into the shopping oasis of **Wangfujing Dajie** (**12**). Take the second left, which leads into a narrow *hútòng*, and turn right into **Wangfujing Snack Street** (**13**; p74), where you can fill up on an exotic dinner-on-a-stick.

Distance 5km **Duration** 4hr ▶ **Start** Ⓜ Hepingmen, then any bus south
⦿ **End** 🚌 Wangfujing

DAY TRIPS
The Great Wall of China at Badaling 八达岭长城 (1, A2; 3)

Twisting and turning for more than 5000km and visible from space, you could once traverse the Great Wall from Shanhai Pass on the east coast to Jiayu Pass in the Gobi Desert. While much of the wall has since crumbled or been blown to dust, a number of sections have been restored and opened to the public.

INFORMATION

70km northwest of Beijing

🚌 Tour Bus 1 from Qianmen (about 1hr)

☎ 6912 1338/1423

💲 Y45/25, plus insurance Y2 (incl entry to the Great Wall Museum & the Great Wall Circle Vision Theatre)

🕐 6am-8pm

The ancient Chinese fortified their cities and states with enormous walls, and by 290 BC these walls dotted the country's northern border. When the Mongolian nomadic peoples began to pose a threat to the ambitious and tyrannical Emperor Qin (221–207 BC), he indentured thousands of labourers to link the existing walls. For 10 years these labourers toiled and by 214 BC the wall was the largest defence mechanism the world had ever seen.

However, by the time of the Sui dynasty (AD 589–1279) the wall was a crumbling mess. It was rebuilt, but the lengthy wall was difficult to man properly and the Mongols swept into China. Years later, the Mings decided to overhaul the again-decaying wall, this time with the aid of bricks and stone slabs, but a century later the wall was again in a state of disrepair.

Of course, this isn't to say that the wall was built in vain. It was the linchpin in unifying China and became an excellent thoroughfare for transporting people and equipment across the mountains. By way of its beacon-tower system, wolf-dung smoke signals quickly sent news of enemy movement back to the capital. In 1972 US President Richard Nixon visited the wall and commented, 'It sure is a great wall'. Beijing's tourism industry hasn't been the same since.

The easiest place to experience the Great Wall is at **Badaling**. This section of the wall was last restored in 1957. At an elevation of 1000m, it affords some magnificent views of the masonry snaking its way through the mountains and gives you an inkling of the wall's enormity. The restored section crawls for about 1km each way; head left up the stairs (south) for the vaguely quieter route. It's worth hiking all the way to the end to see the rather forlorn ruins that carry on over the hill. Good footwear is a must.

Admission also gets you into the **Great Wall Circle Vision Theatre** and the **Great Wall Museum** (🕐 9am-4pm). The latter is definitely worth your time. It's packed with pictures, models, dioramas and (comprehensible!) English captions illustrating the building and history of the wall.

There's no denying that Badaling is swarming with tourists, and vendors who are convinced that everyone needs an 'I Climbed the Great Wall' T-shirt. This is, after all, one of the world's top tourist destinations and you don't come here for serenity but rather the overwhelming 'I am standing on the Great Wall' sensation.

The Great Wall of China at Simatai 司马台长城 (1, C1)

If you really can't face the hubbub of Badaling and consider yourself reasonably fit, give the wall at Simatai a try.

Built by Ming Emperor Hongwu, the views at this 19km stretch are jaw-dropping, and the commanding yet crumbling old watchtowers make sure that you have sturdy shoes with good grip. The steepness of some of the drops and climbs (80 degrees in some places) is so dramatic you will often find yourself on all fours just to stabilise yourself. If that seems daunting, there's also a **cable car** (one way/round trip Y30/Y50; ◷ 8.30am-4.30pm). You'll see very few tourists on this stretch of the wall but be warned that the vendors here are a breed apart. They have a nasty habit of springing out of the watchtowers when you least expect it, usually just as you are about to navigate that one last step that could make the difference between safety and a particularly nasty plunge over the side. If your legs feel like jelly and buying a Great Wall picture book to tote along for the rest of the hike is the last thing on your mind, try to say so firmly and mean it. Hesitate in the slightest and you'll be hiking the rest of the wall with your new best friend. If you are heading down to the bus, you'll notice there's a cable suspended across the river; hand over Y35, slip into the attached harness, and it will deposit you on the opposite bank. There, a boat will collect you to take you back to the parking lot.

Though incredibly expensive, water and soft drinks (and even beer!) are available from vendors prowling the wall. Food, however, is not easy to come by. Make sure to bring enough snacks to last you the day.

INFORMATION

110km northeast of Beijing

🚌 Minibus from Dongzhimen long-distance station (3hr)

☎ 6903 1051

💲 wall Y30, suspension bridge Y5

◷ 8am-5pm

Climbing the Great Wall of China

Ming Tombs 明十三陵 (1, B2)

In many cultures the rituals surrounding death play an important role. For emperors of the Ming dynasty (1368–1644), these ceremonies often reached epic proportions, as did the wealth and attention spent on tombs. In this 40-sq-km area, 13 of the 16 Ming emperors were buried with their wives, concubines and funerary treasures. All of the tombs have been plundered in the past but, following recent restorations, three have been opened to the public.

INFORMATION

50km northwest of Beijing

🚌 Tour Bus 1 from Qianmen; or 845 from Xizhimen subway to Changping (about 1hr), then taxi 10min

☎ 6076 1424

💲 Apr-Oct Y60, Nov-Mar Y40

🕐 8am-5.30pm

ℹ Chinese/English audioguide Y10/30 (available at Ding Ling), deposit Y200

Chang Ling, the resting place of Emperor Yongle, has huge *nánmù* (a type of high-quality wood) halls and displays of unearthed jewellery and clothing. This tomb is the most impressive of the three; it took 18 years to complete and, according to legend, 16 concubines were buried alive with Yongle's corpse. At **Ding Ling**, the tomb of Emperor Wan Li, you can walk through the underground passageways and caverns. These are mainly giant empty rooms, but the imposing marble doors within the tomb are amazing. **Zhao Ling**, where Emperor Longqing rests, is smaller and relatively tranquil. Leading up to the tombs, **Spirit Way** passes a giant tortoise bearing the largest stele in China, followed by 12 sets of fantastic stone animals and 12 stone-faced statues of generals, ministers and officials. Every other animal is in a reclining

Guarding Spirit Way

position, allowing for a 'changing of the guard' at midnight. The 7km Spirit Way is fabulous and well worth encouraging speed-happy tour-bus drivers to stop for a look.

FACE VALUE

Loosely defined as status, ego or self-respect, the concept of 'face' is not unfamiliar to most foreigners. Essentially it's about avoiding being made to look stupid or wrong. What you may find unfamiliar is the lengths Chinese people will go to in order to save face. If a conflict arises, opponents dig in their heels; screaming matches on the streets or in shops are not uncommon. Chinese people will assume that you also want to save face and will hand over one of their ready-to-wear excuses should they feel you need it. Try never to accuse someone directly; unless you love to argue, outright confrontation should be reserved as a last resort.

Marco Polo Bridge 卢沟桥 (1, B3; 8, A6)

Built in 1189, Beijing's oldest marble bridge spans 266m across the Yongding River and is host to 501 uniquely carved stone lions. If you wander along the riverbank, you can get a good view of its 11 arches. En route to the bridge, you'll pass through the ancient city walls of **Wanping**.

While enshrined in the travel logs of the great Italian traveller, the bridge is most famous for the Marco Polo Bridge Incident that occurred in 1937, when Japanese troops illegally occupied a railway junc-

INFORMATION
17km southwest of Beijing
- 🚌 964 from Beijing Xizhan train station (30–45min)
- ☎ 8389 3919
- ✉ 88 Lugouqiaochengnei Xijie, Wanping
- 💲 Y10/5
- 🕐 7am-9pm

tion outside Wanping. Gunfire was exchanged (it's still possible to find shell pits in Wanping's city walls) and Japan had its pretext for attacking Beijing and igniting a full-scale war.

Carved stone lions, Marco Polo Bridge

Nearby, the **Memorial Hall of the War of Resistance** and the **Commemorative Sculpture Garden** will intrigue history buffs.

Tanzhe Temple 潭柘寺 (1, A3)

Beijing's oldest and largest temple reclines amid ancient silver apricot trees, ginkgos and towering pines. Dating back to the 3rd century AD, its great age graces the temple with unique features – dragon decorations, mythical animal sculptures and grimacing gods that are no longer found in temples within the city.

Locals have traditionally come to this atmospheric retreat to pray for rain during droughts or to harvest Cudrania trees, which provide yellow dye and nourish silkworms.

Today the temple grounds retain a calm, spiritual feel. Within the complex, look for the unusual **Tree of Prosperity**, which you can lean against for good luck; the smoky **Guanyin Cave**, where you

INFORMATION
45km west of Beijing
- Ⓜ Pingguoyuan, then bus 931 or taxi (about 45min)
- 🚌 Tour Bus 7 from Qianmen (Y50, 7-8.30am Sat, Sun & holidays Apr-Oct)
- 💲 Y35
- 🕐 8am-6pm Apr–mid-Sep, 8.20am-4.30pm mid-Sep–Mar

can taste eternal springwater tea; and the **Stone Fish**, apparently given to the temple by the Jade Emperor himself.

Outside the temple grounds, **Talin Temple** has a gorgeous collection of intricately detailed stupas.

Chuandixia Village 川底下村 (1, A2)

Nestled in a green valley and overlooked by towering peaks, Chuandixia is an enchanting village forgotten by time. Its cluster of traditional court-yard homes, terraced orchards and beautiful stone alleyways make it a picturesque day trip into rural China. The tiny community has formed a kind of tourism cooperative. In exchange for the small entrance fee to the village, you can have a look inside many of the courtyard buildings (marked with red numbers). The money raised appears to be going back into the village, restoring buildings and improving the roads.

INFORMATION

90km west of Beijing

Ⓜ Pingguoyuan, then bus 929 to Zhaitang, then taxi to Chuandixia (Y10, 10min); or taxi from Pingguoyuan (Y80, 1½-2hr depending on driver's interpretation of the speed limit)

⑤ Y20

As you wander up and around the narrow alleyways, you will likely encounter Maoist graffiti left over from Cultural Revolution days. Slogans such as 'Arm our minds with Mao Zedong Thought' and 'Proletariats of the world unite!' decorate the walls.

Try to fit this special place into your Beijing visit if you can. Even with its remoteness, it seems commercialism may catch up with it eventually. Until very recently, you wouldn't have found a single vendor in this peaceful hamlet, as the villagers continued to go about their days grinding corn or picking apples. Nowadays, however, you may turn a corner and see a villager standing behind a table loaded with multicoloured Chuandixia T-shirts and other paraphernalia.

There's a small teashop up the hill at the far northern end of the village, but otherwise there's not a single shop in this area. You'd be wise to bring along your own water and snacks.

If taking public transport, keep a sharp eye out for your stop. Even if you read Chinese, note that signs to the village are written in classical Chinese and are not easy to recognise.

Take a tour through Beijing's historic *hútòngs*

ORGANISED TOURS

The Chinese government does its best to keep a firm grip on the tourism industry, largely through its incarnation as the China Travel Service (CTS). CTS runs half- and full-day tours around Beijing but they are generally uninspired and often include stops at government-operated shops and restaurants. Unfortunately, there isn't a flood of other options to choose from. Included here are a few companies, mainly operating at large hotels. You're also likely to be approached by 'tour guides' on the street – many offer excellent, personalised tours at good rates, however, be warned that there is always the risk of fraud and theft involved.

China Culture Club
(8, H3)
They aren't exactly a tourist agency, but this club is doing a better job than every official tourist agency in town. The club opened in 2000 and offers cultural programmes, talks and tours for expats and tourists. Whether it's mah jong, cooking, calligraphy or tombs that interest you, this club will likely offer something that will scratch the itch. Check their website for schedules.
☎ 6432 9341 🖳 www .chinesecultureclub.org ✉ 29 Liangmaqiao Lu 💲 varies 🚌 402

China Travel Service
(8, H3)
CTS runs convoys of bus tours to Beijing's biggest sights, including the Great Wall, Ming Tombs, Forbidden City and Temple of Heaven, and to opera and acrobatic performances. The tours are often geared towards Chinese tourists and guides don't always speak English. Tour groups tend to be large and schedules tight. Reserve one day in advance.
☎ 6464 6400, ext 6448/6422 ✉ 2 Beisanhuan Donglu; offices in large hotels, incl Holiday Inn, Novotel & Hilton 💲 Y350-415 🕙 tours vary

Dragon Bus
(4, E5)
Dragon Bus offers tours to the expected sights, catering to business tour groups and offering pre- and post-conference tours.
☎ 8463 4451 ✉ Beijing Hotel, 33 Dongchang'an Jie 💲 Y350-380 🕙 most tours daily

Hello Beijing
(4, C6)
Focusing on the *hútòngs* of Qianmen, this rickshaw tour takes in a kindergarten, a family courtyard home, markets and the Zhengyici Theatre. Book a day in advance to ensure an English-speaking guide and two days in advance if you'd like lunch provided.
☎ 6302 7010 ✉ 13 Danlanying Hutong 💲 from Y160 🕙 9am, 2pm & 5pm or 6pm

Panda Tour
(8, E4)
With smaller tour groups and English-speaking guides, this is a good alternative to CTS. Tours visit popular Beijing sights, *hútòngs*, acrobatic performances and the Mutianyu section of the Great Wall. There are also day trips to Chengde and three-day tours to Xi'an.
☎ 6522 2991 ✉ 36 Nanlishi Lu; counters at St Regis, Kempinski, Jinglun & Shangri-la Hotels 💲 from Y300 (incl lunch) 🕙 most tours daily; Mutianyu Great Wall Sun

River Romance
(4, D2)
River Romance offers candlelit boat tours around Houhai and Qianhai Lakes in a private, Chinese-style gondola. A musician in the bow strumming traditional music adds to the exotic atmosphere.
☎ 6612 5717 ✉ southern end of Qianhai Lake, off Di'anmen Xidajie 💲 per hr Y200, live music Y100 🕙 9am-11pm (evenings best)

Shopping

These days, every other corner of the capital seems to be home to a gleaming new shopping mall or towering department store. Shopping has become a lucrative linchpin in the capital's economic growth and a major pastime for Beijingers. Hard-nosed consumers pound the pavements morning, noon and night. You can't blame them – the shopping here is tops, with everything from the dazzle of Tiffany's to the hustle of the Silk Market. At the rate developers are adding shopping centres to the city, you'll have more choices than you'll know what to do with. However, the real finds in Beijing are still at the antique markets, where discerning eyes can unearth gems.

Shopping Areas

The pedestrianised, southern end of Wangfujing Dajie (4, E5) is *the* place to shop for brand-name goods, with Jianguomenwai Dajie (4, J5) following closely. Sanlitun (5) and the streets around the Workers' Stadium are where the smaller, trendy designer shops are springing up, while Qianmen (6, A1) has some of Beijing's oldest outlets for silk and tea and is packed with clothing stalls. Xidan Beidajie (4, B4) is where young people conglomerate en masse and shop and shop and shop…

Opening Hours

To keep up with their customers' spending sprees, closing time is fading further into the night. Most malls and chain shops are open seven days a week, from 9am or 10am until 10pm, as are many of the boutiques around Sanlitun.

Paying & Bargaining

Prices are fixed in malls and department stores. Markets and tourist and antique shops are another matter, where bargaining is a time-honoured tradition. You'll quickly know if you've tried bargaining in a fixed-price shop by the disappearing backside of the retailer. In older shops, the exchange of money for goods can be a convoluted process: you point out what you want, are given a ticket to give to a cashier who collects your money and gives you a stamped receipt to return to the salesperson in exchange for your purchase. Got it?

SHOPPING CENTRES & DEPARTMENT STORES

China World Shopping Centre
国贸商场 (4, J5)
A mall where you can amble from Gucci to Christian Dior to Salvatore Ferragamo within seconds. Heaven for the well-heeled shopper.
✉ 1 Jianguomenwai Dajie
🕙 9am-10pm Ⓜ Guomao

Friendship Store
友谊商店 (4, H5)
The interior is oppressively drab and the prices higher than elsewhere, but this old standby has all the kites, English-language coffee-table books and Chinoiserie you'll need under one roof. Great for last-minute souvenirs.
✉ 17 Jianguomenwai Dajie
🕙 9am-9pm Ⓜ Yonganli

New World Shopping Mall
新世界商场 (4, F6)
Kids can play in the jungle gym upstairs while you shop below in this colossal multi-level department store. Unlike others of its kind, you'll find plenty here you haven't seen anywhere else.
☎ 6708 0055
✉ 3 Chongwenmenwai Dajie 🕙 9.30am-9.30pm
Ⓜ Chongwenmen ♿

Oriental Plaza
东方广场 (4, E5)
Beijing's finest shopping centre is bright, modern and draws thousands of people daily with labels ranging from Nike to Valentino to Asian labels from abroad. It's also very kid-friendly, with nappy-changing rooms and a playroom downstairs.
☎ 8518 6363
✉ 1 Dongchang'an Jie
🕙 9.30am-10pm
Ⓜ Wangfujing ♿

SOGO Department Store
崇光百货 (4, B6)
Never-ending boutiques are filled with men's and women's clothing from hip Japanese labels you've probably never heard of as well as trendy European brands. And the accessories! The sea of shoes and handbags on the 1st floor is almost too much.
☎ 6310 3388
✉ 8 Xuanwumenwai Dajie
🕙 9.30am-9.30pm
Ⓜ Xuanwumen

FOOD & DRINK

Hongqiao Market
红桥市场 (6, C2)
Scorpions, snake meat, snails, eels in tanks – buy Beijing's delicacies in bulk at this frenzied food market and try to avoid getting splashed.
✉ cnr Tiantan Donglu & Fahuasi Jie 🕙 8.30am-7pm
Ⓜ Chongwenmen, then bus 43 or 610

Jenny Lou's
(4, H4)
Missing your Australian cereal? Russian yoghurt? Arab cheese? This grocery store is an international adventure.
☎ 8563 0626 ✉ 4 Ritan Beilu (northeast cnr Ritan Park) 🕙 8am-10pm
Ⓜ Yonganli, then bus 28

Liubiju
六必居酱园 (6, A1)
The pungent sweet smell coming from this 400-year-old pickle-and-sauce emporium will hit you from the doorway. Inside, let your curiosity lead you from pot to pot, all brimming with colourful and mystifying condiments.
☎ 6303 4278 ✉ 3 Liang-shidian Jie, off Dazhalan Jie
🕙 10am-6pm Ⓜ Qianmen

The exclusive China World Shopping Centre

Paris Patisserie (4, H4)
Diplomats stream in here all day to cart away Western cakes, freshly baked bread and more unusual desserts like green-tea mousse. If you stick around to eat your treats, they come uniquely presented. Even something simple like a glass of milk will come to your table frosty and served in a heavy goblet.
☎ 8562 3355 ⊠ 1 Ritan Donglu ⏲ 7am-10pm Ⓜ Yonganli, then bus 28 or 43

Ten Fu's Tea
天福茗茶 (4, C6)
With branches throughout the city, this is the place to buy top-quality loose tea from all over China. In the time-honoured tradition, a cup of tea is offered to you as soon as you walk inside the shop. Staff at this excellent store are friendly, knowledgeable and generous with the bonbon samples. Expect your pockets to be bulging with jasmine-tea candy and green-tea flavoured gum drops by the time you leave.
☎ 6304 8671 ⊠ 65 Liulichang Dongjie ⏲ 10am-7pm Ⓜ Hepingmen, then any bus south

MARKETS

Beijing Curio City
北京古玩城 (8, H6)
Four floors of scrolls, gifts, ceramics, carpets, furniture and duty-free goods. Your trolling will more than likely be rewarded with top knick-knacks and souvenirs. If you need a life-sized stone elephant or lion for your yard back home, check out the offerings outside.
☎ 6774 7711 ⊠ 21 Dongsanhuan Nanlu ⏲ 9.30am-6.30pm Ⓜ Guomao, then bus 28

Hongqiao (Pearl) Market
红桥市场 (6, C2)
Heaps of pearls and mounds of colourful corals and turquoises await you on the 3rd floor. Freshwater pearls are a great buy in China and the Pearl Market is Beijing's top outlet. You'll also find vendors selling crafts, clothing, electronics and antiques at this market.
⊠ 16 Hongqiao Lu ⏲ 8.30am-7pm Ⓜ Chongwenmen, then bus 43 or 610

Xiushui Silk Market
秀水市场 (4, H5)
Silk galore! Boxer shorts, scarves, shirts, ties, purses and robes line the stalls alongside fake designer goods. Many Beijingers swear this is the best clothing market in the city. Bargaining is a must here, and be sure to keep your senses and your purse about you – this is pickpocket territory.
⊠ Jianguomenwai Dajie ⏲ 9am-sunset Ⓜ Yonganli

Yabao Market
雅宝 (4, H4)
In the market for a swimsuit and, I dunno, maybe a fur coat to throw over it in case there's a chill? This Russian market has an astounding assortment of animal skins and bikinis and very little of anything else. It's definitely worth a stroll, if only to soak up the suburban Moscow atmosphere. Even the Chinese vendors and panhandlers will be yelling to you in Russian.
⊠ off Ritan Lu ⏲ 9.30am-4pm Ⓜ Jianguomen, then bus 44

Zhongguancun Electronics Market
中关村电子商业街 (8, D2)
There's six floors of laptops, MP3 players, cameras, palm pilots and motherboards. And that's just in the first building. Vendors at this market will do anything to get your attention here, from springing in front of you from high boxes to physically pulling you towards their wares. Computer savvy is a must if you're coming here to buy.
⊠ cnr Zhongguancun Lu & Zhongguancun Dajie ⏲ 9.30am-late 🚌 double-decker 4

GAME PLAN
Bargaining is an exhilarating national sport in China and the only real rule (if you want to win) is to be polite. If you're worried about cheating the vendor out of a fair price, don't be – it's nearly impossible. These guys are much better at this game than you. The first price you're offered will be at least double the going rate. Look 'em straight in the eye and cut that number in half. You'll likely end up with something in between. If not, walk away and see what that does to the price.

CLOTHING & ACCESSORIES

Can Cam (5, C2)
Come here for swingy, flimsy, sparkly tops and lace cut jeans from Paris, Italy and Hong Kong. For guys there's shoes, dyed jeans and T-shirts. It's all a little over the top but done in good fun.
☎ 6415 1034 ✉ 40 Sanlitun Lu ☯ 11am-midnight Ⓜ Dongsishitiao, then bus 113 or 115

Feng Ling Fashion Art Design
枫翎原创服装工作室 (5, B2)
Trained as an artist, this controversial designer has taken Mao suits and *qípáos* (traditional Chinese dresses) modern by emblazing them with revolutionary symbols and daring colours. She also has a studio at Factory 798.
☎ 6417 7715 ✉ Tongli Studio, Sanlitun Beilu ☯ noon-9pm Ⓜ Dongsishitiao, then bus 113

Hiersun Diamond Palace
恒信钻石宫殿 (4, E5)
Come press your face against the glass to see the dazzling diamond displays. This place is so packed with glittery jewels it feels like they're winking at you from all over the room.
☎ 8518 5120 ✉ AA29, Oriental Plaza, 1 Dongchang'an Jie ☯ 9.30am-10pm Ⓜ Wangfujing

Jayi Clothing Market
佳亿时尚广场 (8, H3)
This recently renovated indoor complex has a flashy array of stalls selling fake designer goods, sunglasses, bags, shoes and Gore-Tex jackets.
✉ Xinyuan Nanlu, across from Kunlun Hotel ☯ 10am-9pm Ⓜ Dongsishitiao, then bus 701

Mingjingyuan Glasses Wholesale Market
名镜苑眼镜城 (8, H5)
This multi-level wholesale supply store has every colour, shape and size of frame as well as heaps of brand-name knockoffs and lots of deals. Many Beijingers swear this is the place for glasses.
✉ Dongsanhuan Nanlu ☯ 8am-6pm Ⓜ Guomao, then bus 28

Mushi
模西 (4, J4)
French-born Caroline Deleens lived in China as a teenager, studied fashion design in Paris and is now Beijing-based. Her famous fashion line mixes French and Chinese fabrics and styles to create unusual clothes that are still wearable off the runway.
☎ 8529 9420 ✉ Kerry Centre Mall, 1 Guanghua Lu ☯ 10am-8pm Ⓜ Guomao, then any bus north

Nali Mini Mall
那里衣服市场 (5, C2)
Charming rows of brightly painted stalls make up this mall with the look and feel of an out-of-the-way European side street. The vendors are less clingy than in other markets, making it a pleasure to sift through batches of trendy colourful clothing.
✉ lane heading east btwn 44 & 46 Sanlitun Lu ☯ 10am-8pm Ⓜ Dongsishitiao, then bus 113

Neiliansheng Shoes
内联升鞋店 (6, A1)
In business since 1853, this store is famous for its handmade, traditional, multiple-layer cloth shoes. There's a terrific kids' selection and, surprisingly, many of the adult styles look like they belong on a Paris runway. Those with bigger-sized feet, however,

Strike a pose: Can Cam window display

DRESS TO IMPRESS

With its narrow cut and high 'mandarin' collar, the *qípáo* is the most easily recognised traditional Chinese outfit. These days they've raised the hemline, turned up the volume on the material and made the *qípáo* chic all over again. Check out Maggie Cheung in Wong Kar-wai's *In the Mood for Love*. The *qípáo* is practically a character in the film. Find your own version hanging in market stalls, department stores and designer shops, or get one crafted by a tailor.

should prepare themselves for heartbreak.
☎ 6301 3045 ⊠ 34 Dazhalan Jie ⏰ 8am-10pm M Qianmen

Red Phoenix
红凤凰 (5, B1)
If you want a *qípáo* that will turn heads and drop jaws, run to local designer Gu Lin's boutique. Gu's vibrantly coloured ultra-modern versions of the traditional Chinese dress have rabid fans, from movie stars and musicians to those living in the nearby embassy district. Ask to see her catalogue. Most of the clothes are made to order so expect to shell out a wad of cash for her creations.
☎ 6417 3591 ⊠ 30 Sanlitun Lu ⏰ 9.30-11.30am & 1-5.30pm M Dongsishitiao, then bus 113

Sanlitun Yaxiu Clothing Market
三里屯雅秀市场 (5, B2)
This five-storey complex is a mind-whirling kaleidoscope of shoes, bags, outdoor wear, trendy clothes and foreigners shouting '*tài guì!*' ('too expensive!'). If it all gets too much, take your shopping-weary legs up to the top-

floor food court. The choices are endless and there's beer on tap.
⊠ 58 Gongrentiyuchang Beilu ⏰ 9.30am-9pm M Dongsishitiao, then bus 113

SZBR Culture & Art Dress Shop
圣智般若文化艺术服装专卖 (5, B2)
Handmade by a local designer, the women's clothing here is casual and modern and has an ethnic feel. Boxy waist-length jackets with broad slashes of colour are her signature style.
☎ 6415 9442 ⊠ 12 Gongrentiyuchang Beilu ⏰ 9.30am-10pm M Dongsishitiao, then bus 113

Yinshu Jewellery Workrooms
银殊首饰工作室 (8, J1)
Their looks won't work on everyone, but for fresh daring designs you can't do better than here. Earrings are so bold and dramatic they are sold individually to be worn alone. One design is made so long it can wrap around your neck and double as a necklace.
☎ 6437 3432 ⊠ 2 Jiuxianqiao Lu ⏰ 9am-6.30pm 🚌 403

The colourful designs at SZBR Culture & Art Dress Shop

Tailors

Cao Senlin

裁缝曹 (4, F4)

Come get a dress made by the man who once made scholars jackets for Deng Xiaoping and is one of the few traditional *qípáo* makers in the city. This lovely man has been hand-sewing traditional Chinese clothes since 1940 and still turns out beautiful dresses of incredible quality from his tiny courtyard home. You need to bring your own material, a picture or pattern of the dress you want, and, if you don't speak Chinese, a translator too.

☎ 6526 4515 ✉ 25 Shijia Hutong (1st door on left through corridor) 🕐 hit-&-miss; call ahead Ⓜ Dongdan, then any bus north

Sanlitun Yaxiu Clothing Market, 3rd Floor

三里屯雅秀市场, 第三楼 (5, B2)

The silk vendors will be calling to you the moment you get off the elevator. Head to the back where you'll find dozens of tailors waiting to whip up clothes in silk, wool or cashmere. Expect to wait two to four days for the finished product. If you need a rush job come early in the morning: they can be finished by closing the same night. ✉ 58 Gongrentiyuchang Beilu 🕐 9.30am-9pm Ⓜ Dongsishitiao, then bus 113

Wuzhou Friendship Silk Trade Company

五洲友谊丝绸贸易公司 (5, B1)

Favoured by expats for quality work at reasonable rates, this no-frills shop has reams of material to choose from. *Qípáos* can be made in three to four days and suits in a week.

☎ 6532 7913 ✉ Friendship Supermarket, 2nd fl, 7 Sanlitun Lu 🕐 10am-8pm Ⓜ Dongzhimen, then bus 117 or 206

Yongzheng Tailor

永正制衣裁缝店 (4, E4)

Flip through infinite clothing catalogues for your pattern then flick open the traditional Chinese boxes to rifle through swatches of silk. The tailors here do men's and women's clothing and you'll have your dress or suit in about 25 days. Yongzheng Tailor is more upscale and pricier than other tailors.

☎ 6513 7874 ✉ southeast cnr Wangfujing Dajie & Dengshikou Jie 🕐 9am-9pm Ⓜ Wangfujing, then bus 103

CLOTHING & SHOE SIZES

Women's Clothing

Aust/UK	8	10	12	14	16	18
Europe	36	38	40	42	44	46
Japan	5	7	9	11	13	15
USA	6	8	10	12	14	16

Women's Shoes

Aust/USA	5	6	7	8	9	10
Europe	35	36	37	38	39	40
France only	35	36	38	39	40	42
Japan	22	23	24	25	26	27
UK	3½	4½	5½	6½	7½	8½

Men's Clothing

Aust	92	96	100	104	108	112
Europe	46	48	50	52	54	56
Japan	S	M	M		L	
UK/USA	35	36	37	38	39	40

Men's Shirts (Collar Sizes)

Aust/Japan	38	39	40	41	42	43
Europe	38	39	40	41	42	43
UK/USA	15	15½	16	16½	17	17½

Men's Shoes

Aust/UK	7	8	9	10	11	12
Europe	41	42	43	44½	46	47
Japan	26	27	27.5	28	29	30
USA	7½	8½	9½	10½	11½	12½

Measurements approximate only; try before you buy.

FOOT & BLIND MASSAGE

Heping Foot Massage 81
和平健身81 (4, F4)
Don't let the Vegas-style exterior fool you. This is one of the classier massage joints with prices to match. Settle into a plush armchair, flip through a selection of English-language satellite programming on the giant-screen TV, choose a cocktail from the menu and nosh on free watermelon slices. And that's all before the massage even begins.
☎ 6522 8355 ✉ 3 Jinyu Hutong, tucked beside Taiwan Hotel 💲 from Y100 🕐 11am-11pm Ⓜ Wangfujing, then bus 103

Magic Foot Massage
妙手健身中心 (4, E5)
If your Wangfujing shopping spree has got you weary, come in here for pampering from a charming, discreet staff. Besides an array of foot treatments, you can try an 80-minute head and neck massage (Y158) or a 30-minute hand massage (Y50).
☎ 6512 0868 ✉ 6th fl, Gangmei Building, 1 Xiagongfu Jie 💲 80min basic foot massage Y99 🕐 10.30am-11.30pm Ⓜ Dongzhimen, then bus 117 or 206

Qing Song Blind Doctor Massage Centre
真轻松盲人保健按摩中心 (5, A1)
Its pseudo-clinic styling isn't very atmospheric but the foot massages and notoriously powerful Chinese body massages get raves. Prices depend on type and length of treatment.
✉ Chunxiu Lu, just north of Red House Hotel 💲 Y25-60 🕐 10.30am-11.30pm Ⓜ Dongzhimen, then bus 117 or 206

ARTS & CRAFTS

Beijing Arts & Crafts Central Store
工艺美术服务部 (4, E5)
An impressive display of wood and paper fans is on the 2nd floor and most afternoons you can watch the artists hand paint them. This place is also known for its jade and jadeite, but its selection is better than its prices.
☎ 6523 8747 ✉ 200 Wangfujing Dajie 🕐 9am-10pm Ⓜ Wangfujing

Dara
家大家业家居 (8, J1)
The manager greets all customers like long-awaited house guests at this space, which is filled with designer accessories and cushions as well as modern furniture displays. Root around this gorgeous store for unexpected treasures like sculpture-inspired handbags in ornate fabrics. If you don't like what's there, the staff here will whip one up for you in your choice of over 100 fabrics.
☎ 6432 5217 ✉ cnr Jiuxianqiao Lu & Jiuxianqiao Beilu 🕐 9am-6pm 🚌 403

Kuan Yu Gallery
北京关帝艺术馆 (4, C6)
Look up your Chinese name in their book and get it on a chop or a calligraphy painting. Gift boxes that include inks, ink stone, chop, brushes and stands are also for sale starting at Y50. This shop is a great place for picking up souvenirs and its calligraphy brushes are some of the

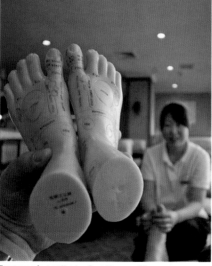
Treat your feet at Heping Foot Massage 81

WHICH BRUSH?

Don't just grab any brush if you've decided to take up Chinese calligraphy or painting. The size and material really does matter. If painting is your thing, make sure you have one weasel-hair brush (the stiff hair is good for details) and one goat's-hair brush (taken from the beard – the softness is considered good for making broad strokes, like when painting leaves). For those wanting to put Chinese script to canvas, a wolf's-hair brush should be the first in your kit. It is known to keep the ideal point, which artists say makes it perfect for calligraphy.

MUSIC & BOOKS

Music comes to you here in Beijing. Walk down Jianguomenwai Dajie or Sanlitun Lu and you'll be approached by street vendors murmuring 'CD? VCD?' and carrying bags full of them. Copyright laws are nowhere to be seen in Beijing, so pirated copies of popular (and not so popular) CDs are mass-produced. China's entry into the World Trade Organization was partly conditional on the trade being cleaned up, but no-one seems to have told the CD vendors.

most reasonably priced on the street.
☎ 6313 1003 ✉ 24 Liulichang Dongjie 🕐 8am-8pm Ⓜ Hepingmen, then any bus south

Qiqiannian Craft Workshop
漆千年 (8, J1)
Workers create sleek lacquer boxes and plates in-store. There's also a gorgeous selection of latticed wood objects like chairs and rocking horses.
☎ 137 0135 3053 ✉ cnr Jiuxianqiao Lu & Jiuxianqiao Beilu 🕐 10am-6pm 🚌 403

Rongbaozhai
荣宝斋 (4, C6)
Beautiful on the outside, typical state-run-store decorating

disaster on the inside. This shop has been selling paper, ink and brushes for decades and has an excellent selection of scrolls, paintings and wood blocks. Check out the giant sauna-sized ink stone.
☎ 6303 6090
✉ 19 Liulichang Xijie
🕐 9am-6pm Ⓜ Hepingmen, then any bus south

Tumasek
大马锡 (4, E5)
Beautiful gleaming goblets, trays and Y26,000 chess sets all made of Malaysian pewter; a little heavy to lug home but totally unique.
☎ 8518 6229 ✉ A108, Oriental Plaza, 1 Dongchang'an Jie 🕐 9.30am-10pm
Ⓜ Wangfujing

Bookworm
书虫 (5, C2)
This charming English-language lending-library has over 11,000 titles to borrow, regular book readings and talks as well as a handful of books for sale. It was bursting at the seams so has recently reopened in a new space just south of the old premises, with a kiddie corner, a restaurant, a café/bar and a rooftop terrace.
☎ 6586 9507 🖥 www.beijingbookworm.com
✉ Bldg 4, east off Nansanlitun Lu 🕐 9am-1am
Ⓜ Dongsishitiao, then bus 113

Cathay Bookstore
中国书店 (4, C6)
If trolling the city hasn't turned up a decent picture book of your favourite Chinese artist, your search is now over. The books at this branch of Cathay Bookstore are exclusively Chinese but the gorgeous pictures need

'READ ALL ABOUT IT!'

There is enough literature on China to see you through the next millennium. Strangely, there's barely enough on Beijing to see you through your flight. In Beijing itself, you can find English copies of *Rickshaw Boy*, a window into the living conditions of rickshaw drivers in the early 20th century. *Dragon Lady: The Life & Legend of the Last Empress of China* by Sterling Seagrave is the fascinating biography of Cixi (see p13). *Twilight in the Forbidden City* is by Reginald F Johnston and describes his days tutoring the last emperor of China. *The Siege at Peking* by Peter Fleming is an excellent account of the Boxer Rebellion in Beijing, while *The Tiananmen Papers* blows away the official smokescreen hanging over 4 June 1989. *Foreign Babes in Beijing: Behind the Scenes of a New China* by American Rachel DeWoskin is a light-hearted memoir of her time working on a Chinese soap opera in the capital.

no explanation. Works range from a Y10 picture book on porcelain to a back-breaking, four-volume work on Chinese master Qi Baishi (Y800).
☎ 6303 2104
✉ 34 Liulichang Xijie
🕙 9am-6pm M Hepingmen, then any bus south

Cool Music World
酷乐唱片 (4, F5)
Craving some Western music? Come here and listen before you buy. It has cool, laid-back staff and CDs are a steal.
☎ 6559 4954 ✉ 92 Dongdan Beidajie 🕙 10am-9.30pm M Dongdan

FAB (4, E5)
DVDs along with rows and rows of Chinese and Western CDs. The store is staffed with music lovers who, although they don't speak much English, are game to suggest CDs if you feel like exploring Chinese pop, rock, rap or jazz.
☎ 8518 8905 ✉ AA02, BB01B Oriental Plaza, 1

Dongchang'an Jie 🕙 9am-10pm M Wangfujing

Foreign Languages Bookshop
外文书店 (4, E4)
If you've finished your novel or are looking for some bedtime stories for the kids, head to this bookshop. There are also maps and travel books (several shelves of Lonely Planets included) for those who are heading further afield. If you need to brush up on your business Chinese or would like to learn a few local phrases, there are rows of books and audiovisual materials to help you as well as heaps of bilingual Chinese-English novels.
☎ 6512 6927 ✉ 235 Wangfujing Dajie 🕙 9am-9pm M Wangfujing

Wangfujing Bookshop
王府井书店 (4, E5)
Head here for maps and a motley collection of English-

language books on the 3rd floor that includes classic literature, translations of Chinese classics and a jarring assortment of modern nonfiction that favours tell-all books by American soap stars.
✉ 218 Wangfujing Dajie
🕙 9am-9pm M Wangfujing

FOR CHILDREN

Children are probably the easiest people to buy souvenirs for in Beijing – mini-parasols, fabulous kites and child-size *qípáos* and scholars jackets are for sale at most markets and at lots of tourist sights.

Jayi Clothing Market
佳亿时尚广场 (4, J1)
In the back right corner of this market you'll find stalls selling original and not-so-original brand-name clothing for kids, as well as toys and shoes. The Baby Mexx stall has the best selection.
✉ Xinyuan Nanlu, across from Kunlun Hotel
🕙 9.30am-9pm
M Dongzhimen, then bus 24

Kid's World
燕沙友谊商城 (8, H3)
They've got Japanese Barbie-type dolls and monstrous toy trucks from Hong Kong. This is a great place to come for toys from all over Asia and the West. You'll also find darling miniature-sized *qípáos* and scholars jackets for kids.
☎ 6465 1188
✉ 2nd fl, Youyi Lufthansa Centre, 50 Liangmaqiao Lu
🕙 10am-10pm
M Dongsishitiao, then bus 701

New China Children's Toy World

新中国儿童用品商店 (4, E4)

'Bleep! Whrrrrr ... Tweet!' After a trip to this maze of whirling toys, gadgets, flashing lights and electronic noises, your kids will be giddy and you may be deaf.

✉ 168 Wangfujing Dajie
🕑 9am-10pm
Ⓜ Wangfujing

ANTIQUES

The best haunt for antique shoppers is Panjiayuan Market (p41).

Cottage

草舍 (4, H4)

Antique Buddha chests, screens and jewellery cases are set out here as if in someone's very cluttered home. It makes opening the drawers, peering inside the boxes and fingering the wares feel somewhat illicit and that much more fun...

☎ 8561 1517
✉ 4 Ritan Beilu
🕑 9.30am-7.30pm
Ⓜ Yonganli, then bus 28

Yidege

一得阁 (4, C6)

Liquid Indian inks have been sold at this store since 1865. Today Yidege is also a treasure chest of antique carvings, scrolls, porcelain and more. Use discriminating eyes.

☎ 6301 7336 ✉ 67 Liulichang Dongjie 🕑 8.30am-7pm Ⓜ Hepingmen, then any bus south

SPECIALIST STORES

Ancient Weapons Shop

古代兵器商店 (8, H6)

An awesome collection of Chinese helmets, lances and spears is on display in this tiny store. A pair of lethal-looking spiked stirrups from Tibet will set you back Y1200. The owner swears everything is at least 100 years old. You be the judge.

☎ 6774 7711, ext 2134
✉ Beijing Curio City, 21 Dongsanhuan Nanlu
🕑 9.30am-6.30pm
Ⓜ Guomao, then bus 28

Daiyuexuan Brush Shop

戴月轩 (4, C6)

Popular with European artists and art restorers, this shop has been perfecting the art of producing sharp-nibbed weasel- and goat-hair brushes since 1916. You can also buy rice paper, ink and ink stones. Then all you'll need is the calligraphy skills.

☎ 6301 4914 ✉ 73 Liulichang Dongjie 🕑 9am-6pm Ⓜ Hepingmen, then any bus south

Fu Shou Tian Artware

福寿田工艺品 (4, C6)

Known as 'chops', stamps are still commonly used throughout China in place of signatures. You'll see their inky effect on paintings and official documents. Everything in this store is beautifully displayed and the shelves here are loaded with jade, marble and stone chops. Some are tiny and others are positively monstrous. Pick one and have your name carved on it in two minutes flat.

☎ 6301 6196
✉ 107b Liulichang Dongjie
🕑 9am-6pm Ⓜ Hepingmen, then any bus south

Herborist

佰草集 (4, E5)

Fragrant jars of bath oil, foot scrubs and facial masks based on 'a modern interpretation of Chinese herbs' promise relaxation and calm. Unfortunately, the browsing experience is anything but. Store employees seem to think service means stalking.

☎ 8518 6573 ✉ BB41, Oriental Plaza, 1 Dongchang'an Jie 🕑 9.30am-10pm Ⓜ Wangfujing

Jiangnan Silk World

江南丝绸 (5, B2)

Part free museum, part hard sell, you'll get a free silk-making tour in English before being unleashed into the arms of eager sales staff and racks of gorgeous pure-silk quilts, carpets and clothes.

☎ 6592 7113 ✉ Workers' Stadium (north entrance), Gongrentiyuchang Beilu ⏰ 9am-7pm Ⓜ Dongsishitiao, then bus 113

Ruifuxiang
瑞蚨祥丝绸店 (6, A1)
Forests of fabric bolts crowd the inside of this century-old shop. There's Shandong silk, satin-silk and brocade silks woven with traditional designs like dragons, bamboo and the *shòu* (long-life) symbol.

☎ 6303 5313
✉ 5 Dazhalan Xijie
⏰ 9am-8pm Ⓜ Qianmen

Ruixiangge Tibet Classical Furniture
瑞祥阁西藏古典家具行 (8, H6)
This place is packed with Tibetan carpets, silverware and richly coloured embroidery and cabinets, and

curiosities like chain-mail vests.

☎ 6773 5926
✉ store 6, 4th fl, Beijing Curio City, 21 Dongsanhuan Nanlu ⏰ 9.30am-6.30pm Ⓜ Guomao, then bus 28

Xinghai Yuehaixuan Musical Instruments
星海乐海轩乐器 (4, C6)
If you're not a fan of traditional Chinese music you'll likely find the instruments easier on the eyes than the ears. Beautiful *èrhú* (fiddles), *gǔzhēng* (zithers) and *pípá* (lutes) are sold here. The souvenirs are in the front; the professional versions made with bamboo, horse hair and snake skin are in the back. Ask to see them, and staff will give you a museum-quality explanation about them.

☎ 6303 1472
📧 lishuping@sina.com.cn
✉ 97 Liulichang Dongjie
⏰ 9am-7pm Ⓜ Hepingmen, then any bus south

Xiongdi Pipe Shop
兄弟烟斗店 (4, D2)
The carvings on these wooden pipes depict monstrous faces and far-away scenes that look like they've been lifted out of a children's fairy-tale book. It will take a little coaxing to get the friendly but shy staff to explain to you what it all means. Pipe and tobacco sets start at Y150.

☎ 6402 3396 ✉ 52 Yandai Xijie ⏰ 9am-late Ⓜ Gulou, then bus 60

Yunhong Chopstick Store
韵泓工艺制品公司 (4, E5)
Glass, plastic, wood; the chopsticks here come in every material and colour imaginable. You can probably cobble together a cheaper set at the markets but this is a great place to browse for inspiration. A simple set of chopsticks with rests is about Y100 to Y200 but some on display go into the thousands.

☎ 6357 3040 ✉ 277 Wangfujing Dajie ⏰ 9am-11pm Ⓜ Wangfujing

Zhaojia Chaowai Market
兆佳朝外市场 (8, H5)
Here you'll find loads of traditional Chinese furniture, from opium beds to barrel-stools. Many stall owners claim their wares date back to the Qing and Ming dynasties – highly unlikely, but prices are reasonable. International shipping offices are on the 1st floor to help you get your spoils back home.

☎ 6770 6402 ✉ 43 Huawei Beilu ⏰ 9am-6pm Ⓜ Guomao, then bus 28

SPORTS & OUTDOOR EQUIPMENT

Golf Store
丹翔 (5, B2)

Nestled in amongst several other stores of its kind, foreign businessmen home in on this one stall to get their knock-off clubs for around Y1300. Ask for Jet and you'll know you are in the right place.

☎ 133 0129 7651 (English) ✉ west side of Sanlitun Yaxiu Clothing Market ⏰ 9am-9pm Ⓜ Dongsishitiao, then bus 113

King Camp
健野户外用品专营店 (5, A3)

Tucked in the wall of the monstrous stadium, this store doesn't look like much on the outside and is easy to miss. But step inside and King Camp lives up to its name, with excellent jackets, footwear and tents.

☎ 6530 1609 ✉ Workers' Stadium (north entrance), Gongrentiyuchang Beilu ⏰ 9am-9pm Ⓜ Dongsishitiao, then any bus east

Sport 100
运动 100 (4, E5)

Egads! Built around a winding, faux indoor jogging track, this place has equipment, gadgets and very *à la mode* outfits for every sport imaginable.

✉ AA67, Oriental Plaza, 1 Dongchang'an Jie ⏰ 9.30am-10pm Ⓜ Wangfujing

Tangjing Tiyu
塘京体育 (4, D2)

This hole-in-the-wall shop in Lotus Lanes is wholly dedicated to table tennis, one of China's most beloved activities. The walls of Tangjing Tiyu are decorated with photographs of Chinese table-tennis champions, as well as ping-pong paddles for sale. The paddles range in price from Y60 to over Y600.

☎ 6616 4829 ✉ Dianmen Xidajie, btwn Lotus Lanes & Qianhai Xijie ⏰ 9am-6.30pm 🚌 13 or 118

Do a lap of the track: Sport 100

Eating

As you squeeze onto a local bus, relax under a tree in the park or whiz past a group of people on your bike, you'll be met by the same greeting: '*Chīfàn le ma?*' ('Have you eaten food yet?'). Food is never far from the minds of Chinese people and eating is the most social activity in town.

Cuisines

Chinese cuisine is divided into four main schools, one for each compass point. While you'll encounter incarnations of them all here, Beijing traditionally subscribes to the northern school. Wheat or millet was originally much more abundant than rice, hence the popularity of *chūnjuǎn* (spring rolls) and *jiǎozi* (boiled dumplings). Beijing's most famous dish, *Běijīngkǎoyā* (Peking duck), is served with typical northern ingredients: wheat pancakes, spring onions and fermented bean paste.

MEAL COSTS

The prices listed in this chapter represent the average cost for one person's main course, excluding drinks.

Y	up to Y50
YY	Y51-100
YYY	Y101-150
YYYY	over Y150

The eastern school abounds with fish and fresh vegetables, and is where the archetypal 'stir-fry' originates. The western school is known to burn your pants off with its red chilli and flower pepper. Further south, the food is much more exotic – there's a saying that the only four-legged thing these people won't eat is the table – and food preparation is far more complex.

Beijing has become truly cosmopolitan in the dining room and you'll be able to satisfy cravings for everything from souvlaki to yakisoba. New restaurants are continuously springing up to keep pace with the ever more affluent, ever more adventurous, hollow-legged populace.

Etiquette

Dining Chinese-style is a steamy, noisy and often messy affair. Eating out is very communal, with huge groups of people crowded around big, round tables and sharing from the many dishes ordered. Dodge, but think nothing of chicken bones spat on the table or floor – this is very acceptable behaviour. And don't worry about being too tidy as you wield your chopsticks; spillage isn't given a second glance.

In all of this chaos, you might think etiquette went out the window with the leftover chicken feet. *Au contraire*. There are some definite do's and don'ts in Chinese dining. First off, don't pour your own drinks. Pour for your hosts and let them fill your cup, otherwise you insinuate that they're not taking care of you. Try not to ask where the rice is – it's often served after the other dishes and you risk insulting the cook's main courses.

Don't stick your chopsticks into your rice bowl while you reach for something else, as this is reminiscent of an offering to the dead. It's polite to finish your rice, but leaving a bit of the main dishes is OK as it lets your host know that you've had enough to eat. Finally, you'll be expected to try to pay, but don't fight too hard. The person who extended the invitation usually foots the bill.

CHAOYANG

Ashandi Restaurant & Wine Bar
阿仙蒂 (4, H2)
Spanish YY
The charming wait staff serve up big helpings of paella in this small, cosy restaurant. Besides mains there's a careful selection of tapas like Galician octopus and eggplant stuffed with chicken and veggies. All go down nicely with sangria or decent bottles of Spanish and South African wine. This is a great place to unwind after a hectic day.
☎ 6416 6231 ⊠ 168 Xinzhong Jie, opposite Workers' Stadium north gate ⏱ 11.30am-2pm & 5.30-11pm Ⓜ Dongsishitiao, then any bus east

Bellagio
鹿港小镇 (5, A3)
Taiwanese YY
It's got a nightclub vibe, spiky-haired wait staff and the most luxurious tasting *bào bīng* (shaved ice desserts) in the city. Next to two of the biggest, snobbiest discos around. Come here to see and be seen.
☎ 6551 3533 ⊠ 6 Gongrentiyuchang Xilu ⏱ 11am-4am Ⓜ Dongsishitiao, then any bus east

Celestial Court
天宝阁 (4, H5)
Cantonese YY
Past the trickling fountain and upscale blue-and-white décor lies one of the best dim sum lunches in town. The set menu (Y108) is all you can eat and comes with soup, veggies and dessert.
☎ 6460 6688, ext 2460 ⊠ St Regis Hotel, 21 Jianguomenwai Dajie ⏱ 11.30am-2pm & 6-10pm Ⓜ Jianguomen

Cherry Tree Café
樱桃园咖啡厅 (4, G2)
European YYY
Settle into a wicker-backed chair at this semi-formal café for a terrific **breakfast buffet** (Y108; ⏱ 6.30-10am) or an à la carte four-course dinner. Don't come here for flash but for calm and excellent service.
☎ 6500 7788 ⊠ Asia Hotel, 8 Xinzhong Xijie ⏱ 6.30am-midnight Ⓜ Dongsishitiao

Dongbeiren
东北人 (4, H2)
Manchurian Y
It's got everything from jellyfish to tofu dishes but the real speciality here is a choice selection of dumplings with fillings like donkey meat or pumpkin and egg, all beautifully presented. The staff don't speak much English but they are keen and make lots of effort.
☎ 6415 2855 ⊠ 1 Xinzhong Jie, off Dongzhimenwai Dajie ⏱ 11am-10pm Ⓜ Dongzhimen

Far Away Café
遥远西餐巴 (5, A3)
Mediterranean Y
This very friendly Western-style café specialises in steak and seafood dishes. Their two- and three-course set lunch menus (Y58/68) include a glass of red wine and there's live jazz and blues Friday and Saturday nights.
☎ 6551 3529 ⊠ 7 Gongrentiyuchang Xilu ⏱ 11am-2am Ⓜ Dongsishitiao, then any bus east

Jiang Hu Club
江湖会馆 (8, J1)
French/Chinese YYY
This place is pricey but serves a range of pasta and French dishes like snails in brandy sauce. It has an extensive French wine list and is a pleasant place to relax after a day of exploring Factory 798 (p18).
☎ 6431 5190 ⊠ 4 Jiuxianqiao Lu ⏱ 10am-midnight 🚌 403

Meizhou Dong Po
眉州东坡酒楼 (5, A2)
Sichuanese YY
This place has a generic interior but it's always full and is a good place to sample some of China's spiciest cuisine. The blistering-hot bean curd with chilli or dried chilli beef will have you screaming for water.
☎ 6417 1566 ⊠ 7 Chunxiu Lu ⏱ 11am-10.30pm Ⓜ Dongzhimen, then any bus east

Old Dock
老船坞 (4, G2)
Cantonese YYYY
Tuck into the elegantly presented dishes while floating in a traditional Chinese riverboat anchored in this restaurant's shallow indoor pond. A great place for a leisurely, romantic dinner served by smooth, professional wait staff. There's also more exotic fare like goose heads marinated in rice wine and a range of birds' nest dishes. Reserve ahead for a boat.
☎ 6500 7788 ⊠ Asia Hotel, 8 Xinzhong Xijie, off Gongrentiyuchang Beilu ⏱ 11.30am-2pm & 5.30-10pm Ⓜ Dongsishitiao

Outback Steakhouse
澳拜客 (5, B2)
Australian YYY
While more theme-park American than authentic down-under atmosphere, this family-style restaurant is a hoot nonetheless. The place to go for 'Prime Minister's Prime Rib', 'Wallaby Darned' cocktails and thick burgers with names like the 'Out-backer' and 'Mad Max'.
☎ 6506 5166 ✉ Workers' Stadium (north entrance), Gongrentiyuchang Beilu ☽ 5-10.30pm Mon-Fri, 11am-11pm Sat & Sun Ⓜ Dongsishitiao, then any bus east ♿

Tasty Taste
泰笛黛斯 (5, A2)
Cakes Y
Scarf down pillowy forkfuls of sour cherry cheesecake or chisel your way through the deliciously dense chocolate-brownie cake. The service at Tasty Taste swings wildly between impatiently overattentive and criminally indifferent. But the sweets list is endless and the coffee is the best in the neighbourhood.
☎ 6551 1822 ✉ cnr Gongrentiyuchang Beilu & Gongrentiyuchang Xilu ☽ 9am-11pm Ⓜ Dongsishitiao, then any bus east

Tongrenju Restaurant
同仁居酒家 (5, B3)
Sichuanese YYY
A casual restaurant to come to for a delicious meal surrounded by noisy locals. Do not miss the *shuǐ zhǔ yú* (fish buried in blazing chillies).
☎ 8561 9040 ✉ cnr Gongrentiyuchang Donglu & Gongrentiyuchang Nanlu, across from bus stop ☽ 11am-2pm & 5-10pm 🚌 118 or 403

W Sports and Music Restaurant & Bar
维京锐点 (5, C3)
Swedish YY
Part owned by Swedish ping-pong king Jan-Ove Waldner and hockey player Michael Nylander, the ambience here is bright and fun. This is the place to come when you're craving *köttbullar* (meatballs in cream sauce) and *pytti-panna (*fried diced meat with onions and potatoes). Popular sports events are broadcast on two giant-screen TVs and Swedish musicians are brought in regularly.
☎ 6585 6945 ✉ 120 Sanlitun Nanlu ☽ 10am-2am 🚌 43

Xinjiang Red Rose Restaurant
新疆红玫瑰餐厅 (5, A2)
Uyghur YY
Not to be confused with Xinjiang Restaurant on the main road, this traditional Muslim restaurant serves every lamb dish imaginable and gets wild with boisterous eaters and belly dancing after 8pm.
☎ 6415 5741 ✉ Xingfuyicun ☽ 11am-11pm Ⓜ Dongsishitiao, then any bus east

Indulge at Tasty Taste

CHONGWEN & XUANWU

Bianyifang Roast Duck Restaurant

便宜坊烤鸭店 (4, F6)

Beijing YY

Around since the Qing dynasty, come to Bianyifang for noise, bustle and sinfully rich duck with all the trimmings: pancakes, onions, cucumber, sauce, duck soup and buns. A wonderful place to watch Beijingers toast each other endlessly over tables groaning with food.

☎ 6712 0505 ⊠ 2a Chongwenmenwai Dajie ⏰ 11am-10pm Ⓜ Chongwenmen

Duyichu

都一处 (6, A1)

Beijing/Shandongese Y

With a history going back to 1752, this restaurant is known for its *shāomài*, a delicate, money-bag shaped dumpling with filling peeking out the top. Choose from meat, seafood or veggie options.

☎ 6760 6235 ⊠ 36 Qianmen Dajie ⏰ 10.30am-9pm Ⓜ Qianmen Ⓥ

Fengzeyuan

丰泽园 (6, A1)

Shandongese YY

A Beijing institution, this is where locals go to celebrate over Shandong specialities like sea cucumber with scallion or sautéed fish slices. Don't be surprised if diners next to you are busy toasting with round after round of snake wine.

☎ 6318 6688, ext 212 ⊠ 83 Zhushikou Xidajie ⏰ 11am-2pm & 5-9pm Ⓜ Qianmen, then bus 59

DON'T TRY THIS AT HOME

Once an imperial delicacy, Peking duck went mainstream after the fall of the Qing dynasty and scores of royal chefs opened restaurants after finding themselves on the street without work. The public quickly fell in love with the duck dish. But it's not easy to make. First, the duck is inflated by blowing air between its skin and body. The skin is then pricked and the duck is doused in boiling water. Finally, it's hung up to air dry before being roasted. When cooked, the duck's skin is crispy on the outside and juicy on the inside and served with sauce, pancakes, green onions and cucumber.

First Floor Restaurant

第一楼 (6, A1)

Beijing Y

This restaurant has the best *tāngbāo* (soup buns) around. It's not all that beautiful but it's bustling and a favourite hangout for locals.

☎ 6303 0268 ⊠ 83 Qianmen Dajie ⏰ 9am-10.30pm Ⓜ Qianmen

Gongdelin Vegetarian Restaurant

功德林素菜馆 (6, A2)

Vegetarian Y

Devoid of decoration and with a tiny booklet menu that looks about 30 years old, this vegetarian restaurant draws a loyal band of expats and proves you don't need flash or decoration for a warm, satisfying dining experience. Service is shy but charming.

☎ 6702 0867 ⊠ 158 Qianmen Nanjie ⏰ 10.30am-8.30pm Ⓜ Qianmen, then bus 17 Ⓥ

Goubuli

狗不理 (6, A1)

Beijing Y

It's noisy and the service is sloppy but this famous Tianjin *bāozi* outlet is a great place to try big, plump dumplings stuffed with crab or pork. Shoppers pour in here all day long for refuelling.

☎ 6315 2389 ⊠ 29-31 Dazhalan Jie ⏰ 9am-10.30pm Ⓜ Qianmen

Mian ai Mian

面爱面 (6, A1)

Japanese Y

Nourishing servings of steaming noodle soup, sushi and Japanese dumplings are beautifully presented and arrive at your table in minutes. The window seats are a great place to watch the buzzing street life around Qianmen.

☎ 6303 5816 ⊠ cnr Qianmen Xidajie & Qianmen Dajie ⏰ 8am-9pm Ⓜ Qianmen

Purple Vine Teahouse

紫藤庐 (7, A3)

Chinese Teahouse YY

There's a fountain trickling gently in the entrance and warm, attentive service. Menus are printed on gorgeous fans; there's one for tea and one for food. Located just outside the Forbidden City's west gate, this Chinese teahouse is a lovely place to

Quanjude Roast Duck Restaurant

unwind after a day fighting the crowds.

☎ 6606 6614 ✉ 2 Nan-chang Jie 🕑 noon-2am
Ⓜ Tiananmen Xi, then bus 5

Qing Feng Guan
清风馆 (7, A4)
Chinese Teahouse Y

The atmospheric Qing Feng Guan is cosy, intimate and beautifully decorated with dark furniture. Feel your body relax the moment you walk through the door of this teahouse. The owner here speaks English and will patiently explain the Chinese-only menu to foreigners.

☎ 6603 5979 ✉ Nanchang Jie, north of Dayanyue Hutong 🕑 10am-1am
Ⓜ Tiananmen Xi

Quanjude Roast Duck Restaurant
全聚德烤鸭店 (4, E4)
Beijing YYY

This multi-floored restaurant is one of the storied chain's better branches, and is conveniently located near Wangfujing Dajie. Since 1864 it's been serving that perfect combination: juicy duck and crisp scallions slathered in unctuous sauce and wrapped in velvety crepe. Get a seat near the 4th-floor wall and peer in at the cooks as they sling the birds in the oven. The ducks are lovingly carved at your table.

☎ 6525 3310
✉ 9 Shuaifuyuan Hutong
🕑 11am-2pm & 4.30-9pm
Ⓜ Wangfujing

Tianhai Canting
天海餐厅 (4, D6)
Traditional Beijing Y

With its New Orleans–meets-China look, this bistro serves sausage, duck, hotpot and lamb stew. A must for the atmosphere alone. There's black-and-white photos of old Beijing, a gramophone, and jars of snakes on the counter.

☎ 6304 4065 ✉ 37 Dazha-lan Jie 🕑 9.30am-11pm
Ⓜ Qianmen

Yong He
永和大王 (6, A1)
Chinese Fast Food Y

Don't be confused by this chain's freakish Colonel Sanders–like mascot. It has nothing to do with fried chicken and everything to do with dumplings, rice bowls and its wildly popular breakfast fare like hot soy milk and deep-fried bread. Go to the cash register for the foreigners' picture menu. This chain thinks of everything and outlets run like well-oiled machines.

☎ 8844 0088 ✉ Old Station Bldg, Qianmen 🕑 24hr
Ⓜ Qianmen

PICKY EATER

Royal dining was hefty work. Twice a day, Empress Dowager Cixi was presented with well over 100 dishes prepared by an army of 450 kitchen workers. The dishes had to nourish and be pleasing to the eye. Each one was tested by a eunuch for poison. If chowing down on endless courses sounds like fun, you too can dine like the empress at Fangshan Restaurant (opposite) or Li Family Restaurant (p73).

DONGCHENG

Baguo Buyi
巴国布衣 (4, E2)
Sichuanese YY
Done up like a Chinese inn of yore, this place is colourful and theatrical, with superior food at both ends of the price spectrum. There's tofu with chilli (Y12) or stewed soft-shell turtle in taro (Y168). Live *biàn liǎn* (a dazzling Sichuan face-change performance) each night at around 8.10pm.
☎ 6400 8888 ✉ 89-3 Di'anmen Dongdajie
🕒 11am-2pm & 5-9.30pm
🚌 118

Be There or Be Square
不见不散 (4, E5)
Cantonese Y
It's not exactly the classiest location, but with MTV on the monitors and super-animated staff wearing lime green and orange, Be There or Be Square always has a kind of energy about it. Give the Western dishes a miss in favour of some Canto favourites like *cha siu*

(barbecue pork) and *chun kuen* (spring rolls).
☎ 8518 6518
✉ BB71, Oriental Plaza, 1 Dongchang'an Jie
🕒 24hr Ⓜ Wangfujing

Courtyard
四合院 (7, D3)
Fusion YYYY
The dining room looks out on the Forbidden City's moat and the European dishes flash with Asian touches. There's lamb chops with spices from China's northwest and ginger-lemongrass-soy *crème brûlée*. Choose from one of the 500 selections on the wine list. About as perfect as upscale dining can get.
☎ 6526 8883
✉ 95 Donghuamen Dajie
🕒 6-10pm Mon-Sat, 11.30am-2pm & 6-10pm Sun
Ⓜ Tiananmen Dong

Donghuamen Night Market
东花门夜市 (4, E4)
Beijing, Hui & Uyghur Y
Gastronomic adventurers won't be able to get enough of the grasshoppers, scorpions

and bullfrogs impaled on sticks. For others, there's more familiar fare like noodles and kebabs. Polish it off with a fruit skewer dessert. Feel your teeth shatter the hard candy shell and plunge into sweet, plush-like morsels of strawberry inside. Divine!
✉ Donganmen Dajie
🕒 5.30-10.30pm
Ⓜ Wangfujing

Fangshan Restaurant
仿膳饭庄 (4, C3)
Imperial YYYY
You'll have all you need to feel just like Cixi. There's 800 regal dishes to choose from, doting wait staff and a dining room decorated with more gold and red than the eye can comfortably take in. 'A' menus are designed with foreigners in mind and include dishes like Beijing duck. The more exotic 'B' menus are geared to local tastes and include fare like forest-frog fat and camel-hump meat.
☎ 6401 1889 ✉ Jade Islet, Beihai Park (east gate)
🕒 11am-1.30pm & 5-8pm
Ⓜ Fuchengmen, then bus 101

Donghuamen Night Market

VIEWS TO DINE FOR

While Beijing has a lot of restaurants high in the sky, their food isn't always as tops as their views. It's well worth reserving for those that do satisfy. For an excellent fusion meal overlooking the moat, edged with the golden splendour of the Forbidden City, book at the Courtyard (p71). Or, let yourself be pampered by the superior wait staff at the Summit Club (p79) while you spin around at dizzying heights for 360-degree views of northern Beijing.

Gonin Byakusho
五人百姓 (4, E5)
Japanese YYY
This is a quiet and simply decorated restaurant that specialises in *nimono* (boiled) and *yakimono* (baked or roasted) Japanese dishes, as well as ornately presented sushi, tempura and sashimi.
☎ 6513 7766, ext 666
✉ 1st fl, Beijing Hotel, 33 Dongchang'an Jie
🕒 11.30am-2pm & 5.30-9.30pm Ⓜ Wangfujing

Green Tianshi Vegetarian Restaurant
绿色天食素菜馆 (4, E4)
Vegetarian YY
They've got everything from imitation fish to 'Peking duck' at this slightly gaudy but immensely pleasant restaurant. The lobster dishes are unconvincing but you can't go wrong with any of the 'chicken' or 'beef' choices. There's no alcohol but they have a tempting selection of milkshakes with flavours like pineapple and coconut.
☎ 6524 2349
✉ 57 Dengshikou Dajie
🕒 10am-10pm
Ⓜ Wangfujing, then bus 103 or 104 Ⓥ

Kaorouji Restaurant
北京烤肉季 (4, D2)
Muslim Y
Unfortunately, whoever painted the elaborate exterior never made it inside; the interior of this restaurant couldn't be more drab. But this place has been serving up dishes like lamb in ginger and braised lamb hooves since the Qing dynasty.
☎ 6404 2554 ✉ 14 Qianhai Dongyan 🕒 11am-11pm Ⓜ Gulou

Kosmo (4, D2)
Café Y
Come here to Kosmo, on the bank of Qianhai Lake, for its delectable juices like cucumber, celery, pear and pineapple, or drinks with muesli, yoghurt and low-fat milk. There's a limited food and sweets menu but it always offers up something new and different, such as white sesame cheesecake or curried noodles with chicken.
☎ 6657 0007 ✉ No 5, west bank of Qianhai Lake 🕒 10am-1am Ⓜ Gulou, then bus 60

A waiter from the Fangshan Restaurant (p71)

Li Family Restaurant
厉家菜 (4, C1)
Imperial YYYY

Step into the unpretentious home of the Li's, where Mrs Li creates masterpieces. Gastronomists take note: she can only squeeze three or four tables into her front room, dining is by reservation only and in summer she can be booked up for weeks in advance.
☎ 6618 0107
✉ 11 Yangfang Hutong
🕑 4.30-10pm 🚌 58

Liujia Guo
刘家锅 (4, E4)
Hunanese YY

This restaurant serves toned-down Hunan cuisine – only one handful of chillies instead of two. There's grilled beef and braised pork and more daring fare like stir-fried soft-shell turtle. Vegetarians can tuck into the mock mutton or 'peasant family'–style eggplant.
☎ 6524 1487 ✉ 19 Nan-heyan Dajie 🕑 10am-noon & 5-10pm Ⓜ Tiananmen Dong Ⓥ

Red Capital Club
新红资俱乐部 (4, F2)
Beijing YYY

Dine on Chairman's Favourite Roast Pork or Chiang Kai-shek's Balls (rice stuffed with peanuts and black sesame paste). With its 1950s Politburo-meeting props, this restored Qing-styled courtyard is high camp at its best. Dishes aren't so much listed on the menu as leisurely revealed in pages of coy, poem-sized prose. Not for the impatient or the very hungry. Reservations are required.
☎ 6402 7150, nights 8401 8866 ✉ 66

Dongsi Jiutiao 🕑 6-11pm
Ⓜ Dongsishitiao, then bus 113 or 115

Sichuan Fandian
四川饭店 (4, C2)
Sichuanese YYY

As the city's oldest Sichuanese restaurant, this place is famous among locals and Chinese tourists. Service and décor are a little drab but when it comes to food, this eatery delivers the fiery goods. Try the duck that's been marinated in wine for 24 hours, covered in tea leaves and cooked over a charcoal fire.
☎ 6615 6924 ✉ 14 Liuyin Jie 🕑 11am-2pm & 5-9pm 🚌 60 or 118

South Silk Road
茶马古道 (4, D2)
Yunnanese YY

This is one of Lotus Lanes' standouts. Opened by artist Fang Lijun, enjoy the ultra-hip décor and artfully presented dishes as the boats float by on Qianhai Lake. Don't miss the winning combination of fiery Yunnan sausage with an ice-cold beer.
☎ 6615 5515 ✉ Rooms 12-13, 19a Qianhai Xiyan
🕑 10am-1.30am
Ⓜ Gulou, then bus 60

Tiandi Yijia
天地一家 (7, D5)
Imperial YYYY

The staff's cool demeanour matches this restaurant's

Sign for the divine Li Family Restaurant

airy, minimalist space. The menu is done up like ancient parchment and the list of dishes is endless and includes delicacies like abalone and shark's fin 'to your taste' (Y1248).

☎ 8511 5556
✉ 140 Nanchizi Dajie
🕙 11am-2pm & 5-11pm
Ⓜ Tiananmen Dong

Wangfujing Snack Street
王府井小吃街 (4, E5)
Snacks Y
This pedestrianised street is a jumble of atmosphere and flavour. Stalls are bursting with food from all over China, including flat bread, oodles of noodles and pancakes. It's elbow-to-elbow and definitely worth a look.
✉ Wangfujing Jie 🕙 11am-8pm Ⓜ Wangfujing

Xu Xiang Zhai Vegetarian Restaurant
叙香斋 (4, F1)
Vegetarian YY
The fare at this newly-opened restaurant tastes so authentic that many meat-lovers can't tell they aren't eating the real thing. The daily lunch and dinner buffets are not to be missed. The dishes are endless, beautifully laid out, and you can wash it all down with exotic drinks like watermelon juice.
☎ 6404 6568 ✉ 26 Guozijian Jie 🕙 11.30am-2pm & 5.30-9pm Ⓜ Yonghegong-Lama Temple Ⓥ

Yuanfu Kaiten Sushi
元绿回转寿司 (4, E5)
Japanese Y
Settle in at the counter as the artfully conceived sushi dishes snake by on the conveyer belt and just try to control yourself.
☎ 8518 6817 ✉ AA73A, Oriental Plaza, 1 Dongchang'an Jie 🕙 10.30am-10pm Ⓜ Wangfujing

JIANGUOMENWAI EMBASSY AREA

Ah Yat Abalone Restaurant
阿一鲍鱼酒家 (4, J5)
Cantonese YYYY
Pictures of the chef staring out from wall photos and stacks of promotional material make the décor of this banquet-style restaurant a little off-putting. However, the eatery is favoured by Cantonese visitors and has some of the freshest abalone in town.
☎ 6508 9613 ✉ 1a Jianguomenwai Dajie 🕙 10.30am-10.30pm Ⓜ Guomao

Bleu Marine
蓝玛利 (4, J5)
French YY
It's well located and the menu changes often but you'll always have French comfort food like cod in lemon-butter sauce and beef tenderloin in three-pepper sauce. In summer, multicoloured lights are strewn about its outdoor terrace and it's a wonderful place to sit and take in the neighbourhood buzz.
☎ 6500 6704 ✉ 5 Guanghua Xilu 🕙 11am-11pm Ⓜ Yonganli

Danieli's
丹尼艾丽意大利餐厅 (4, H5)
Italian YYY
It's got fresh homemade pasta, bright elegant surroundings and one of the more interesting assortments of regional Italian wines in town. There's also a set business lunch on weekdays. Very pricey but very worth it.
☎ 6460 6688, ext 2440 ✉ 2nd fl, St Regis Hotel, 21 Jianguomenwai Dajie 🕙 11.30am-2pm & 6-10pm Mon-Fri, 6-10pm Sat & Sun Ⓜ Jianguomen

Elephant
大笨象 (4, H4)
Russian Y
This sombre restaurant is about as authentic as you can get. Russian expats hunker down at the tables as Soviet-era period dramas beam out from the bar's TV. Don't miss the borscht: it's got succulent beef pieces and is perfectly flavoured with dill.
☎ 8561 4013 ✉ 17 Ritan Beilu 🕙 11.30am-1am 🚌 44

Justine's
杰斯汀 (4, J5)
French YYYY
This French cuisine is the real thing – goose liver, fresh oysters, caviar, cheese and champagne and slightly snobby wait staff to serve it all.
☎ 6500 2233 ✉ Jianguo Hotel Beijing, Jianguomen-wai Dajie 🕙 6.30-9.30am, noon-2.30pm & 6-10.30pm Ⓜ Yonganli

Lemongrass
香兰叶餐厅 (4, J5)
Indian & Thai YY
Generic ambience, fantastic food and eager service are this restaurant's hallmarks. Dishes like red-curry beef and pumpkin and tandoori dishes are beautifully pre-

sented. Even the rice comes in a tiny wooden barrel. A takeaway menu is available. ☎ 6591 3100 ✉ 17 Jianguomenwai Dajie ⏰ 10am-2am Ⓜ Jianguomen Ⓥ

Makye Ame
玛吉阿米 (4, H5)
Tibetan Y
Slurp back some yak-butter tea and dine on mutton as glowing lanterns swing above. This atmospheric restaurant is always packed. Dinner reservations are recommended. ☎ 6506 9616 ✉ 2nd fl, 11 Xiushui Nanjie ⏰ 11am until the last person leaves Ⓜ Jianguomen

Phrik Thai
泰辣椒餐厅 (4, H4)
Thai YY
Lots of tasty Thai barbecue, curries and soups, and pleasant, nonintrusive staff. The papaya salad is one of the most popular in town. ☎ 8561 5236 ✉ Gateway Bldg, 10 Yabao Lu (running

south off main Yabao Lu, across from Bank of China bldg) ⏰ 11.30am-2.30pm & 5.30-10.30pm Ⓜ Jianguomen, then any bus north

Steak and Eggs
喜来中 (4, H5)
American Y
If you are craving eggs, bacon, sausage, toast and pancakes, you can't do better than this place. It's an authentic American greasy-spoon experience from the food on down to the Aunt Jemima syrup on each tabletop. The rest of the day you'll find anything from milkshakes to steak and mashed potatoes. ☎ 6592 8088 ✉ 5 Xiushui Nanjie ⏰ 7.30am-10.30pm Sun-Thu, 7.30am-midnight Fri & Sat Ⓜ Yonganli

Taj Pavilion
泰姬楼印度餐厅 (4, J5)
Indian YYY
This restaurant in the China World Shopping Centre has

it all: great food, a relaxed atmosphere and, best of all, Jasmeet, a manager so welcoming it feels like he's been waiting all day just for your arrival. House specialities like deep-fried vegetables and spinach stuffed with cottage cheese in special tomato-and-onion sauce should not be missed. ☎ 6505 5866 ✉ L128, West Wing, China World Shopping Centre, 1 Jianguomenwai Dajie ⏰ 11.30am-2.30pm & 6-10.30pm Ⓜ Guomao Ⓥ

Xiheyaju Restaurant
義和雅居餐厅 (4, H4)
Sichuanese YY
Enjoy excellently prepared dishes like hotpot or pork ribs in bamboo in this leafy, bright conservatory. This place is a longstanding favourite of both locals and the expat business crowd. ☎ 8561 7643 ✉ northeast cnr of Ritan Park ⏰ 11am-2pm & 5-10pm Ⓜ Yonganli, then bus 28

Yak meat at Makye Ame

SANLITUN EMBASSY AREA

1001 Nights
一千零一夜 (5, C2)
Middle Eastern Y

There's a choice selection of *merguez* (spicy sausage) dishes as well as vegetarian fare like falafel and tabouleh. The restaurant is a touch too cavernous during the day, but it leaves plenty of room for the nightly belly dancers to shimmy between the tables. There's a small bakery in the entrance where you can buy pastries with nuts, honey and rose water.

☎ 6532 4050 ✉ Gongrentiyuchang Beilu ⏰ 11am-2am Ⓜ Dongsishitiao, then bus 113 Ⓥ

Alameda (5, C2)
Brazilian YY

This is a chic, confident little gem tucked off one of Sanlitun Lu's side streets. The set menus are small but creative and change daily. With plenty of windows and simple décor, this restaurant is bright and airy in the afternoon and still manages to be cosy and intimate in the evenings.

☎ 6417 8084 ✉ Sanlitun Beijie, beside Nali Mini Mall ⏰ noon-3pm & 6-10.30pm Mon-Sat Ⓜ Dongsishitiao, then bus 113

Athena Greek Restaurant
雅典娜 (5, B1)
Greek YY

Whitewashed walls, splashes of blue, Greek music and warm, welcoming service make this a pleasant Sanlitun pit stop. The lunch buffet (Y58), 11.30am to 2pm Monday to Friday, is a great place to fill up before an afternoon of sightseeing.

☎ 6464 6036 ✉ 1 Sanlitun Xiwujie ⏰ 11.30am-10pm Ⓜ Dongzhimen

Beijing Dadong Roast Duck Restaurant
北京大董烤鸭店 (8, H3)
Beijing YY

If your patience isn't tried by the ever-present table queues, you will be rewarded with succulent duck with one of the crispiest skins in town. English-speaking servers are hustled to foreigners' tables for a quick duck tutorial when they order this city staple. A good choice for first-time duck eaters.

☎ 6582 2892 ✉ 3 Tuanjiehu Beikou, off Dongsanhuan Beilu ⏰ 11am-10pm Ⓜ Dongsishitiao, then bus 406

Bella's
贝拉西餐厅 (5, B2)
Café Y

Escape the frenzy of the next-door market in this un-assuming café. No marks for atmosphere but they've got sandwiches, coffee and serve soft drinks in multicoloured vase-like glasses.

✉ 58 Gongrentiyuchang Beilu (next to Sanlitun Yaxiu Clothing Market) ⏰ 8am-9pm Ⓜ Dongsishitiao, then bus 113 Ⓥ

Berena's Bistro
伯瑞娜酒家 (5, B3)
Chinese YY

This warm Chinese restaurant is a long-time favourite. It's done up like a European brasserie but the food leans towards Sichuan and can be heavy on the chilli. The sizzling beef platter or seafood in oyster sauce are both good choices as you taste your way through the bar's many imported beers.

☎ 6592 2628 ✉ 6 Gongti Donglu ⏰ 11.30am-midnight Ⓜ Dongsishitiao, then bus 113

Golden Elephant
金象 (5, B1)
Thai & Indian YY

It's cancelled its popular lunch buffet and the dining room is nondescript. But this restaurant still packs them in with gracious service, quality meals and desserts like sweet potato and taro cubes in coconut milk. Takeaway menu available.

☎ 6417 1650 ✉ Sanlitun Houjie, west of Sanlitun Lu ⏰ 11am-midnight Ⓜ Dongsishitiao, then bus 113 Ⓥ

Gustomenta (5, B1)
Café Y

With an eye-popping décor of lime green, deep purple and gleaming white, this

---

FROZEN GOODIES

There's a dazzling choice of ice-cream bars for you to try in Beijing. Besides the more familiar chocolate and juice varieties, you can get yours with red-bean paste, green tea or corn kernels. Taro, a root vegetable, pops up in many varieties as well – try the kind mixed with extra-large plump raisins.

newly opened Italian eatery is a breath of fresh air on Sanlitun Lu. Come here for gelato, sundaes drizzled with liqueur, light meals and, of course, a killer espresso.
☎ 6417 8890 ✉ 24 Sanlitun Lu ☷ 9am-2am Ⓜ Dongsishitiao, then bus 113

Java & Yangon (5, B1)
Indonesian & Myanmar Y
A unique little gem with an exciting menu showcasing the best of the two countries' cuisines. Chicken in coconut gravy, pig-ear salad and choice meats marinated in Indonesian spices and lemongrass are just some of the dishes. Go on a weekday and you'll be elbow-to-elbow with workers from the nearby embassies who flock to the restaurant for its terrific set-lunch menu (Y38). There's also free delivery.
☎ 8451 7489 ✉ Sanlitun Xiwujie, lane behind Friendship Store ☷ noon-2.30pm & 5-10.30pm Ⓜ Dongzhimen, then bus 416

Kiosk (5, C2)
Serbian Y
The fries are voluptuous velvet mouthfuls on the inside covered by a brittle-crisp deep-fried skin. The monstrous burgers and sandwiches are embedded with sweet-hot chillies and served on crusty bread with maximum mouth feel. All this from a food stand the size of a bedroom closet. Do NOT leave the city without a visit.
☎ 6413 2461 ✉ Sanlitun Beijie, hut next to Jazz-Ya ☷ 10.30am-9.30pm Tue-Sun Ⓜ Dongsishitiao, then bus 113

Mediterraneo
美丽海西餐厅 (5, B2)
Mediterranean YY
This restaurant serves up a great choice of risottos, pastas and couscous dishes, along with some terrific seafood like cod baked in tahini sauce. Best of all, there's a patio out the front which is surrounded by shrubbery. It's a great place to hide out in the afternoons to write postcards with a cold chardonnay. At night, it transforms into a buzzing outdoor terrace.
☎ 6415 3691 ✉ Bldg 8, 1a Sanlitun Lu ☷ 11.30am-10.30pm Sun-Thu, 11.30am-11.30pm Fri & Sat Ⓜ Dongsishitiao, then bus 113 Ⓥ

Scholtzsky's Deli
斯乐斯基 (5, C2)
American Y
The place to go for American-sized meat sandwiches, salads and sweets. Except for blips like the bizarrely cookie-shaped sourdough and wheat breads by the counter, this place does deli food well.
☎ 6539 3922 ✉ Unit 102, Pacific Century Place, 2a Gongti Beilu ☷ 8am-9pm Ⓜ Dongsishitiao, then bus 113 Ⓥ

Serve the People
为人民服务 (5, B1)
Thai YY
So, the service isn't always the most proactive... You'll

The menu outside the entrance to Mediterraneo

have forgotten about it by the time you've eaten your way through the *tom yam* (spicy, lemongrass-flavoured soup), pungent curries and the banana poached in coconut. This is the city's hippest Thai eatery.

☎ 8454 4580 ✉ 1 Sanlitun Xiwujie ☼ 10.30am-10.30pm Ⓜ Donzhimen, then bus 416 Ⓥ

Xiao Wang's Home Restaurant
小王府 (5, B2)
Chinese YY
Look for the giant water wheel and follow the arrow to the home-style cuisine at Xiao's place. Their famous Xinjiang-style chicken wings are a must.

☎ 6592 8777 ✉ 4 Gongti Donglu ☼ 10am-11pm Ⓜ Dongsishitiao, then bus 113

SANLITUN NORTH

Louisiana
路易斯安那 (8, H3)
American YYYY
Not to be outshone by a famous wine list, the kitchen's food menu changes frequently, turning out the best of Creole and Cajun favourites like jambalaya and fried oysters. The service is first rate and, even on weeknights, this place draws crowds.

☎ 5865 5050 ✉ 2nd fl, Hilton Hotel, 1 Dongfang Lu, off Beisanhuan Donglu ☼ 6-10pm 🚌 403 or 405

Paulaner Brauhaus
普拉那啤酒坊 (8, H3)
German YYY
Come to Paulaner Brauhaus to hunker down with towering pints of frosty beer and meat plates stacked with sausages, sauerkraut

and lashings of mashed potatoes. Finish it off with a slab of terrific central European–style apple strudel for the most authentic German eating experience in the city. A children's menu is available.

☎ 6465 3388, ext 5732 ✉ Youyi Lufthansa Centre, 50 Liangmaqiao Lu ☼ 11am-1am Ⓜ Donsishitiao, then bus 701

Red Basil
紫天椒 (8, H3)
Thai YYY
Don't let the gaudy neon sign and dreary exterior fool you. Inside is a sleek, elegant restaurant with pleasant wait staff and tempting choices of mild and hot curries.

☎ 6460 2339 ✉ Sanyuan Dongqiao, west side ☼ 11am-2pm & 5-10pm 🚌 403 Ⓥ

Sorobal
萨拉伯你 (8, H3)
Korean YY
Excellent *bànfàn* (rice, egg, meat, veggies and hot pepper sauce) and *páigǔ* (roast spareribs) are served at this slightly stuffy restaurant.
☎ 6465 3388, ext 5720 ✉ Youyi Lufthansa Centre, 50 Liangmaqiao Lu ⏱ 10am-10pm Ⓜ Dong-sishitiao, then bus 701

Sui Yuan
隋园 (8, H3)
Cantonese YYY
This friendly restaurant is renowned for its endless all-you-can-eat dim sum

lunch (Y68). Located on the 2nd floor of the Hilton Hotel, it's also an excellent place for seafood as well as gastronomic adventures such as 'bean curd topped with luffa melon and dried scallops'.
☎ 5865 5030 ✉ 2nd fl, Hilton Hotel, 1 Dongfang Lu, off Beisanhuan Donglu ⏱ 11.30am-2pm & 5.30-10pm Mon-Fri, 11am-3pm & 5.30-10pm Sat & Sun 🚌 403

Summit Club
顶峰俱乐部 (4, J1)
Mixed YYYY
Indian, Chinese, Western and afternoon tea every day –

there's a little bit of everything on this pricey menu. The service is masterful and the views at night to die for.
☎ 6590 3388, ext 5406 ✉ Kunlun Hotel, 2 Xinyuan Nanlu ⏱ 6.30-9.30am, 11.30am-2pm & 4-11pm Ⓜ Dongzhimen, then bus 413

Trattoria La Gondola
意大利威尼斯餐厅 (8, H3)
Italian YY
It's a cosy space with a quality menu of basic pastas and pizzas. There's no surprises here but dishes like squid-ink pasta with seafood and fusilli in traditional tomato sauce won't disappoint. Touches like red candles melting over the wine bottles give this place a nice touch of little Italy.
☎ 6465 3388, ext 5707 ✉ Youyi Lufthansa Centre, 50 Liangmaqiao Lu ⏱ 11.30am-2.30pm & 5.30-11pm Ⓜ Dongsishitiao, then bus 701 🚻 Ⓥ

MEAL DEALS
If you're looking to impress your clients (or clients-to-be), take them to the classy and relatively quiet Xiheyaju Restaurant (p75). For a more Western atmosphere, try Danieli's (p74), which also has one of the best business-lunch menus around. For drinks, look no further than Centro (p85), *the* place for upscale wheeling and dealing over martinis.

WORTH THE TREK

Jiuhuashan Roast Duck Restaurant

九花山烤鸭店 (8, D4)

Beijing YY

There's kids running around the tables. The wait staff carry away dirty dishes by sweeping them into small bathtubs and carrying them out in teams of two or three. This restaurant is an absolute madhouse but its duck has heavy succulent meat and skin that crunches like autumn leaves. Duck connoisseurs swear this is the way it's meant to be done.

☎ 6848 3481 ⊠ Ziyu Hotel, 55 Zengguang Lu

🕑 11am–2pm & 5–9pm

Ⓜ Fuchengmen or Chegongzhuang, then 4km by taxi

Xinghuayuan Restaurant

星花园酒店 (8, E2)

Beijing Homestyle Y

The décor isn't much but you will be seduced by the perfect dishes, including pork in tofu crepes and pork with crispy noodles. Whatever the dish, this restaurant seems to nail everything from the taste to the texture to the temperature. The menu is only in Chinese so go, take in the beautiful dishes, and point. It's an adventure that will be well rewarded.

☎ 6672 2399

⊠ 17 Huayuan Lu

🕑 9.30am–9.30pm

Ⓜ Xizhimen, then bus 702

STREET FOOD

If you are looking for food on the run, line up with the rest of Beijing for some street food. The giant crepe-like *jiānbǐng* is crunchy and filled with egg, green onions and spices and sold from the backs of tricycles. You can have yours *là* (hot) or *bú là* (mild). There's also *mántóu* (steamed buns) or *ròubǐng* (cooked bread stuffed with chopped pork). If you have a sweet tooth try *tánghúlu* (sugar-coated haws on a stick). You can prowl Donghuamen Night Market (p71) and Wangfujing Snack Street (p74) for even more exotic choices.

Entertainment

Is it the Olympics? A more daring generation of venue owners? A more discerning crowd of culture vultures? Whatever the reason, nightlife is revving up in the capital and a new breed of Beijingers is heading out in droves to sop it all up. Whether you're interested in watching puppets, listening to live jazz, sipping a martini or trolling the city's underground punk clubs, you'll likely be impressed by what Beijing has to offer. New bars and clubs are cropping up all over town, run by a young, more worldly generation that includes artists and musicians. These venues have plenty of atmosphere, play cutting-edge music and are quickly overtaking the stale karaoke-pumping, *báijiǔ*-slinging drinking holes of the past. On any given night there are also scores of Chinese opera and acrobatics performances and these traditional entertainment forms should not be missed.

> ## TOP SPOTS
> Sanlitun is synonymous with Beijing nightlife. But proving nothing is sacred, city planners recently demolished everything along Sanlitun Nanlu, wiping out some of the city's more interesting bars and live venues. Running north, 'Sanlitun Bar Street' (Sanlitun Lu) is filled with cookie-cutter clubs. Skip them. The best bars and discos are found in the warren of alleyways off the main drag. East of here, the area around Chaoyang Amusement Park has gems like Latinos (p87) and the World of Suzie Wong (p88), Beijing's best club. The banks of Qianhai and Houhai Lakes are also packed with clubs and discos and are among the best places to party down in summer.

Theatre is the only art form that hasn't quite found its audience. The Cultural Revolution didn't exactly help it along and stage drama has never fared well against the competition from opera and DVD. These days there are a growing number of theatres where you can check out local thespians. Though performances are almost exclusively in Chinese, they are worth a visit, if only to rub elbows with the city's small yet devoted group of theatre fans.

Entrance into the majority of clubs and bars is free from Monday to Friday with weekend cover charges of up to Y50. But keep in mind that weekday clubbing in Beijing still hasn't quite taken off. Don't be surprised if, even late on a Thursday night, the staff outnumbers the partiers at some of the city's hippest nightspots. Beijingers seem to prefer saving up for Friday and Saturday nights when many clubs are open to dawn.

Information

There's a thriving expat press putting out free English-language listings and entertainment magazines so it will be no problem to find out what's going on in the city. The most complete is *that's Beijing*, a well-written monthly magazine with independent, opinionated listings. *Time Out Beijing* has fewer listings but their reviews are more detailed and include regular features on shopping and culture. Others to keep an eye out for are *Beijing This Month* and the bi-weekly *City Weekend*. It's a good idea to check these listings, especially for bars and clubs, before you head out. Even Beijing's most popular nightspots are known to shut inexplicably or swap locations with each other without much warning.

BARS

Bar Blu (5, B2)
This bar has something for everyone: there's a dance floor, a lounge and a gorgeous rooftop terrace. Don't miss its Flaming Lamborghini cocktail – five 'secret' liqueurs stacked in three separate glasses and set alight for Y90.
☎ 6416 7567 ⊠ 4th fl, Tongli Studios, Sanlitun Beilu ◷ 4pm-late Ⓜ Dongsishi-tiao, then bus 113

Black Ant Bar
黑蚁吧 (5, C3)
Its day job selling camping equipment has been put on the back burner, but you can still come here for hip-hop and cheap beer in a grungy college atmosphere.
☎ 6502 1385 ⊠ 3 Baijiazhuang Lu ◷ 8pm-2am Ⓜ Yonganli, then bus 43

Bridge Bar
桥吧 (4, D2)
Nothing beats perching on the rooftop terrace at Bridge Bar with a tea or beer and taking in the views over the Silver Ingot Bridge. Come here and make a day of it. There's sandwiches and pizza served during the day and hip-hop and Y30 cocktails at night. You won't have to leave your roost 'til closing.
☎ 6615 1366 ⊠ 14 Yinding Qiao ◷ 2pm-2am Ⓜ Gulou, then bus 60

Buddha Café
不大 (4, D2)
With black-and-white photographs of Beijing's *hútòngs*, wooden benches and a great drinks menu, Buddha Café is a comfortable place to relax. In summer its lakeside tables are deserv-edly popular. The smaller

branch a few doors down serves food.
☎ 6617 9488 ⊠ 2 Yind-ing Qiao ◷ 11am-11pm Ⓜ Gulou, then bus 60

Bus Bar
大蓬车 (5, A2)
Yes, it's just what it sounds like, and no, it's not exactly the destination of choice for Beijing hipsters. However, the drinks are cheap, the atmosphere pleasantly gritty, and, if you're feeling claustro-phobic, there are tables and chairs outside in the summer. Besides, how often do you get to party on a gutted, paint-splattered bus?
⊠ parking lot across from Workers' Stadium north gate ◷ 6pm-late Ⓜ Dongsishi-tiao, then bus 113

Charlie's Bar
查理酒吧 (4, J5)
This place was one of the city's most popular bars

Relax outside Buddha Café

SPECIAL EVENTS

Late January/early February *Chinese New Year* – 29 January 2006 and 18 February 2007; the biggest festival of the year, celebrated with three days of temple fairs (visit Lama Temple, Ditan Park and White Cloud Temple) and family bonding

Lantern Festival – 12 February 2006 and 4 March 2007; 15 days after Chinese New Year, this colourful festival parades through the evening streets in search of airborne spirits

March *International Women's Day* – 8 March; a public holiday with little fanfare

Birthday of Guanyin, Goddess of Mercy – 19th day of second moon; a great time to visit Buddhist and Taoist temples

April *Tomb Sweeping Day* – 5 April (4 April in leap years); a day for worshipping ancestors by cleaning gravesites and burning ghost money

Late April/early May *Tianhou Festival* – Taoists celebrate the birth of the Goddess of the Sea and Protector of Fishermen

May *International Labour Day* – 1 May; the entire city, particularly Tiananmen Square, is blanketed in flowers

June *Children's Day* – 1 June; kites blot out the sky

July *Anniversary of the Founding of the Chinese Communist Party* – 1 July; official flag waving in Tiananmen Square

August *Anniversary of the Founding of the People's Liberation Army* – 1 August; more official flag waving in Tiananmen Square

Ghost Month – when ghosts from hell walk the earth; it's considered a bad time to swim, travel, marry or move house

September *Mid-Autumn Festival* – 6 October 2006 and 25 September 2007; also known as Moon Festival; families get together and chow down on moon cakes

October *National Day* – 1 October; marching bands come rolling out

Confucius' Birthday – 27 October; aptly celebrated at Confucius Temple

November *International Jazz Festival* – groove to the rhythms of jazz bands from around the globe

back in the day. It's a little yesteryear now, but it remains a favourite of nearby embassy staff.

☎ 6500 2233 ✉ Jianguo Hotel, 5 Jianguomenwai Dajie 🕒 9am-12.30am Ⓜ Yonganli

Den
敦煌 (5, B2)

There's a giant TV screen, a great Western menu and rosy-cheeked expats perched on the stools. It's packed on weekends with people listening to pop music and mingling.

☎ 6592 6290
✉ 4 Gongtiyuchang Donglu 🕒 24hr Ⓜ Dongsishitiao, then bus 113

Guangfuguan Greenhouse
广福观的温室 (4, D2)

This former Taoist temple has been transformed into a restful bar. Climb the steep stairs (ladder?) to the roof for intimate seating and a first-row view of the street theatre below on one of Qianhai Lake's most manic lanes.

☎ 6404 2778 ✉ 37 Yandai Xiejie 🕒 5pm-late
Ⓜ Gulou, then bus 60

Hou Hai Café & Bar
后海吧 (4, D2)

This café and bar has a low-key atmosphere and is beautifully decorated. It has large rattan chairs and serves teas, coffees, beers and liqueurs. Kick back and enjoy watching the cyclists, vendors, sightseers and locals wandering past Houhai Lake.

☎ 6613 6209 ✉ 20 Houhai Nanyan 🕒 noon-2am
Ⓜ Gulou, then bus 60

Lush
成府路 (8, D1)

This is the linchpin of Wudaokou's mushrooming student-driven club scene. Go during the day to nosh on great focaccia sandwiches as laptop-toting students practice Chinese and vent about life in the capital. Go at night for great drinks as the same students vent about the West and exchange visa-extension tips.

☎ 8286 3566
✉ 2nd fl, 1 Huaqing Jiayuan, cnr Chengfu Lu & Zhongguancun Donglu 🕒 24hr Ⓜ Wudaokou

Nanjie
南街 (5, A2)

The drinks have names like Viagra Shot and On My Ass and shooters are sold by the dozen (Y100 for rack of 12). If you are looking for a wild night you know where to come.

☎ 6413 0963
✉ small alley opposite Workers' Stadium north gate 🕒 5pm-late Ⓜ Dongsishi-tiao, then bus 113

No Name Bar
白枫 (4, D2)

Sit yourself down here at one of the oldest bars on Qianhai Lake and peer through the jungle of greenery and wind chimes. Amidst the chaos of the Houhai club scene, this place has kept much of its original charm: there's still no sign out the front, the staff are still super laid back and loyal crowds still come here to wind down their Friday and Saturday nights.

☎ 6401 8541 ✉ 3 Qianhai Dongyan 🕒 noon-2am
Ⓜ Gulou, then bus 60

Passby Bar
过客 (4, E2)

Catering to tumbleweed travellers, this courtyard bar is relaxed, friendly and has a useful library of travel books. Its food is outstanding and the sangria unforgettable.

☎ 8403 8004
✉ 108 Nanluogu Xiang 🕒 9am-2am Ⓜ Dongsishi-tiao, then bus 115

Press Club
记者俱乐部酒吧 (4, H5)

This intimate, wood-panelled bar has the posh air of a pri-

vate, old boys' club. There's afternoon canapés and warm and attentive service. The business set will feel right at home.

☎ 6460 6688
✉ St Regis Hotel, 21 Jianguomenwai Dajie ⏱ 2pm-late Ⓜ Jianguomen

Propaganda (8, D1)

A little darker and a little seedier, with lots of hook-ups; Propaganda is where you go when your night at Lush doesn't seem to be going anywhere.

☎ 136 9137 6777
✉ Zhongguancun Donglu, about 150m south of Lush
⏱ 9am-2am Ⓜ Wudaokou

Tree

隐蔽的树 (5, B2)
One of the South Sanlitun demolition victims, this bar (formerly the famous 'Hidden Tree') has reopened in Beisanlitun Lu with its Belgian beers and the best pizzas around.

☎ 6415 1954
✉ 43 Beisanlitun Lu, beside You Yi Youth Hostel
⏱ 11am-late Mon-Sat, 1pm-late Sun Ⓜ Dongsishitiao, then bus 113

LOUNGES

Aperitivo

意式餐吧 (5, B2)
Foreigners on long-term postings to the capital flock to this sophisticated yet casual European-flavoured lounge. It's not exactly a pick-up joint, but it draws a lot of solo business travellers and sparks have been known to fly.

☎ 6417 7793
✉ 43 Sanlitun Beilu
⏱ 10am-late Ⓜ Dongsishitiao, then bus 113

Centro

炫酷 (4, J4)
It's swish. It's got live jazz. It's got the best martinis around. No place in the city has better, or more deserved, buzz than here. Those in town on business should reserve at least one night to drop by and see what the fuss is about.

☎ 6561 8833
✉ Kerry Centre Hotel, 1 Guanghua Lu ⏱ 24hr
Ⓜ Guomao

Courtyard

四合院 (7, D3)
Upstairs from the restaurant is a tiny cigar room

where you can sip port in a leather chair and take in the perfectly framed view of the Forbidden City's east gate and the surrounding moat. A perfect end to a meal.

☎ 6526 8883
✉ 95 Donghuamen Dajie
⏱ 6pm-10pm
Ⓜ Tiananmen Dong

Jazz-Ya

爵士 (5, C2)
Expats love this Tokyo-style bar/bistro with the black-clad wait staff, wooden tables and killer jazz soundtrack. Asian and Western food is also served.

☎ 6416 2063 ✉ 18 Sanlitun Beilu ⏱ 11.30am-2am
Ⓜ Dongsishitiao, then bus 113

Rive Gauche

左岸 (4, D2)
A swanky but quiet wine bar, Rive Gauche has huge leather couches, local art on the walls, a great wine list and a collection of fishbowls, flowers and potted plants.

☎ 6401 2302 ✉ south end of Jinding Qiao near post office ⏱ 11am-late
Ⓜ Gulou, then bus 60

PUBS

Black Jack Garden
幸福花园 (5, A2)
With Harley-Davidson paintings, faux-wood panelling and beer on tap. A cosy place to settle in for the night, shoot pool and belt back the beer.
☎ 6417 4628
✉ small alley opposite Workers' Stadium north gate
🕙 5pm-2am Ⓜ Dongsishitiao, then any bus east

Club Football Centre
万国群星足球俱乐部 (5, A2)
A comfy pub crowded with football paraphernalia, trophies and sports fans crowded around games on the satellite TV.
☎ 6416 7786 ✉ Red House Hotel, 10 Chunxiu Lu 🕙 11am-midnight
Ⓜ Dongzhimen

Frank's Place
万龙 (5, B3)
Sports on the big screen, Carlsberg and Guinness on tap and pool tables at the back; Frank provides a recognisable 'slice of home' for North Americans. It's very popular with expats who come here after a hard round of golf. You can fill up on buffalo

Shoot pool at Frank's Place

wings and burgers and breakfast is available round the clock.
☎ 6507 2617
✉ Gongrentiyuchang Donglu 🕙 10am-2am Ⓜ Dongsishitiao, then bus 113

Goose & Duck Pub
鹅和鸭 (8, H3)
It's got pool, darts and a giant-screen TV. Come kick back at this cavernous but friendly pub. The service is refreshingly proactive and drinks are two for one from 4pm to 8pm.
☎ 6538 1691
✉ 1 Bihuju Nanlu
🕙 24hr Ⓜ Dongsishitiao, then bus 117

Huxley's
德彼酒吧 (4, D2)
Like the Tree, Huxley's has picked itself up, dusted itself off and reopened. Now near Qianhai Lake, the new and improved Huxley's is cosier and darker than its Sanlitun incarnation but its local and expat crowd remain the same.
☎ 6402 7825
✉ 16 Yandai Xiejie
🕙 6pm-late
Ⓜ Gulou, then bus 60

ROCKET FUEL
Báijiǔ (white spirit) is the Chinese answer to Russian vodka or Mexican tequila. It's sweet and clear and goes down like rocket fuel. Beijing men (and, increasingly, women) drink it by the bucketful with meals, to celebrate or just to pass the time. For less than Y10, *báijiǔ* will make your world fuzzy, play havoc with your motor skills and cause you to forget your own name. Erguotou is the 'connoisseurs' brand; it comes in handy 5L plastic drums.

CLUBS & DISCOS

Babyface (5, A3)
It's monstrous, trendy and one of the snobbiest clubs in town. You don't see many expats but young, hip, fashionable locals flock here in droves to dance, mingle and catch glimpses of the city's high rollers and the odd celebrity. Wear heaps of attitude and your hottest club gear.
☎ 6551 9081
✉ 6 Gongtiyuchang Xilu
$ notoriously variable, usually about Y50
☻ 8pm-4am Ⓜ Dongsishitiao, then bus 113

Club 70s
生于**70** 年代 (8, H3)
It's never going to draw the crowds like famous neighbour Suzie Wong's does, but this is a beautiful space with a dance floor done up in red and black and with plenty of beds and curtains to relax in. It brings in some of the city's best DJs on weekends, pleasing hip-hop and house fans.
☎ 6508 9799
✉ 1a Nongzhanguan Lu, west of Chaoyang Park
$ usually about Y50
☻ 8pm-8am Ⓜ Dongsishitiao, then bus 117

Club Banana
吧那那 (4, H5)
Part of the dreary Scitech complex, this club doesn't look like much on the outside. But step inside for an explosion of colour, guest DJs and music that runs from chill-out to techno.
☎ 6528 3636
✉ Scitech Hotel, 22 Jianguomenwai Dajie $ Y20-30

☻ 8.30pm-4.30am Mon-Fri, 8.30pm-5am Sat & Sun
Ⓜ Jianguomen or Yonganli

Club Mix (5, A2)
Mix is much maligned in expat circles but the proof is on the dance floor. Beijingers love this place and keep it packed while nearby clubs are almost empty. Favouring hip-hop, house and R&B, there's also a 2nd floor that attracts an older business-type crowd with its fancy appetisers and view of the dance floor.
☎ 6530 2889
✉ inside Workers' Stadium north gate $ Fri & Sat Y50
☻ 8pm-late Ⓜ Dongsishitiao, then bus 113

Cross Club
法雨 (5, C3)
Reminiscent of the bars favoured in Sean Connery–era James Bond movies, come here to relax in the comfortable, traditional Chinese lounge with a cigar and spirit. Occasional live jazz.
☎ 6586 5020
✉ 78 Sanlitun Nanlu
☻ 8pm-late
Ⓜ Yonganli, then bus 43

Kai
开 (5, B2)
If the chaos at Poachers is getting to you, this is a

smaller, more intimate space. Join the dancers by the bar (yes, that is the dance floor) or join the chatting crowd outside as they gesticulate wildly with their drinks. It's got a house party vibe that draws loyal crowds.
☎ 6416 6254 ✉ Sanlitun Beijie, around the cnr from Poachers ☻ 6pm-2am Mon-Fri, 6pm-4am Sat & Sun
Ⓜ Dongsishitiao, then bus 113

Latinos (8, H3)
One of the few exceptions to the 'Beijingers-don't-go-out-on-weeknights' rule, this club is always full of happy, hip-shaking dancers. There's terrific live bands from South America and a night here feels like being at a big friendly festival. If you're inspired by the moves on the floor, call them about their dance classes.
☎ 6507 9898 ✉ Chaoyang Amusement Park south gate
$ Fri & Sat Y50
☻ 8pm-late Tue-Sun
Ⓜ Dawanglu, then bus 31

Loft
藏酷酒吧 (5, C3)
Looking a bit like LA in the '80s, this popular and comfortable club has an outdoor garden, an art gallery and a dance floor for those moved

by the jazz, techno and house music.
☎ 6586 7877
✉ 4 Gongrentiyuchang Beilu (down alley next to Pacific Department Store)
🕐 11am-2am Ⓜ Dongsishitiao, then bus 113

Poachers Inn
友谊青年酒店 (5, B2)
With pop music bouncing off the high ceilings and a young crowd of foreigners and locals dancing on the tabletops, this is a great place for a long sweaty night. One of the loudest places in town.
☎ 6417 2632
✉ 43 Beisanlitun Lu
🕐 8pm-late Ⓜ Dongsishitiao, then bus 113

Public Space
白房 (5, C2)
One of Sanlitun's longest-standing residents. It's managed to maintain its atmosphere and remains popular with the 'see-and-be-seen' crowd. DJs spin house music in the evenings.
☎ 6416 0759
✉ 50 Sanlitun Lu
🕐 10am-2am Ⓜ Dongsishitiao, then bus 113

Tango
糖果 (8, G3)
A multi-floored fun house for adults. Bump and grind to hip-hop in the sleek 1st-floor disco. Head upstairs at 11pm for live house music in a bar decked out with illuminated statues, red sofas and diaphanous curtains. If you have any energy left, there are karaoke rooms for rent in the basement.
☎ 6428 2288
✉ Ditan Park south gate
💲 Y30 🕐 24hr Ⓜ Yonghegong-Lama Temple

Vic's
威克斯 (5, B2)
This club has couches, a pool table and a sweaty dance floor. Decorated in black and red, Vic's draws diverse crowds; most nights the music is R&B, hip-hop and pop. Ladies' night on Wednesday is a somewhat sordid affair.
☎ 6593 6215
✉ inside Workers' Stadium north entrance 💲 Sun-Thu Y30, Fri & Sat Y50
🕐 8.30pm-late Ⓜ Dongsishitiao, then bus 113

World of Suzie Wong
苏西黄 (8, H3)
Stepping into Suzie Wong's is like walking onto the set of an Enrique Iglesias video but with cooler music. The dance floor throbs with beautiful people moving to house, techno, pop and rock. Meanwhile, other even more beautiful people flop into giant couches or drape themselves across the traditional wooden beds piled high with silk cushions. But despite it all, there is nothing snobbish about this Shanghai-opium-den-cum-chic-lounge-styled space. Suzie's remains what it's been from day one – four floors and one patio of opulent décor, friendly faces from around the globe, attentive table service and superb cocktails. It's like being at the party of your dreams.
☎ 6593 7889
🖥 www.suziewong.com.cn
✉ Chaoyang Amusement Park west gate (through Club 70s entrance)
🕐 7pm-late Ⓜ Dongsishitiao, then bus 117

CINEMAS

Pirated DVDs and VCDs spill into Beijing so quickly that you can easily get your hands on films that have only had their US screen launch a day or two before. This does not do wonders for cinemas. To top it off, only a handful of Western films get the authorities' stamp of approval each year, making film-going for non-Chinese speakers somewhat dire. Nevertheless, if you're hungry for the big screen, the following cinemas are worth checking out. If you are going to a commercial cinema be aware that some Beijingers see movie-going as a social outing more than a time to sit silent in a dark theatre. Though the situation has been improving somewhat, ringing mobile phones and the subsequent conversations should be expected add-ins to the movie soundtrack. The click-click of people text messaging should also be taken as a given.

Centre Culturel Français
法国文化中心 (5, A3)
If you like your films with a certain *je ne sais quoi*, movies from France and China are screened here regularly. The cinema has both afternoon and evening showings.
☎ 6532 2627
🖥 www.centreculturelfrancais.com.cn
✉ 18 Gongrentiyuchang Xilu
💲 Y20/10 Ⓜ Dongsishitiao, then bus 113

Cherry Lane Theatre
友厅公司 (8, H3)
Popular with expats, this theatre shows Chinese films with English subtitles every Friday and Saturday evening.
☎ 139 0113 4745
🖳 www.cherrylanemovies
.com.cn ✉ 29 Liangmaqiao
Lu ⑤ Y50 ⏱ 8pm 🚌 402

Goethe Institute Inter Nationes
哥德学院北京分院 (8, D2)
Run, Lola, run to regular screenings of German movies with Chinese or English subtitles.
☎ 8215 2909 🖳 www
.goethe.de/os/pek/deindex
.htm ✉ 17th fl, 2 Zhong-
guancunnan Dajie
🚌 double-decker 4

Maple Garden Drive-Inn Cinema
枫花园汽车电影院 (8, J3)
More Beijingers are buying cars than ever before and this '50s throwback is thriving. Come as much for the atmos-phere as the newly released Western and Chinese films.

Best of all, unlike in regular theatres, you won't hear your neighbours' mobile phones going off every five minutes.
☎ 6432 9884
✉ 21 Liangmaqiao Lu
⑤ per car Y120
⏱ 7.30pm-late
🚌 south side of Guo Park

Star Cinema City
新世纪影城 (4, E5)
This will remind you of your snazzy multiplex back home. Come here to watch newly released foreign movies with subtitles.
☎ 6527 4420 🖳 www
.xfilmcity.com ✉ Oriental
Plaza, 1 Dongchang'an Jie
Ⓜ Wangfujing

Sundong'an Cinema City
新东安影城 (4, E4)
This cinema usually shows at least one Hollywood feature. If you're into Hong Kong flicks and can figure out the plot minus the subtitles, you've got a few of those to choose from as well.
☎ 6528 1988
✉ 5th fl, Dongan Shopping
Centre, Wangfujing Dajie
⑤ Y40 Ⓜ Wangfujing

ROCK, JAZZ, BLUES & POP

2 Kolegas
两个好朋友 (8, J3)
Opened by two music-crazy friends from western China who were lured to Beijing by its comparatively thriving music scene, this bar is a great place to hear under-ground rock and punk acts at ear-blistering volumes.
☎ 8196 4820
✉ 21 Liangmaqiao Lu (in-side Maple Garden Drive-Inn
park) ⑤ varies ⏱ 7.30pm-
late 🚌 402 or 418

Big Easy
快乐站 (8, J3)
The Big Easy has the feel of a Mississippi riverboat both inside and out. With live jazz and blues, gumbo and blackened tuna steaks, it's a favourite with foreigners.
☎ 6508 6776
✉ Chaoyang Amusement
Park south gate
⏱ 4pm-2am Sun-Thu,
3pm-2am Fri & Sat
Ⓜ Dawanglu, then bus 31

CD Jazz Cafe
森帝爵士俱乐部 (8, H3)
Owned by saxophonist Liu Yuan (whose band plays Fri-day and Saturday nights), this club has regular live shows. Monday is swing night.
☎ 6506 8288
✉ 16 Dongsanhuan Beilu
(south of Agricultural Centre,
tucked in by the overpass)
⏱ 4pm-late
Ⓜ Guomao, then bus 421

What? Bar
什么? 酒吧 (7, A3)
The owners of this tiny space favour rock but are committed

GOING SOLO

Chinese tend to go out en masse; the idea of going to the local bar alone (never mind one halfway around the world) is balked at by many locals. Unless you speak Chinese, finding yourself alone in a bar surrounded by crowds of people clinking *báijiǔ* can be a lonely experience. Solo women in particular will draw curious stares. But it's not all so dire. Try the World of Suzie Wong (p88), Poachers Inn (p88), Rive Gauche (p85) or the bars along the western shore of Qianhai Lake. Frank's Place (p86) and Passby Bar (p84) cater almost exclusively to foreigners and are good, non-pick-up places to meet people.

to showcasing anything and everything from the Beijing music scene. Friday or Saturday nights hear bands play anything from blues to goth to punk to Brit pop.
☎ 133 4112 2757
✉ 72 Beichang Jie
$ gig nights (incl 1 beer) Y20 ⏱ 3pm-midnight
Ⓜ Tiananmen Xi, then bus 5

Yugong Yishan
愚公移山 (5, A2)
You'll find anything from DJs to alt-rock to blues at this low-ceilinged, spacious club. Serious music fans can't get enough of this place. There's a good mix of locals and expats.
☎ 6415 0687 ✉ 1 Gong-rentiyuchang Beilu (in back

of parking lot) ⏱ 3pm-late
Ⓜ Dongsishitiao, then bus 115

THEATRE

Going to the theatre can set you back the price of a bowl of noodles or nearly as much as your hotel room. Prices vary dramatically, depending on who takes the stage. Always call in advance to check.

Beijing North Theatre
北剧场 (4, E2)
This theatre is a good place to see not only local troupes but also travelling companies from all across

China. It's got a good mix of comedies, experimental theatre and Chinese folk productions.
☎ 6404 8021
✉ 67 Jiaodaokou Nanjie, at Beibingmasi Hutong
Ⓜ Andingmen, then bus 104

Capital Theatre
首都剧院 (4, E3)
Contemporary Chinese productions can be seen here six days a week. Call for a schedule.
☎ 6524 9847
✉ 22 Wangfujing Dajie
⏱ 7pm Tue-Sun
Ⓜ Wangfujing

Central Academy of Drama Theatre
中央戏剧学院剧场 (4, E2)
The academy's students regularly perform here. This is where Gong Li and Zhang Ziyi, big names on the big screen, learned their art.
☎ 6642 5702
✉ 39 Dongnianhua Hutong
Ⓜ Andingmen, then bus 108

Central Experimental Drama Theatre
中央实验话剧院 (4, D2)
Off in a quiet *hútòng*, this theatre has regular experi-

The Capital Theatre by night

mental and avant-garde Chinese-language theatre.
- ☎ 6403 1099
- ✉ A45 Mao'er Hutong
- Ⓜ Gulou, then bus 60

Chang'an Grand Theatre
长安大戏院 (4, G5)

While opera tends to get centre stage here, the theatre occasionally puts on classical Chinese plays.
- ☎ 6510 1309
- ✉ 7 Jianguomennei Dajie
- Ⓜ Jianguomen

People's Art Theatre
人艺小剧场 (4, E3)

Find out who's walking the floorboards of Beijing's thespian scene by taking in one of the People's regular performances.
- ☎ 6525 0123
- ✉ 22 Wangfujing Dajie (behind Capital Theatre)
- Ⓜ Wangfujing

CLASSICAL MUSIC

Beijing Concert Hall
北京音乐厅 (4, C5)

This elaborate concert hall has nightly performances of classical Chinese music plus international repertoires including Western classical music.
- ☎ 6605 5812 ✉ 1 Beixinhua Jie 💲 Y50-500
- 🕐 usually 7.30pm Ⓜ Xidan

Century Theatre
世纪剧院 (8, H3)

The violin, cello and flute get centre stage here with top symphony orchestras. It also has occasional ballet performances.
- ☎ 6466 4805
- ✉ 40 Liangmaqiao Lu
- 💲 generally Y100-500
- 🕐 usually 7.30pm 🚌 402

Forbidden City Concert Hall
中山公园音乐堂 (7, B4)

This concert hall in Zhongshan Park showcases classical and traditional Chinese music nightly. There are also occasional opera performances.
- ☎ 6559 8285
- ✉ Zhongshan Park
- 💲 Y50-500 🕐 usually 7.30pm Ⓜ Tiananmen Xi

National Library Concert Hall
国图音乐厅 (8, D3)

New interpretations of classical Chinese tunes as well as classical pieces from around the world are performed here.
- ☎ 6848 5462 ✉ 33 Zhongguancun Nandajie
- 🕐 usually 7.30pm
- Ⓜ Xizhimen, then 10min taxi ride

Poly Plaza International Theatre
保利大厦国际剧院 (4, G2)

You can find a wide range of music performances here, from Chinese folk to the China Philharmonic Orchestra.
- ☎ 6500 1188, ext 5127
- ✉ Poly Plaza, 14 Dongzhimen Nandajie
- 💲 Y100-680 🕐 usually 7.30pm Ⓜ Dongsishitiao

Sanwei Bookstore & Teahouse
三味书屋 (4, B5)

After browsing through the bookshop, head upstairs to the teahouse for live traditional Chinese music Saturday nights. Reservations recommended.
- ☎ 6601 3204 ✉ 60 Fuxingmennei Dajie
- 💲 Y30 🕐 9.30am-10.30pm
- Ⓜ Xidan

ACROBATICS & KUNG FU

Chaoyang Theatre
朝阳剧场 (8, H4)

Visiting acrobatic troupes fill the stage with plate-spinning and hoop-jumping while vendors prowl the seats selling things like ice-cream bars.
- ☎ 6507 2421
- ✉ 36 Dongsanhuan Beilu
- 💲 from Y80 🕐 7.30pm
- Ⓜ Chaoyangmen, then bus 101

Heaven & Earth Theatre
天地剧场 (4, G2)

Young performers from the China Acrobatic Circus mesmerise the crowd with joint-popping, mind-bending routines. This is a favourite with tour groups; book ahead. You can also visit the **circus school** (☎ 6502 3984) to see the performers training.
- ☎ 6416 9893 ✉ 10 Dongzhimen Nandajie
- 💲 Y60-200 🕐 7.15pm
- Ⓜ Dongsishitiao

Liyuan Theatre
梨园剧场 (8, F5)

Over the centuries, the monks of Songshan Mountain Temple have developed 'Shaoling Kung Fu' to protect their sacred grounds. The performance here demonstrates these ancient moves to a lunch-munching crowd.
- ☎ 6301 6688, ext 8860
- ✉ Jianguo Hotel Qianmen, 175 Yong'an Lu 🕐 performance 12.30pm, box office 9am-8pm Ⓜ Hepingmen, then any bus south

Wansheng Theatre
万胜剧院 (6, A2)

The Beijing Acrobatics Troupe is considered to give the best

acrobatic performance in Beijing. Catch it nightly.
☎ 6303 7449
✉ 95 Tianqiao Market St, at east end of Beiwei Lu
🕑 7.15pm Ⓜ Qianmen

OPERA

Chang'an Grand Theatre
长安大戏院 (4, G5)
Come here for an authentic Chinese opera experience. Members of the audience chatter knowledgably and slurp tea loudly while the stage is filled with giant operatic presences.
☎ 6510 1309
✉ 7 Jianguomennei Dajie
💲 Y40-150 🕑 7.15pm
Ⓜ Jianguomen

Chaoyang Theatre
朝阳剧场 (8, H4)
The audience here is almost exclusively bewildered-looking foreigners. Take your cues from the front row musicians. They erupt into applause and standing ovations themselves if the subtleties of a particular scene have been missed by the audience. Those in the expensive seats get free tea and movie-style popcorn.
☎ 6507 2421
✉ 36 Dongsanhuan Beilu
🕑 several performances nightly Ⓜ Chaoyangmen, then bus 101

Huguang Guild Hall
湖广会馆 (8, F5)
Elaborately decorated with balconies surrounding the canopied stage, this theatre hosts nightly Beijing opera performances. It's also the site where the Kuomintang was established in 1912.
☎ 6351 8284
✉ 3 Hufang Lu
💲 Y100-380 🕑 7.15pm
Ⓜ Hepingmen, then bus 14

Lao She Teahouse
老舍茶馆 (4, D6)
The performances here are a combination of opera, crosstalk and acrobatics. There's **matinées** (Y10-60; 🕑 3-4.30pm) on Saturdays and Sundays. Reservations two days in advance are recommended.
☎ 6303 6830 🖳 www .laosheteahouse.com
✉ 3rd fl, 3 Qianmen Xidajie
💲 Y40-130 🕑 7.30pm, occasional shows 3pm
Ⓜ Qianmen

Liyuan Theatre
梨园剧场 (8, F5)
Traditional operas are staged each night in Liyuan Theatre's far-from-traditional setting.
☎ 8315 7297, 6301 6688, ext 8822 ✉ Jianguo Hotel Qianmen, 175 Yong'an Lu
🕑 performance 7.30pm, box office 9am-8pm Ⓜ Hepingmen, then any bus south

Prince Gong's Residence
恭王府 (4, C2)
The gorgeous Grand Opera House in the west of this residency dates back to the Qing dynasty and is a fantastic place to appreciate traditional Beijing opera. It's a good idea to reserve in advance.
☎ 6618 6628 ✉ 14 Liuyin Jie 💲 Y80-120 (incl tea & snacks) 🕑 7.30pm Mar-Oct
Ⓜ Gulou, then bus 60

Zhengyici Theatre
正乙祠剧场 (4, C6)
Undergoing renovations at the time of writing, China's oldest wooden theatre is ornately decorated and a superb place to experience Beijing opera. The theatre, originally a temple, was bought privately and revived in 1995 and has been going strong ever since.
☎ 8315 1649 ✉ 220 Xiheyan Jie Ⓜ Hepingmen

Take in some Chinese opera at Zhengyici Theatre

GAY & LESBIAN BEIJING

The Chinese Psychiatric Association has declassified homosexuality as a mental disorder but the gay and lesbian scene in Beijing, though growing, is largely underground. Authorities still take a dim view of homosexuality, considering it a 'Western problem'. As a gay foreigner in China you are a potential target for discrimination. While very unlikely, it is not beyond the authorities to send you packing if you display what they perceive as 'overt homosexual behaviour' in public. Nevertheless, authorities generally turn a blind eye to the bars and clubs. That means gays and lesbians have a better choice of nightlife than ever before. For newcomers to the city, finding gay or gay-friendly nightclubs can be a challenge, as few places explicitly advertise gay and lesbian nights. When you check out the expat listings make sure to read between the lines. You can also check www.utopia-asia.com/tipschin.htm for tips on where to go.

Destination
目的地 (5, A3)
It's grey, it's barren, but on weekends every man in Beijing seems to be in here working up a sweat. For guys new to the capital, this is your first stop.
☎ 6551 5138 ✉ 7 Gongrentiyuchang Xilu $ Y20 ☾ 6pm-late M Dongsishitiao, then bus 113

On/Off Bar
上下线 (5, A2)
Low lighting, comfy lounge seating and red and silver décor make this a great place for a drink. It's frequented by gay crowds and the staff is welcoming and enthusiastic. Don't miss one of their frequent fashion shows.
☎ 6415 8083 ✉ 5 Xingfuyicun Lu $ varies ☾ 7.30pm-2am M Dongsishitiao, then bus 113

Pipe's Café (5, B3)
Lesbian friendly all week, this bar comes alive with locals and expats on ladies night, held each Saturday. Don't come for slickness – the dance floor is tiny, the same songs are replayed umpteen times in the course of two hours and as the night wears on music will be determined by whatever CDs are knocking around in your fellow partiers' bags. Pipe's loyal crowd swears it's all part of its charm and newcomers will find this a friendly, chill place to spend an evening.
☎ 6593 7756 ✉ Workers' Stadium south gate, 100m east of Blue Zoo $ weekends Y20 ☾ 6pm-2am M Yonganli, then bus 43 or 120

Rainbow Bar
水晶彩虹 (8, J3)
Step through the cylindrical glass door and over the little bridge to get to this club's pole-bedecked dance floor. Friday is lesbian night.
☎ 6466 6800 ✉ cnr Xingba Lu & Nuren Jie, look for the rainbow sign over the door $ Y20 ☾ evenings until late 🚌 402 or 413

West Wing
西厢房 (8, F3)
Inside an old watchtower, this lounge is lively on weekends, laid back on weekdays and is a favourite with the city's lesbian crowd. Buy your drink on the 1st floor then head downstairs for sofas, darts or to take your frustrations out on the punching bag.
☎ 8208 2836 ✉ inside Deshengmen tower, north of Houhai & Xihai Lakes ☾ 10am-2am 🚌 44

SPORTS

With the exception of football, ask a Beijinger where you can see some sports and you'll be given a perplexed shrug of the shoulder. A sports-bar waiter will simply point at the TV. At the moment spectator sports are absent on the Beijing scene but it can only be assumed that, as the 2008 Olympics approach, this will all change. Keep your eyes on the **National Olympic Sports Centre** (8, F2; 1 Anding Lu).

Football

The Chinese wowed themselves by making it into the FIFA World Cup and Beijingers have gone football crazy, packing out the stadiums. National games are played at the **Workers' Stadium** (5, A3; ☎ 6501 6655; Gongrentiyuchang Beilu) on Sunday and Wednesday. You can buy tickets at the north entrance a couple of days before each match or from hawkers around the stadium on game night.

Taichi

Technically taichi is not a spectator sport, but it is the thing that gets Beijingers up and out in the morning with a string of interested tourists behind them. The ancient art form is about energy flow and, while it looks like practitioners are going about it in slow motion, it is also a form of self-defence. Judging from the folks you see bending and stretching, it will also keep you limber well into your 90s. Good places to see taichi early in the morning are Jingshan Park (p37) and Temple of Heaven Park (p14).

Sleeping

Travellers have never had it better when it comes to looking for lodging in Beijing.

Top-end and deluxe hotels are sprouting up all over the city to accommodate the flood of tourists expected in the run-up to the 2008 Olympic Games. Deluxe hotels have all the amenities you would expect in the West, including tours, business services and Internet access. It's a plus for those looking for familiarity but a disappointment for those looking for something with a flavour of China.

Midrange and budget hotels are often somewhat frayed around the edges. However, a number of the city's atmospheric courtyard hotels fall within this price range. Steeped in history and with personal service, these are the most unique accommodation options. Reservations are a must in summer. Rooms in these popular hotels are often booked weeks in advance.

For those on more of a budget, the law barring foreigners from most of the city's midrange and budget accommodation was recently abolished. Not all hotels seem to have gotten the news, however, and some places still turn foreigners away. But overall the frugal-minded traveller has more options than ever before.

Never assume the hotel's listed rates are its actual prices. Hotels usually slash these by 40% to 50% in all but the busiest times of the year. The peak season for Chinese tourists is July and August, when midrange and budget hotels are very busy. The high season for foreign travellers is September and October, when top-end hotels tend to fill up and charge closer to their posted rates. In the dead of winter you can often bargain fantastic deals in all hotels. If you're going to be in Beijing over Chinese New Year, book ahead, as many hotels close down.

ROOM RATES

These categories indicate the cost per night of a standard double room.

Deluxe	Y2000 & over
Top End	Y1250-1999
Midrange	Y600-1249
Budget	Y599 & under

Deluxe and top-end hotels add a 15% service charge to quoted rates. Many midrange and budget hotels add a 10% charge. Dorm beds in hostels will set you back Y45 to Y90.

The grand entrance of the Hyatt (p96)

DELUXE

Ascott
北京雅诗阁 (8, H4)
It seems no detail goes unattended to at this chic, discreet hotel. There's secretarial, limousine and courier services and the swish, serviced apartments have every amenity imaginable, down to bedside reading that ranges from murder mysteries to books on doing business in China.
☎ 6567 8100 🖳 www.theascottbeijing.com
✉ 108b Jianguo Lu
Ⓜ Guomao 🍴 Taj Pavilion (p75) ♿

China World Hotel
中国大饭店 (4, J5)
This luxurious hotel has elegant rooms, confident service and free yoga classes in the fitness centre. The subway and dizzyingly opulent China World Shopping Mall are just steps away.
☎ 6505 2266
🖳 www.shangri-la.com
/beijing/chinaworld/en/
✉ 1 Jianguomenwai Dajie
Ⓜ Guomao
🍴 Taj Pavilion (p75)

Grand Hyatt Beijing
北京东方君悦大酒店 (4, F5)
This hotel is so gorgeous it's practically a sight in and of itself. Rooms have floor-to-ceiling windows and marble bathrooms. The indoor pool, done up like a tropical lagoon, has to be seen to be believed.
☎ 8518 1234
🖳 www.beijing.grand.hyatt.com ✉ Oriental Plaza, 1 Dongchang'an Jie
Ⓜ Wangfujing
🍴 Courtyard (p71) ♿

Kempinski Hotel
凯宾斯基饭店 (8, H3)
Business-floor accommodation is filled with memorable flourishes like complete Chinese tea sets and silk slippers for women executives. The Youyi Lufthansa Centre is perched next door so the amenities and choice of restaurants are endless.
☎ 6465 3388 🖳 www.kempinski-beijing.com
✉ 50 Liangmaqiao Lu
Ⓜ Dongsishitiao, then bus 701 🍴 Red Basil (p78), Trattoria La Gondola (p79)

Kerry Centre Hotel
嘉里中心饭店 (4, J4)
With elegant service and lushly coloured, ultra-modern décor, the Kerry Centre Hotel is a complete stunner. There's also a rooftop jogging track, children's playground and a massive indoor swimming pool. Internet access is available in the hotel's lobby, restaurants and pubs.
☎ 6561 8833 🖳 www.shangri-la.com/beijing/kerrycentre/en/
✉ 1 Guanghua Lu
Ⓜ Guomao ♿

Kunlun Hotel
昆仑饭店 (4, J1)
Like Versailles, the Kunlun Hotel is cavernous, endless

Fantasy becomes reality: the indoor tropical lagoon at the Grand Hyatt Beijing

and unapologetically lavish. The well-equipped business centre is open around the clock and deluxe executive rooms have flat-screen TVs perched above the bathtubs.
☎ 6590 3388
🖳 www.hotelkunlun.com
✉ 2 Xinyuan Nanlu
Ⓜ Dongsishitiao, then bus 701 ☒ Summit Club (p79)

Peninsula Palace Hotel
王府饭店 (4, F4)
The marble bridge and soaring lobby fountain are just the beginning. Recently renovated rooms now have fax machines, plasma TVs and sleek furnishings right out of an upscale décor magazine. For those that need still more luxury, Tiffany & Co and Chanel are just some of the big names found in the attached shopping arcade. The hotel also boasts two excellent restaurants.
☎ 8516 2888 🖳 www .beijing.peninsula.com
✉ 8 Jinyu Hutong
Ⓜ Dongdan
☒ Courtyard (p71)

St Regis
北京国际俱乐部饭店 (4, H5)
The slick, self-assured service and fantastic restaurants set this hotel apart from other deluxe accommodation in Beijing. The pool is open 24 hours and butler and massage services are also available around the clock.
☎ 6460 6688
🖳 www.stregis.com/beijing
✉ 21 Jianguomenwai Dajie
Ⓜ Jianguomen
☒ Danieli's (p74)

TOP END

Asia Hotel
亚洲大酒店 (4, G2)
This hotel has the most beautiful lobby in the city, minimally decorated with sleek modern sculpture. The staff are not very confident with English but this hotel has a great location near nightlife and the embassy district.
☎ 6500 7788
🖳 www.bj-asiahotel.com.cn
✉ 8 Xinzhong Xijie
Ⓜ Dongsishitiao
☒ Old Dock (p67), Cherry Tree Café (p67) ♿

Beijing Hotel
北京饭店 (4, E5)
Dating back to 1900, Beijing's oldest hotel has deluxe rooms with views across Tiananmen Square and the Forbidden City and is steps away from the Wangfujing shopping district.
☎ 6513 7766, ext 777
🖳 www.chinabeijinghotel .com.cn ✉ 33 Dongchang'an Jie Ⓜ Wangfujing
☒ Gonin Byakusho (p72), Wangfujing Snack Street (p74)

Friendship Hotel
北京友谊宾馆 (8, D2)
Built in the 1950s to house 'foreign experts', this hotel is a sprawling complex of

buildings surrounded by lush gardens and countless trees. There's a pool, fitness centre and an outdoor beer garden in summer. It's a bit of a trek from downtown but its popularity persists with tourists.
☎ 6849 8888
🖳 www.bjfriendshiphotel .com ✉ 1 Zhongguancun Nandajie 🚌 double-decker 4 ☒ Jiuhuashan Roast Duck Restaurant (p80)

Grand View Garden
大观园酒店 (8, E6)
There's a lovely atmosphere at this pagoda-roofed hotel. Traditional Chinese music wafts through the halls and your room key gets you free access to the hotel's namesake garden (p37) in the back. There's also bowling and a beautiful indoor pool.
☎ 6353 8899
🖳 www.gvghotel.com
✉ 88 Nancaiyuan Jie 🚌 56

Marco Polo
马可波罗酒店 (4, B5)
One of the newer hotels on the scene, the Marco Polo's plain rooms are spotless but a bit of a letdown after coming through the sleek minimalist lobby. However, the rest of the hotel rises to the occasion: service is precise and

STAYING AWHILE?

If you're looking for a serviced apartment, there are a number of options. The Ascott (p96) has deluxe two-bedroom flats starting at Y2200 per day. Spacious two-bedroom flats at the Asia Hotel (p97) start at Y3000 per day. Suites at the Red House Hotel (p100) include kitchenettes and laundry facilities (Y480 per day). Book ahead for reduced rates.

---

unfussy, the exercise facilities and trainers rival those of a commercial gym's, and the business district, Xidan shopping district and tourist sites are all nearby.

☎ 6603 6688 ☐ www .beijing.marcopolohotels .com ✉ 6 Xuanwumennei Dajie Ⓜ Xidan

Oriental Garden Hotel
东方花园饭店 (4, G2)

Recent renovations have given this hotel its second wind. It looks brand new, the business services are terrific and even the staff seem rejuvenated.

☎ 6416 8866; fax 6415 0638 ✉ 6 Dongzhimen Nandajie Ⓜ Donsishitiao

Poly Plaza Hotel
保利大厦酒店 (4, G2)

With a great location near the Sanlitun bar area, the rooms here are comfortable and beautifully accented in blues and yellows. Nab a corner room if you can.

☎ 6500 1188 ☐ sales-polyplaza@163.net ✉ 14 Dongzhimen Nandajie Ⓜ Dongsishitiao

Presidential Plaza
国宾酒店 (8, E4)

This hotel caters to business travellers with laptop rental, business-card printing and translation services.

The décor is slightly old-fashioned but the staff is truly outstanding.

☎ 6800 5588 ☐ www .stateguesthotel.com ✉ 9 Fuchengmenwai Lu Ⓜ Fuchengmen

Red Capital Residence
新红资客栈 (4, F2)

This place oozes with retro-kitsch communist décor. Stay in the chairman's suite, a concubine's boudoir or an author's study. The Bomb Shelter Bar, accessed through a rockery in the courtyard, plays Long March propaganda films and serves cigars and port. It all cleverly teeters on the burlesque and is so worth a visit.

☎ 8403 5308 ☐ www .redcapitalclub.com.cn ✉ 9 Dongsi Liutiao

Ⓜ Dongsishitiao, then bus 115 or 118 ✗ Red Capital Club (p73)

Swissotel
瑞士酒店 (4, G2)

After the palatial lobby, the rooms, though smart, are a bit of a letdown. But executives love this place and there are business services and meeting facilities galore. There's also an outdoor tennis court.

☎ 6553 2288 ☐ www.beijing.swissotel .com ✉ 2 Chaoyangmen Beidajie Ⓜ Dongsishitiao

Wangfujing Grand
王府井大饭店 (4, E3)

Business facilities at this hotel are tops. Perks for executive-floor guests include free 'health pillows' stuffed with fillings like silkworm excrement or buckwheat shell, said to heal neck pain and improve sleep. Located between the Wangfujing shopping district and the Forbidden City.

☎ 6522 1188 ☐ www .wangfujinghotel.com ✉ 57 Wangfujing Dajie Ⓜ Wangfujing, then bus 103 or 803 ✗ Courtyard (p71)

Guest sitting room, Red Capital Residence

MIDRANGE

Jianguo Hotel

Comfort Inn
凯富饭店 (5, C2)
This hotel is well located near the Sanlitun bar area and embassy district. Its rooms are nondescript but comfortable. Bonuses include discounts for kids and seniors with reservations.
☎ 8523 5522
⌨ www.choicehotels.com
✉ 6 Gongrentiyuchang Beilu
Ⓜ Dongsishitiao, then bus 113 ✕ Serve the People (p77), Mediterraneo (p77) &

Haoyuan Binguan
昊园宾馆 (4, F4)
Guarded by two stone lions in a quiet *hútòng* (alleyway), this courtyard hotel dates from the late period of the Qing dynasty. The standard and deluxe rooms have traditional décor and the room rate includes breakfast.
☎ 6512 5557
⌨ www.haoyuanhotel.com
✉ 53 Shijia Hutong
Ⓜ Dongdan
✕ Green Tianshi Vegetarian Restaurant (p72)

Holiday Inn Lido
丽都假日饭店 (8, J2)
This hotel is so full of conveniences and amenities it could qualify as a city-state. From corporate offices and Starbucks to bowling and baby-

sitting – it's got everything. The only downside is a remote location near the airport.
☎ 6437 6688 ⌨ http:// beijing-lido.holiday-inn.com
✉ cnr Jichang Lu & Jiangtai Lu ⛟ shuttle to & from downtown & the airport &

Jianguo Hotel Qianmen
前门建国饭店 (8, F5)
This hotel is slightly yesteryear but charming nonetheless. It's nicely located for visits to Tiananmen Square and the Forbidden City. The Liyuan Theatre on the 1st floor means the lobby is always buzzing.
☎ 6301 6688 ⌨ www .qianmenhotel.com
✉ 175 Yong'an Lu Ⓜ Hepingmen, then any bus south

Novotel Xinqiao Hotel
松鹤新桥大酒店 (4, F6)
For a midrange hotel this place has plenty of perks, including an outdoor tennis court and staffed business centre. Tiananmen Square

and the Temple of Heaven are within striking distance.
☎ 6513 3366
⌨ www.novotel.com
✉ 2 Dongjiaomin Xiang
Ⓜ Chongwenmen

Sports Inn
工体运动酒店 (5, B3)
Tucked into the eastern side of the mammoth Workers' Stadium, this inn's generic rooms are clean and bright. Just don't come here for quiet. Football games and major rock acts all pass through this stadium. The crowds' every cheer and moan vibrates through the building.
☎ 6501 6655
⌨ reserve@gongtihotel.com
✉ Beijing Workers' Stadium, east gate Ⓜ Dongsishitiao, then bus 113

Taiwan Hotel
台湾饭店 (4, F4)
There's nothing fussy about this well-run hotel in the heart of the Wangfujing shopping district. It's a favourite with Chinese tour groups and European couples in town adopting Chinese babies. Many major tourist sights are within walking distance.
☎ 6513 6688
⌨ www.btwhotel.com
✉ 5 Jinyu Hutong
Ⓜ Dongdan

CONSTRUCTION HEADACHE
Don't underestimate Beijing's building boom. When booking your hotel *make sure* you ask if there is construction being done nearby and ask to be guaranteed a room as far away from the racket as possible. Consider booking with a hotel directly; toll-free operators are often in call centres rather than in the hotel itself, so won't know about any nearby constructions sites.

BUDGET

Bamboo Garden Hotel
竹园宾馆 (4, D1)
This sumptuous courtyard hotel has traditionally decorated rooms and gardens that belonged to a eunuch in Empress Cixi's entourage. The occasionally high-strung service can be off-putting but this hotel remains a popular budget option.
☎ 6403 2229 ☐ www
.bbgh.com.cn ✉ 24 Xiaoshiqiao Hutong Ⓜ Gulou Dajie

Far East International Youth Hostel
远东国际青旅
舍 (8, F5)
Full of character, this is the city's best dorm accommodation. It has well-kept rooms and, providing you can pry hostel staff off them, computers with Internet (Y10 per hour) and phones for free local calls. The courtyard buzzes in the summer with travellers drinking cheap beer and swapping stories.
☎ 5195 8811 ☐ www
.fareastyh.com ✉ 90 Tieshu Xiejie Ⓜ Hepingmen

Friendship Guesthouse
友谊宾馆 (4, E2)
Built in 1875, this large courtyard hotel was home to Chiang Kai-shek in the 1940s. The décor is dated but the suites are colossal and come

with complimentary tea and slippers.
☎ 6403 1114; fax 6401 4603 ✉ 7 Houyuan'ensi Hutong Ⓜ Andingmen

Hademen Hotel
哈德门饭店 (4, F6)
This weathered hotel has comfortable rooms that are fantastic value for money. The subway's nearby and shopping galore is at your doorstep.
☎ 6711 2244 ☐ www
.hademenhotel.com ✉ 2a Chongwenmenwai Dajie Ⓜ Chongwenmen

Home Inn
如家快捷酒店 (4, J1)
This inn has the feel of an American motel. Rooms are spotless, bright, excellent value and, not surprisingly, almost always full.
☎ 6597 1866 ✉ 8 Xinyuan Nanlu Ⓜ Dongzhimen, then bus 413 ✗ Summit Club (p79), Red Basil (p78)

Lusongyuan Binguan
侣松园宾馆 (4, E2)
Five-star service sets this courtyard hotel apart

from the pack. Built by a Mongolian general during the Qing dynasty, the hotel has retained much of its character. Limited dorm accommodation is available for around Y80.
☎ 6404 0436; fax 6403 0418 ✉ 22 Banchang Hutong Ⓜ Andingmen, then bus 104 or 113 heading south

Red House Hotel
瑞秀兵馆 (5, A2)
It looks like a cross between a giant barn and a fire station, but this hotel has high ceilings and air-conditioning and is near shopping and Sanlitun. Breakfast is included with the room rate.
☎ 6416 7810, 6416 7500 ☐ www.redhouse.com.cn ✉ 10 Chunxiu Lu Ⓜ Dongzhimen ✗ Meizhou Dong Po (p67)

You Yi Youth Hostel
友谊青年酒店 (5, B2)
You like the nightlife? You like to party? This clean, spacious dorm accommodation is attached to Poachers Inn (p88), one of the loudest and most popular pubs in town. Laundry service and breakfast are included in the room price.
☎ 6417 2632, 6417 2597 ☐ www.poachers.com.cn ✉ 43 Beisanlitun Lu, off Sanlitun Lu Ⓜ Dongsishitiao, then bus 113 ✗ Golden Elephant (p76)

Noticeboard, Far East International Youth Hostel

About Beijing

HISTORY
Long, Long Ago
Peking Man, believed to be one of the first people to call Earth home, dwelled in the neighbourhood of Beijing some 500,000 years ago. The earliest recorded settlement in this area dates from about 1000 BC, after which Beijing developed as a trading town for Mongols, Koreans and tribes of people now known as China's ethnic minorities. Positioned on the edge of the North China Plain, the city became a strategic pawn during the Warring States Period (475–221 BC) and conquerors began to quarrel over it. In AD 1215 Genghis Khan, the great Mongol warrior, descended on the city; his grandson Kublai eventually became ruler of the largest empire the world's ever known, with Beijing (then known as Dadu) as its capital. This was China's Yuan dynasty (1279–1368), brought to an end by the world's first case of paper-currency inflation and a few natural disasters.

Imperial Heyday
The Ming dynasty (1368–1644) saw the city and its walls refurbished and the Forbidden City and Temple of Heaven erected. The basic grid of present-day Beijing was born. The Mings overhauled the Great Wall to try to keep out the Manchus, who waltzed into town anyway, overthrew the Mings and established the Qing dynasty (1644–1911). The Qings further renovated the city and added summer palaces, pagodas and temples. During the final years of Qing rule, invaders and rebels launched repeated strikes against Beijing. The Second Opium War (1856–60), the Taiping Rebellion (1851–64) and the Boxer Rebellion (1900) all took their toll on the capital, as did the Qing's last true leader, Empress Dowager Cixi (see the boxed text, p13).

Inside the Forbidden City

RECENT DYNASTY RUNDOWN

Tang dynasty (618–907) Art and literature flourishes, refinement of Confucian government exams

Song dynasty (960–1279) Zhao Kuangyin (927–976) founds the dynasty and becomes emperor; rise of the merchant class, strong central government, growth of cities

Yuan dynasty (1271–1368) Kublai Khan (1215–94) founds the first Mongol dynasty and becomes emperor; sees continued trade, international links, growing influence of Islam in the west

Ming dynasty (1368–1644) Orphan and former Buddhist novice Zhu Yuanzhang (r 1368–98) founds the dynasty and becomes Emperor Hongwu; the Great Wall is reshaped and extended, the basic layout of contemporary Beijing is established; Emperor Yongle (r 1403–25) moves the capital to present-day Beijing and oversees the construction of the Forbidden City and the Temple of Heaven

Qing dynasty (1644–1911) Manchus found the dynasty; outer Mongolia is conquered, territorial expansion in the west, foreign invasion, weakening of the central government; in 1908 Empress Dowager Cixi (1835–1908) bequeaths power to two-year-old Puyi, the last emperor of China

Revolt!

When Cixi died she bequeathed power to two-year-old Puyi, China's last emperor. The Qing dynasty, brutal and incompetent at the best of times, was now rudderless and it quickly collapsed. The revolution of 1911 paved the way for the Kuomintang to take power and the Republic of China was declared, with Sun Yatsen as president. Warlords continued to carve up and rule the north of the country and foreigners controlled important economic zones in major ports like Shanghai and Tianjin.

Crippling poverty and splintered rule was a recipe for further rebellion. Beijing University bubbled with dissent and it was here that Karl Marx's *The Communist Manifesto* found its way into the hands of a library assistant named Mao Zedong (1893–1976). The Communists soon emerged and pensively joined with the Kuomintang to wrestle power from the northern warlords. The Kuomintang turned on the Communists a year later (1927) and slaughtered them en masse. Communist survivors fled to the countryside and launched a civil war.

The Japanese invaded Beijing in 1937 and overran the east of China for the duration of WWII, causing the Kuomintang to flee west. After Japan's defeat by Allied forces in 1945, the Kuomintang returned to Beijing but its days were numbered; by this time the Chinese Civil War was in full swing and the Communists, under the leadership of Mao, cheered 'Victory!' in 1949. As the Kuomintang fled to Taiwan, the People's Liberation Army (PLA) marched into Beijing, where Mao proclaimed the People's Republic of China.

Aftermath

After 1949 came a period of catastrophic historical destruction in Beijing. The huge city walls were pulled down, hundreds of temples and monuments were destroyed and buildings were flattened. In 1966 Mao launched the Cultural Revolution and China was to remain in the grip of chaos for a decade. Anything considered antiproletarian was destroyed – from temples to the education system to countless people. Everyone was suspected of harbouring 'capitalist-roadster' thoughts, neighbours turned on one another and Mao's youth army, the Red Guard, terrorised the nation.

Mao died in 1976 and Deng Xiaoping, his former protégé, launched a modernisation drive. The country opened up and Westerners were given the chance to see what the Communists had been up to for the past 30 years. The 1980s and '90s saw the restoration of temples, monuments and schools. Glittering towers and high-rises erupted. China decided to embrace modernity without altering politically. In 1989 pro-democracy student demonstrations took place in Tiananmen Square; the government's brutal retaliation sent shivers through the world. Today there's a conspicuous absence of protest in Beijing. Political dissent exists, but unrelenting government coercion has consigned it to a deeply subterranean level. Beijing is straddling two very different currents – communism and capitalism – as it takes its place on the world stage.

ENVIRONMENT

With one of the world's largest city populations and a rapidly expanding economy, Beijing's environment feels the strain. Beijing also boasts an increasing number of lush green spaces; however, with water resources stretched to their limits and drought taking over much of the country, residents (and visitors) are urged to conserve every last drop. Air pollution is also a problem and sometimes gets so bad the smog can clog your lungs and wafts from drains can nearly asphyxiate you. But Beijing is making an effort to clean up its act. In addition to increasing numbers of green spaces in the city, recycling bins dot Tiananmen Square, officials

MIXED LEGACY

Beijing was a kind of giant grey village when Deng Xiaoping, a sheriff's son from Sichuan province, took over the nation's helm in 1979. Nevertheless, his modernisation drive that launched the nation onto the global stage also pushed the capital towards global city status. However, many Beijingers never forgave their 'Paramount Leader' for ordering soldiers to stop the 1989 Tiananmen Square demonstrators. It was a blemish on his record that haunted him until his death in 1997, aged 92 years.

trumpet a target of 90% of buses and 70% of taxis running on natural gas by 2007, and industries prone to pollution are being relocated out into the suburbs. China's entry into the World Trade Organization (WTO) and an Olympic mandate to purify the air before 2008 are largely responsible for Beijing's sudden green campaign. The International Olympic Committee says Beijing is doing enough, but with starry Beijing nights still an exotic event, it remains to be seen how much impact the new environmental measures will have on air quality.

GOVERNMENT & POLITICS

Communist by name if not entirely by nature, China's central government has its quarters in Beijing, although precious little is known about

its inner workings. Political competition is not tolerated in China and political debate in public has long been a dangerous and therefore infrequent activity. Beijing is an independent municipality within Hubei province, with its own mayor; however, like many national capitals, the municipality is directly under the control of the central government.

ECONOMY

After two decades of intense development, China's current annual economic growth of 9% is considered relatively slow. While the number of shops and shoppers in Beijing make the economic picture look shiny and bright, unemployment is on the rise and you will encounter the urban poor as well as the rural poor who have taken to the city in an attempt to find work.

Increasingly, state-owned enterprises are being bought out or shut down; many laid-off workers feel the government has abandoned them to the market economy, and social unrest is beginning to rumble. In an attempt to stimulate the economy, the government is pouring money into public-works projects and welcoming foreign investment. While

Chairman Mao: still hanging around in Tiananmen Square

some predict the Chinese economy will be the world's largest by 2020, it's difficult to know what the true picture is: mass corruption leads to catastrophically inaccurate statistics and also sends around 13% to 17% of GDP into unlawful ends.

SOCIETY & CULTURE

Over 95% of Beijingers are Han Chinese, with only a scattering of representatives from China's 56 official ethnic minorities. Chinese culture took a severe beating during the Cultural Revolution; the older generations carry many scars from the past and their way of thinking is often in complete opposition to the worldliness and fearlessness of younger Beijingers. While Beijing is a modern metropolis, traditional ideas and ways continue to live on in the lifestyles of many of its residents.

Religion

In recent years Beijingers have been returning to restored temples with armfuls of incense to appease their gods and ancestors. The dominating religions of Confucianism, Taoism and Buddhism have influenced each other and society for centuries.

Buddhism and Taoism give reverence to gods and goddesses who

STRINGS ATTACHED

Guānxì, or 'connections', string together much of Chinese society; you're either in the loop or you're not. It's the old practice of 'you scratch my back and I'll scratch yours'. In business it's referred to as 'going through the back door' and it can lead to anything from tickets on an oversold train to a job you have no qualifications for. When you meet Chinese people, the conversation may turn to what you've got to offer and how they can help you – they're throwing you the *guānxì* line.

preside over earth and the afterlife. Confucianism is more of a philosophy than a religion, dealing with the affairs of life but not of death. Confucianism defines codes of conduct and a patriarchal pattern of obedience; respect flows upwards from child to adult, woman to man and subject to ruler. Not surprisingly, it was adopted by the state for two millennia.

These days the government is nondenominational and is not overly concerned with religious groups unless they are believed to challenge state doctrine, as was the case with the quasi-Buddhist exercise regime Falun Gong, whose thousands of practitioners have been menaced into obscurity.

> **DID YOU KNOW?**
> • About 15 million people live in Beijing.
> • The average Beijinger's salary is Y15,600 (about US$1900) a year.
> • Around 70,000 taxis prowl the city streets.
> • The city will host 16,000 officials and athletes during the 2008 Games.
> • Beijing plans to have 19 subway lines covering 570km by 2020.
> • Beijing residents have access to 10,593 cubic feet of water a year (the world average is 35,310).

Feng Shui

Literally meaning 'wind and water', feng shui is a collection of ancient geomantic principles that see bodies of water and landforms directing the cosmic currents of the universal *qi* (energy). To follow feng shui guidelines is to create a positive path for *qi*, which can maximise a person's wealth, happiness, longevity and fertility. Ignoring the principles

Inside the Ancient Observatory (p27)

and blocking the flow can spell disaster. Temples, tombs, houses and even whole cities have been built in feng shui fashion to harmonise with the surrounding landscape. Within a building, the order of rooms and arrangement of furniture can also inhibit or enhance *qi* flow. The barging through of railways and roads and the construction of high-rises has incensed some residents, who believe the balance of the geography is being disturbed.

Family

Family has traditionally been the smallest unit in Chinese society and the more recent emergence of the individual has challenged its values. The traditional Chinese family is interdependent; younger generations depend on older generations for wisdom and guidance, and older generations depend on the young for subsistence and care. China's One-Child Policy (see p40) is changing the shape of families, creating a 4-2-1 balance (four grandparents, two parents and one child); if traditional values and practices survive, today's children will each potentially have six elderly dependents.

Etiquette

Many frustrations experienced by foreigners in China are based on cultural misunderstandings; what might be considered rude in the West may well be normal behaviour in China. For example, you queue for a subway ticket only to have customer after customer barge in front of you. After finally getting onto the train, someone practically sits on top of you. You glare at them only to be met with a grin. Keep your cool. In China, where queues are unheard of and privacy exists in the mind and not in the space around you, this is normal, not rude.

There are, however, a few things that are considered rude. When given a business card or piece of paper, always receive it with both hands. When writing something, use any colour ink but red, as it denotes unfriendliness. When giving gifts, money is insulting but imported goods carry much prestige and will win you points. You can smoke when you like but always offer the pack (not single cigarettes) around first.

ARTS
Acrobatics

Chinese acrobatic troupes will blow you away. Young contortionists turn themselves inside out and upside down while plate-spinners whiz countless plates through the air. Circus acts have a long history in China, dating back 2000 years. Routines were developed using simple everyday objects like sticks, hoops, chairs and jars. Difficult acts to follow include 'Peacock Displaying its Feathers' (a dozen or more people balanced on one bicycle) and 'Pagoda of Bowls' (a performer does everything with her torso except tie it in knots, while balancing a stack of bowls on her foot, head, or both).

Martial Arts

Martial arts combine discipline, flexibility, spirituality and defence. Practised in China for centuries, three of the most common forms are *tàijíquán* (usually called taiji or taichi), *gōngfu* (kung fu) and *qìgōng*. In all forms, respect and responsibility are considered paramount, while fighting is seen as a last resort. Taichi is very slow and fluid and its motions mirror everyday actions like gathering water. *Gōngfu* has become popular through Hong Kong action films, and focuses on self-defence. *Qìgōng* is a form of energy management aimed at maintaining good mental and physical health.

Music

Musical instruments have been unearthed from Shang dynasty tombs, and Chinese folk songs can be traced back at least this far. Today, traditional musical concerts are on the boom in Beijing. Performances feature the *shēng* (reed flute), the *èrhú* (two-stringed fiddle), the *húqín* (two-stringed viola), the moon-shaped *yuèqín* (four-stringed guitar), the *gǔzhēng* (zither), the *pípá* (lute) and the ceremonial *suǒnà* (trumpet). These instruments are also the musical stars of Chinese opera.

China has a thriving contemporary-music scene, largely initiated by Beijing's face of rock, Cui Jian. He laid the groundwork for punk bands like Underground Baby and metal groups like Tang Dynasty and Black Panther. These days, musicians from all over the country settle in the capital, attracted by its reputation as China's rock-music mecca. Fans have their choice of almost any style, from the manic grunge trio Cold Blooded Animal (Lengxue Dongwu) to ska-band Dirty Mind (Nao Zhuo).

Opera

Beijing opera is China's most famous form of theatre. With a history of some 900 years, the opera stage has brought together disparate art forms like acrobatics, martial arts, poetic arias and stylised dance. Traditionally, opera performers were male only and at the very bottom of the social ladder, on a par with prostitutes and slaves. Despite this, opera remained a popular form of entertainment, included in festivals, marriages and even funerals.

Most performances were open-air, compelling performers to develop a piercing style of singing that could be heard above the crowds, and to wear garish costumes that could be seen through the poor lighting of oil lamps. Performances continue to be loud and bright, with singers taking on stylised roles instantly recognised by the audience. The four major roles are the female role, the male role, the 'painted-face' role (for gods and warriors) and the clown.

'HI, I'M A STUDENT,...'

You'll probably have been approached at least a dozen times with that phrase by the time you leave Beijing. Usually it will be followed by an invitation to an art exhibition they're having nearby. Some people who go along enjoy meeting the students and buy a painting or two. They even say they've gleaned useful tourist information or received mini tours. Others are disappointed when they arrive at the exhibition and find that the 'student art' is actually just mass-produced commercial copies the students are shilling for. Most people come away feeling bullied into buying something and seriously ripped off.

Painting

A traditional Chinese painting may be achieved following much thought and total conception of the piece in the artist's mind beforehand. The brush line, which varies in thickness and tone, is the important feature; shading is regarded as a foreign technique and colour plays only a minor symbolic and decorative role. Figure painting dominated the scene from the Han dynasty (206 BC–AD 220) until Taoist painters began landscape painting in the 4th and 5th centuries.

It wasn't until the 20th century that there was any real departure from tradition. In the early days of communism, artistic talent was used to glorify the revolution. These days you'll find a flourishing avant-garde art scene in Beijing, with young artists gaining critical acclaim worldwide.

Literature

Over time, Beijing has both produced and attracted well-known authors. Lao She, a novelist of the early 20th century, penned numerous novels in the capital, including *Rickshaw Boy*, a social critique of the living conditions of rickshaw drivers in Beijing. Other important 20th-century writers who resided in Beijing include Lu Xun, Mao Dun and Guo Moruo.

When the Communists came to power, writing became a hazardous occupation and many writers did not survive. These days the situation has improved somewhat; writers continue to skirt around politically taboo issues but do explore social realities. Author Zhang Jie has been labelled China's first feminist writer for her internationally acclaimed *Love Must Not Be Forgotten*, while Wang Shuo's short stories express the realities of Beijing's unemployed and disaffected youth.

Quotations – and more quotations – from Mao

ARRIVAL & DEPARTURE

Direct flights from Europe, the Americas and Asia vie for touchdown at Capital International Airport. Competition within the airline industry means good deals are available, particularly in the low season (October to May). Trains chug in from Russia along the Trans-Siberian Railway or you can take a longwinded train journey from Hong Kong or Vietnam. You can also get pretty close to Beijing by sea from South Korea or Japan to Tianjin.

Air
INFORMATION
General Inquiries (☎ 6456 3604)

Flight Information
Air Canada (☎ 6468 2001)
Air France (☎ 400 880 8808)
American Airlines (☎ 6517 1788)
British Airways (☎ 8511 5599)
Japan Airlines (☎ 6513 0888)
Korean Air (☎ 8453 8888)
Lufthansa Airlines (☎ 6465 4488)
Qantas Airways (☎ 6467 3337)
Singapore Airlines (☎ 6505 2233)

Hotel Booking Service
The information desk at the international arrivals hall has a hotel booking service. You pay a deposit here and the hotel returns it to you upon your arrival.

AIRPORT ACCESS
Bus
You can buy tickets from the desk inside the terminal for Y16. Bus journeys into Beijing take anywhere from half an hour to an hour and head to points all over the city.

Three of the buses follow express routes into town. Route A is the most popular; it passes by the Youyi Lufthansa Centre, Dongzhimen and Dongsishitiao subway stops and terminates downtown at the Beijing International Hotel.

Returning to the airport, you can catch a shuttle from Xidan subway station, outside the Civil Aviation Administration of China (CAAC) booking office.

Taxi
Getting a taxi into town should cost about Y85, including the Y15 expressway toll, and only takes around 20 minutes if you don't get caught in a traffic jam. Dodgy taxi operators will attempt to lure you into a Y300 ride while you are still in the terminal. Ignore them, head out to the taxi queue and find a driver willing to use the meter.

Train
Domestic trains arrive and depart at Beijing train station (4, G6) or Beijing West train station (8, D5). Tibet is the only Chinese province not covered by the country's extensive network. Trains for Moscow, Pyongyang and Ulaan Baatar arrive and depart from Beijing train station, while trains for Hong Kong and Vietnam use Beijing West train station.

Domestic train tickets (hard seat, soft seat or sleeper) can be bought up to four days in advance from the station or, for a small surcharge, from your hotel. Try to avoid travelling during holidays, particularly Chinese New Year: tickets are rare and trains are congested.

Monkey Business (5, H2; ☎ 6591 6519), which is located in the Red House Hotel, room 35, and the **Beijing Tourism Group** (4, G5; ☎ 6515 8565; 7th fl, 28 Jianguomenwai Dajie) sell tickets for the Trans-Siberian, Trans-Manchurian and Trans-Mongolian Railways. Note that visas can be quite complicated for these trips.

Travel Documents
PASSPORT
All visitors to Beijing require a visa and therefore a passport. Passports must be valid for at least three months longer than the expiry date of the visa.

VISA
Nationals of all countries require a visa to visit China (with the exception of those from

Hong Kong and Macau). Visas must be arranged at embassies or consulates before arriving in China; they take about three days to process if you apply in person and are valid for one to three months.

The 'valid until' date on the visa is the date by which you must enter the country, not the date upon which your visa expires. Information and printable visa application forms can be found at www.china-embassy.org.

RETURN/ONWARD TICKET
You may need to show your return ticket when applying for your visa.

Customs
As a tourist, customs officers are unlikely to pay you much attention. If you're trying to take out anything considered an antique (ie made before 1949), you'll require a certificate and a red seal, obtainable from the **Relics Bureau** (4, H5; ☎ 6401 4608; Friendship Store; ⏱ 1.30-4.30pm Mon-Fri). It is illegal to take home antique objects from Tibet or antiques made before 1795.

Left Luggage
Left-luggage facilities are on the ground floor of the international terminal. Luggage can be stored for up to seven days. You'll be charged according to the size of your bag.

GETTING AROUND
Beijing is so sprawling that even after arriving at the bus or subway stop nearest your destination, you may still have a good 30- to 45-minute walk ahead of you. Especially for those on short trips to the capital, consider taking a taxi, rickshaw or pedicab the rest of the way. In this book, the nearest subway station or bus route is noted after the Ⓜ or 🚌 in each listing.

Travel Passes
Bus and subway passes exist but are off limits to tourists. If you have a student or work visa, however, you can try to get a bus pass (one-month student pass Y10, three-month adult pass Y120) from any of the major bus stations by showing your passport.

Bus
The tangle of Beijing's bus routes can be bewildering for short-stay travellers and traffic can slow buses to an infuriating crawl. Bus maps can be handy but are also fairly cryptic, with numbers disappearing at one end of town and reappearing at the other. Buses run from 5am to 11pm and tickets cost around Y1 to Y2. At almost any time of day, buses can be packed to the gills; your chances of getting a seat are just about nil.

Buses displaying one- and two-digit route numbers operate in the city centre. Those beginning with '3' are part of the suburban line. Private minibuses follow many of the main bus routes; they're slightly more expensive than city buses and can be slower and more dangerous. Double-decker buses do loops around the city centre and are much less traumatic. A ticket costs Y2 and you are almost guaranteed a seat.

Subway
Subway delays are rare and it only gets seriously crowded during the 5pm rush hour. Trains run every few minutes from 5am to 11pm. There are presently four lines. Most major tourist sites are served by Lines 1 or 2 and a ticket is Y3. Line 13 is a light-rail line that snakes through the northern suburbs but is useful for getting near sights in the city's northwest. A ticket is Y3. A combo subway–light-rail ticket is Y5. The Batong line is east off the Sihuidong stop and costs Y2 but won't be of interest to most tourists. The city is ambitiously planning another four lines to be opened before the 2008 Olympics.

To spot a subway station, look for the blue capital 'D' with a circle around it. Platform signs are in Chinese and Pinyin. Stops are in Chinese and Pinyin and announcements are in Chinese and English.

Bicycle

Beijing is fairly flat and has lots of bike lanes. However, the thick traffic and bad drivers can make them extremely dangerous. You can rent bikes at hotels or rental shops. Theft can be a problem in Beijing; lock your bike and park it in a patrolled bike parking lot. Few bikes are equipped with lights; helmets are nowhere to be seen.

Taxi

Unless there's a rainstorm or it's rush hour, you should have no problem hailing a taxi. If you don't speak Chinese, try to have your destination written down in Chinese characters.

As in any big city, taxi drivers may attempt to take you on a wild goose chase; hold onto a map and look like you know where you're going. Most Beijing taxi drivers are fair and efficient; in the unlikely event that they don't want to use the meter, insist that they do or get out. Don't expect rear seatbelts in any but the best taxis, and watch out for exhausted drivers.

Look for the sticker on the side rear window showing the taxi's rate per kilometre: it varies depending on the model. Between 11pm and 6am there's a 20% surcharge added to the flag-fall metered fare.

Car

If you're willing to brave Beijing's mad traffic, you can hire a car. However, given the restrictions and the recklessness you'll see on the roads, it can hardly be recommended. Rather than do the driving yourself, it's much less hassle to hire a chauffeur-driven car.

RENTAL

One of the best (and only) places to hire a car is from **Hertz China** (4, J5; ☎ 6595 8109, 800 810 8883; www.hertz.net.cn; Jianguo Hotel). **Beijing Car Solutions** (☎ 135 0138 0047; www.car-solution.com) also offers car rental and assistance. Chauffeur-driven cars can be arranged at major hotels and travel agencies.

ROAD RULES

You will quickly begin to wonder if there are any; the most consistent rule seems to be carelessness. The majority of cars drive on the right, as required by law, and seat belts are compulsory for front-seat passengers. Speed limits are posted. Tolerance for drinking and driving is zilch.

DRIVING LICENCE & PERMIT

You will require an International Driving Licence if you plan to drive in Beijing. Even with this licence, you're only allowed to drive within Beijing and Tianjin proper and cannot set out further afield.

PRACTICALITIES
Business Hours

Businesses are generally open Monday to Friday from 8.30am or 9am to 5pm or 6pm. Most close for an hour over lunch and many are open on Saturday morning. Shops are often open on Saturday and Sunday. While many shops don't open until 10am, they stay open until 10pm seven days a week.

Restaurants are usually open from 11am to 2pm and 6pm to 10pm. Most sights are open from 9am to 4.30pm or 5pm; almost all are open over the weekend and a few are closed on Monday. Most ticket offices stop selling tickets anywhere from 30 minutes to one hour before closing time. Almost all parks are open daily from 6am to 9pm.

Climate & When to Go

The best time to visit Beijing is in autumn (mid-September to November), when it has blue skies and manageable temperatures.

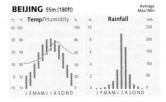

BEIJING 55m (180ft)

Summer (June to mid-September) can be absolutely scorching and humid, making sightseeing a sweaty affair. It's also high season for Chinese tourists and sights are often packed.

Spring (April to May) is quiet, but sand storms that sweep in from Inner Mongolia can be blinding. Winter (December to March) is glacial but brings the best deals at hotels.

Disabled Travellers

Beijing will be a major obstacle course if you are disabled. Pavements are crowded and in appalling condition, and high curbs prevent wheelchair access. Many streets can only be crossed via multi-stair underground walkways, and subways and buses are not accessible.

As wheelchairs are prohibitively expensive for most disabled people in China, attractions and buildings are not designed with access in mind. In this book, the ♿ symbol has been awarded only to places with ramps and lifts (elevators), and where wheelchairs can be manoeuvred. Those with sight, hearing or walking disabilities must be extremely cautious of traffic, which almost never yields to pedestrians.

INFORMATION & ORGANISATIONS

It can be useful to contact the travel officer of your national support organisation before leaving home; they can sometimes offer travel literature to help with planning and can put you in touch with appropriate tours. In the UK the **Royal Association for Disability & Rehabilitation** (Radar; ☎ 020-7250 3222; radar@radar.org.uk; Unit 12, City Forum, 250 City Rd, London EC1V 8AF) produces fact-packs for disabled travellers. In the USA try the **Society for the Advancement of Travel for the Handicapped** (SATH; ☎ 212-447 7284; www.sath.org; Suite 601, 347 Fifth Ave, New York, NY 10016).

In France try the **Comité National Français de Liaison pour la Réadapta-tion des Handicapés** (CNFLRH; ☎ 01 53 80 66 66; 236 bis rue de Tolbiac, Paris).

Discounts

Kids under 1.2m often get into sights for half-price, as do students and seniors with recognised ID.

The Beijing Museum Ticket is valid for one year and will get you into around 60 museums for a huge discount. They are released at the end of December but sell out quickly. The ticket is sold at participating museums and at the Wangfujing train station.

STUDENT & YOUTH CARDS

Students with ISIC or STA cards receive discounts at many of Beijing's major sights. Unfortunately, discounts don't extend to travel.

SENIORS' CARDS

Discounts for seniors are often given but not listed at attractions. Show some ID that has your date of birth – you may be pleasantly surprised.

Doing Business

Obtaining licences, hiring employees and paying taxes can generate mind-boggling quantities of red tape in China. It's a 'who you know' system and it can take a lot of persistence to find a cooperative official.

The trade section of your embassy in Beijing may be able to get you started, as can one of the many Trade Promotion Organisations like the **American Chamber of Commerce** (☎ 8519 1920; www.amcham-china.org.cn), the **China Council for the Promotion of International Trade** (☎ 6802 0229; www.ccpit .org) or the **British Chamber of Commerce** (☎ 8525 1111; www.britcham .org/bj). They can also suggest English-speaking lawyers and accountants.

Business centres in major hotels can provide office equipment, secretarial assistance, conference rooms, printing help and translation services.

Electricity

Beijing's electric current is 220V, 50Hz AC. Most plugs will take four designs: three-pronged angled pins (as in Australia), three-pronged round pins (as in Hong Kong), two flat pins (US style, without the ground wire) and two narrow round pins (European style). Conversion plugs are widely available in Beijing.

Embassies

Embassies in Beijing:

Australia (5, B1; ☎ 5140 4111; www .austemb.org.cn; 21 Dongzhimenwai Dajie)
Canada (5, B1; ☎ 6532 3536; www.beijing .gc.ca; 19 Dongzhimenwai Dajie)
France (5, C2; ☎ 6532 1331; www .ambafrance-cn.org; 3 Sanlitun Dongsan Jie)
New Zealand (4, H4; ☎ 6532 2731; www .nzembassy.com/china; 1 Ritan Dong Erjie)
Russia (4, G1; ☎ 6532 2051; fax 6532 4851; 4 Dongzhimen Beizhongjie)
Thailand (4, G4; ☎ 6532 1749; fax 6532 1748; 40 Guanghua Lu)
UK (4, H4; ☎ 5192 4000; www.british embassy.org.cn; 11 Guanghua Lu)
USA (4, H4; ☎ 6532 3831; www .usembassy-china.org.cn; 3 Xiushui Beijie)

Emergencies

The consequence for crime against foreigners is steep in China (often death), so hardened criminals will pay very little attention to you. Pickpocketing, however, is a big problem in crowded places like buses or markets, and especially in Tiananmen Square, so carry your bag in front of you. Also keep some small change in an accessible pocket to avoid having to open up your wallet. Don't walk alone along empty streets at night and don't wander off by yourself into deserted areas of parks.

Beggars are numerous in areas frequented by foreigners. Many of them, usually women or children, do get aggressive. Though desperate, they're not known to be harmful.

Technically, spitting is illegal in Beijing, but many locals continue to gob with gusto. Do your best to keep out of the line of fire.
Ambulance (☎ 120)
Fire (☎ 119)
General Emergency (☎ 999)
Police (☎ 110)

Fitness

There are a number of clubs and recreational facilities around town.

FITNESS CLUBS

Evolution Fitness (8, H4; ☎ 6567 3499; www.evolution-fitness.com; 2 Dongsanhuan Nanlu)
Nirvana Fitness & Spa (5, C2; ☎ 6597 2008; www.nirvana.com.cn; 2 Gong-rentiyuchang Beilu)

GOLF

Beijing International Golf Club (1, B2; ☎ 6076 2288) Located 35km north of Beijing, on the north side of the Ming Tombs reservoir.

SWIMMING

Dongdan Sports Centre (4, F5; ☎ 6523 1241; 2a Dahua Lu; Y30; ☽ noon-10pm Mon, 10am-10pm Tue-Fri, noon-9.30pm Sat & Sun)

Gay & Lesbian Travellers

While there is greater tolerance of homosexuality in Beijing than in China's more rural areas, it's not recommended that gays and lesbians be too open about their sexual orientation in public. Gay clubs appear to function without official harassment, although they tend to be low profile.

See p93 for gay and lesbian bars.

INFORMATION & ORGANISATIONS

The rarely updated www.utopia-asia.com /tipschin.htm can provide some tips on travelling China, as well as listings of gay bars and clubs nationwide. You can also contact the

International Gay and Lesbian Travel Association (☎ 954-776 2626; www.iglta .com) in the USA.

Health
IMMUNISATIONS
No vaccination requirements exist for entry into China, except for yellow fever if you are coming from an infected area. As a basic precaution, check that your tetanus, diphtheria and polio vaccinations are up to date. Vaccinations against hepatitis A and B are also worth considering, as is one against influenza, particularly for senior travellers. Malaria is not a risk in Beijing.

PRECAUTIONS
Beijing is a relatively healthy place, but influenza is almost synonymous with China, particularly in the winter months.

Travellers are also prone to diarrhoea, usually brought on by ingesting food and water foreign to your body. Drink bottled water (make sure bottles are sealed when you buy them) and peel all fruit and vegetables. Avoid eating raw vegetables in all but the most foreigner-friendly restaurants.

Travellers after current health advisories for China should check the World Health Organization website www.who.int.

MEDICAL SERVICES
Hospitals with 24-hour accident and emergency departments include the following:
Beijing International Medical Centre (8, H3; ☎ 6465 1561/2/3; Room S106-S111, Youyi Lufthansa Centre, 50 Liangmaqiao Lu; Ⓜ Dongzhimen, then bus 701)
Beijing Union Hospital (4, F4; ☎ 6529 5284, emergency 6529 5269; 53 Dongdan Beidajie; Ⓜ Dongdan)
Hong Kong International Medical Clinic (4, G2; ☎ 6501 4260; 9th fl, Hong Kong Macau Centre, Swissotel, Gongrentiyuchang Beilu; Ⓜ Dongsishitiao)

DENTAL SERVICES
If you chip a tooth or require emergency treatment, head to the Beijing International Medical Centre or the Hong Kong International Medical Clinic (see left).

PHARMACIES
Pharmacies are everywhere and they usually sell both traditional and Western medicines.

Try the following places:
Golden Elephant Pharmacy (4, B5; ☎ 6607 7021;114 Xidan Beidajie; ☽ 24hr)
Wangfujing Medicine Shop (4, E4; ☎ 6524 0122; 267 Wangfujing Dajie; ☽ 8.30am-9pm)

Holidays
New Year's Day 1 January
Chinese New Year Late January/early February (three days)
International Women's Day 8 March
International Labour Day 1 May
Youth Day 4 May
Children's Day 1 June
Anniversary of the Founding of the Chinese Communist Party 1 July
Anniversary of the Founding of the People's Liberation Army 1 August
National Day 1 October

Internet
Internet cafés are not easy to find. They rarely have signs or even formal names. Try and memorize the characters for Internet café (网吧; *wǎngbā*) and keep your eyes peeled, or try the cafés below.

INTERNET CAFÉS
Internet Café (5, A2; south of Red House Hotel, northeast of Xingfucun Lu; per hr low-/high-usage times Y3/4; ☽ 24hr)
Internet Café (4, A6; in alley west off Chanchun Jie; per hr low-/high-usage times Y3/4; ☽ 24hr)
Internet Café Qianmen (6, A1; Old Station Building, southeast of Tiananmen Square; per hr Y20; ☽ 9am-11pm)

USEFUL WEBSITES

Lonely Planet's website (www.lonelyplanet .com) offers a speedy link to many of Beijing's websites. Other websites to try include:

Beijing Page (www.beijingpage.com)
Beijing Tourism Administration (www .bjta.gov.cn)
China Online (www.chinaonline.com)
Fly China (www.flychina.com)
Wild China (www.wildchina.com)

Lost Property

Unfortunately, if you've lost it in Beijing it's likely gone for good. Your chances of recovering your property are slightly better if you lost it in a taxi. Make sure you always ask your driver for a receipt, which will have the cab number on it. Your hotel can call the taxi company and they will locate the driver.

Metric System

China officially uses the international metric system. See the conversion table below. You may also encounter China's ancient weights and measures system of *liǎng* and *jīn*. One *jīn* is 0.6kg (1.32lbs), and one *liǎng* is 37.5g (1.32oz); there are 16 *liǎng* to the *jīn*.

TEMPERATURE
°C = (°F - 32) ÷ 1.8
°F = (°C x 1.8) + 32

DISTANCE
1in = 2.54cm
1cm = 0.39in
1m = 3.3ft = 1.1yd
1ft = 0.3m
1km = 0.62 miles
1 mile = 1.6km

WEIGHT
1kg = 2.2lb
1lb = 0.45kg
1g = 0.04oz
1oz = 28g

VOLUME
1L = 0.26 US gallons
1 US gallon = 3.8L
1L = 0.22 imperial gallons
1 imperial gallon = 4.55L

Money
CURRENCY

Chinese currency is called Renminbi (RMB) or 'people's money', and is issued by the Bank of China. Its basic unit is the *yuán* (Y), also referred to as *kuài*, the equivalent slang to 'buck' or 'quid'. The *yuán* is divided into 10 *jiǎo* (pronounced *máo*) and the *jiǎo* is divided into 10 *fēn*. These days, *fēn* are worth next to nothing and are disappearing from use.

Paper notes are issued in denominations of one, two, five, 10, 20, 50 and 100 *yuán*; one, two and five *jiǎo*; and one, two and five *fēn*. Coins are in denominations of one *yuán*; one, two and five *jiǎo*; and one, two and five *fēn*.

TRAVELLERS CHEQUES

Travellers cheques from most of the world's leading banks and issuing agencies (the most obvious being Citibank, Amex and Visa) are easily cashed in Beijing, even though they are a pain to unload in the rest of China.

You can exchange cheques at the main branch of the **Bank of China** (4, E5; Oriental Plaza), exchange desks at the airport, and at some of the larger tourist hotels.

CREDIT CARDS

Most four- and five-star hotels, fancy restaurants and major department stores accept credit cards. If you use your credit card for a cash advance at the Bank of China or CITIC Bank you will be levied with a steep 4% commission.

ATMS

A growing number of ATMs are springing up in Beijing. Cards with GlobalAccess, Cirrus, Interlink, Plus and Star are all commonly accepted. You can also get cash advances on Visa, MasterCard and Amex at many ATMs. It's always good to have a backup and not depend solely on your bankcard, as ATMs are often out of service or out of money.

CHANGING MONEY

Foreign currency can be exchanged at the Bank of China, exchange desks at the airport, CITIC Bank and tourist hotels. Banks give the official rate, as do most hotels, though many hotels add a small commission and some will only exchange money for their own guests.

Hold onto at least a few of your exchange receipts as, theoretically, you'll need them if you want to exchange any remaining RMB at the end of your trip.

Newspapers & Magazines

The Chinese government's favourite English-language mouthpiece is the **China Daily** (www.chinadaily.net), which you can pick up for free in hotel lobbies or buy for Y1. Magazines and newspapers from North America and Europe are available in major tourist hotels and the Friendship Store but are sometimes trimmed of opinion; for the uncensored version visit the newspapers' websites.

Photography & Video

Colour-print film, including Kodak and Fuji, is readily available in Beijing. Kodak shops are on every other corner, although some are better at developing film than others.

China subscribes to the PAL video standard, which is the the same as Australia, New Zealand, the UK and most of Europe. DVDs and VCDs are more widely used in China than videotapes.

Post

You'll see small green post offices all over Beijing but the most efficient is the **Beijing Main Post Office** (4, G5; Jianguomen Beidajie; ☽ 8am-7pm Mon-Sat). You can also send parcels from here, but don't seal them up before you have them inspected by the postal staff.

To send anything considered an antique, you'll need the correct paperwork (see p112).

POSTAL RATES

Postage for airmail letters (up to 20g) sent to anywhere outside China costs Y5.40 to Y6. Postcards cost Y4.50.

Radio

You can pick up the BBC World Service on 17760, 15278, 21660, 12010 and 9740 kHz. Voice of America can be found at 17820, 15425, 21840, 15250, 9760, 5880 and 6125 kHz.

Telephone

You can make local calls for around 2 *jiǎo* from orange public pay phones or domestic phones at kiosks. Long-distance international calls can also be made from orange phone booths, but they're pricey (around Y15 per minute to the USA or Europe). Between midnight and 7am calls are 40% cheaper. International calls can be made from main telecommunications offices.

PHONECARDS

There are a range of phonecards available. The best deal is Internet Phone (IP); rates are Y2.40 per minute to North America, Y1.50 per minute to Hong Kong, Macau or Taiwan and Y3.20 per minute to all other countries. They can be purchased at most hotels and kiosks.

Lonely Planet's global phonecard, specifically aimed at travellers, provides competitive international call rates, messaging services and free email. Log on to www.lonelyplanet.ekit.com for details.

MOBILE PHONES

Check whether your mobile phone has a setting for use in China. If not you can rent one from business centres in top-end hotels or try **Phone Rent** (☎ 6586 6669; www.phone rent.com).

COUNTRY & CITY CODES

Beijing (☎ 010)
People's Republic of China (☎ 86)

USEFUL PHONE NUMBERS

Note that there is a 50% chance that the people at the other end of these lines do not speak English.

International Directory Inquiries (☎ 115)
Local Directory Inquiries (☎ 114)
Time (☎ 117)
Weather (☎ 121)

INTERNATIONAL DIRECT DIAL CODES

Dial ☎ 00 followed by:

Australia (☎ 61)
Canada (☎ 1)
Japan (☎ 81)
New Zealand (☎ 64)
UK (☎ 44)
USA (☎ 1)

Television

Channel CCTV9 is Beijing's English-language channel, offering painfully dull drivel and propaganda news. CCTV4 occasionally carries more interesting English-language programmes on travel in China, and CCTV5 has sports in Chinese. Many tourist hotels have ESPN, CNN and HBO.

Time

Despite covering numerous world time zones, all of China is on Beijing Standard Time, which is eight hours ahead of GMT/UTC. At noon in Beijing it's 8pm the previous day in Los Angeles, 11pm the previous day in New York, 4am in London, 5am in Paris, 2pm in Melbourne and Sydney and 4pm in Wellington.

Tipping

Most top-end hotels and many of the city's classier restaurants will add a 10% to 15% service charge to your bill but tipping is neither customary nor expected in Beijing. Porters are the notable exception and will expect something.

Toilets

China's loos can be a heinous assault on the senses. But Beijing's toilets are pristine compared to those in China's countryside. In most tourist hotels you'll find Western-style toilets; at sights and restaurants you'll find squat-style toilets in a variety of conditions.

If you're down a *hútòng* and need the loo, you'll experience truly public toilets. Located every block or so, these are what the locals use – to find them just follow your nose.

Toilet paper is not often available, so carry some with you. Also, Beijing's sewerage system can't handle toilet paper; just drop it in the basket beside the toilet.

Tourist Information

Chinese tourist offices haven't quite got the hang of public service. You'll get information on their own tours from them but little else. You're better off asking the concierge at your hotel for city info. In Beijing, neighbourhood-based tourism offices are somewhat better but English skills are extremely limited. The **Xuanwu branch** (8, F5; ☎ 6351 0018; 3 Hufang Rd; 9am-6pm) is marginally more helpful. Tours and train and plane tickets can be booked at the **Beijing Tourism Group** (4, G5; ☎ 6515 8565; fax 6515 8192; 1st fl, 28 Jianguomenwai Dajie).

The English-language 24-hour **Beijing Tourism Hotline** (☎ 6513 0828) can answer questions and listen to complaints.

Women Travellers

Respect for women is deeply ingrained in Chinese culture and foreign women are unlikely to suffer sexual harassment here.

There have been a few reports of foreign women being hassled in parks or when walking or cycling at night; take a whistle or alarm with you. Beijing is very cosmopolitan, and shorts, tank tops and shorter skirts are worn by local women.

Tampons are not readily available in China but you'll find some at Watson's Drugstores (there's a branch in Oriental Plaza; 4, E5) and a few foreigner-friendly supermarkets. It's also best to bring your own contraceptive pills.

LANGUAGE

The official language of the People's Republic of China is Putonghua, based on (but not identical to) the Beijing Mandarin dialect.

Written Chinese script is based on ancient pictograph characters that have been simplified over time; while over 56,000 characters have been verified, it is commonly held that a well-educated Chinese person knows and uses between 6000 and 8000 characters. Pinyin has been developed as a Romanisation of Mandarin using English letters, but many Beijingers cannot read it.

A growing number of Beijingers speak some English; in tourist hotels and restaurants and at major sights you'll get along OK without Mandarin. But if you venture into shops, neighbourhoods or conversations that are off the tourist track, you may find yourself lost for words. For a user-friendly guide, with pronunciation tips and a comprehensive phrase list (including script that you can simply show to people rather than speak), get a copy of Lonely Planet's *Mandarin phrasebook*.

Social
MEETING PEOPLE

Hello.	nǐ hǎo
Goodbye.	zàijiàn
Please.	qǐng
Thank you.	xièxie
Thank you very much.	tài xièxie le

Yes.	shìde
No. (don't have)	méi yǒu
No. (not so)	búshì
Do you speak English?	nǐ huì shuō yīngyǔ ma?
Do you understand?	dǒng ma?
I understand.	wǒ tīngdedǒng
I don't understand.	wǒ tīngbudǒng

Could you please ...?	nǐ néng bunéng ...?
repeat that	chóngfù
speak more slowly	shuō màn diǎnr
write it down	xiě xiàlái

GOING OUT

What's on ...?	... yǒu shénme yúlè huódòng?
this weekend	zhège zhōumò
today	jīntiān
tonight	jīntiān wǎnshang

Where are the ...?	... zài nǎr?
clubs	jùlèbù
gay venues	tóngxìngliàn chángsuǒ
places to eat	chīfàn de dìfang
pubs	jiǔbā

Is there a local entertainment guide?	yǒu dāngdì yúlè zhǐnán ma?

Practical
QUESTION WORDS

Who?	shuí?
What?	shénme?
When?	shénme shíhou?
Where?	nǎr?
How?	zěnme?

NUMBERS & AMOUNTS

1	yī/yāo
2	èr/liǎng
3	sān
4	sì
5	wǔ
6	liù
7	qī
8	bā
9	jiǔ
10	shí
20	èrshí
30	sānshí
40	sìshí
50	wǔshí
60	liùshí
70	qīshí
80	bāshí
90	jiǔshí
100	yìbǎi
1000	yìqiān

DAYS

Monday	xīngqīyī
Tuesday	xīngqīèr
Wednesday	xīngqīsān
Thursday	xīngqīsì
Friday	xīngqīwǔ
Saturday	xīngqīliù
Sunday	xīngqītiān

BANKING

I'd like to ...	wǒ xiǎng ...
change money	huàn qián
change travellers cheques	huàn lǚxíng zhīpiào
cash a cheque	zhīpiào

Excuse me, where's the nearest ...?	qǐng wèn, zuìjìnde ... zài nǎr?
ATM	zìdòng guìyuánjī
foreign exchange office	wàihuì duìhuànchù

POST

Where's the post office?	yúojú zài nǎlǐ?

I'd like to send a ...	wǒ xiǎng jì ...
letter	xìn
fax	chuánzhēn
package	bāoguǒ
postcard	míngxinpiàn

I'd like to buy (a/an) ...	wǒ xiǎng mǎi ...
aerogram	hángkōngyóujiǎn
envelope	xìnfēng
stamps	yóupiào

PHONE & MOBILE PHONES

I want to buy a phone card.	wǒ xiǎng mǎi diànhuà kǎ

I want to make ...	wǒ xiǎng dǎ ...
a call (to ...)	diànhuà (dào ...)
a reverse-charge /collect call	duìfāng fùfèi diànhuà

Where can I find a/an ...?	nǎr yǒu ...
I'd like a/an ...	wǒ xiǎng yào ...
mobile/cell phone for hire	zūyòng yídòng diànhuà or zūyòng shǒujī
prepaid mobile/ cell phone	yùfù yídòng diànhuà or yùfù shǒujī
SIM card for your network	nǐmen wǎngluò de SIM kǎ

INTERNET

Is there a local Internet café?	běndì yǒu wǎngbā ma?
Where can I get online?	wǒ zài nǎr kěyǐ shàng wǎng?
Can I check my email account?	wǒ chá yīxià zìjǐ de email hù, hǎo ma?

computer	diànnǎo
email	diànzǐyóujiàn (often called 'email')
Internet	yīntèwǎng/hùliánwǎng (formal name)

TRANSPORT

What time does ... leave/arrive?	... jǐdiǎn kāi/ dào?
the bus	qìchē
the train	huǒchē
the plane	fēijī
the boat	chuán

When is the ... bus?	... qìchē jǐdiǎn kāi?
first	tóubān
next	xià yìbān
last	mòbān

Is this taxi available?	zhèi chē lā rén ma?
Please use the meter.	dǎ biǎo

How much (is it) to ...?	qù ... dūoshǎo qián?
I want to go to ...	wǒ yào qù ...
this address	zhège dìzhǐ

Food

breakfast	zǎofàn
lunch	wǔfàn
dinner	wǎnfàn
snack	xiǎochī
eat	chī
drink	hē

Can you recommend a ...?	nǐ néng bunéng tuījiàn yíge ...?
bar/pub	jiǔbā/jiǔguǎn
café	kāfēiguǎn
restaurant	cānguǎn

Is service/cover charge included in the bill?	zhàngdān zhōng bāokuò fúwùfèi ma?

Emergencies

It's an emergency!	zhèshì jǐnjí qíngkuàng!
Could you help me, please?	nǐ néng bunéng bāng wǒ ge máng?

Call the police/ a doctor/ an ambulance!	qǐng jiào jǐngchá/ yīshēng/ jiùhùchē!
Where's the police station?	jǐngchájú zài nǎr?

Health

Excuse me, where's the nearest ...?	qǐng wèn, zuìjìnde ... zài nǎr?
chemist	yàodiàn
chemist (night)	yàodiàn (yèjiān)
dentist	yáyī
doctor	yīshēng
hospital	yīyuàn

Is there a doctor here who speaks English?	zhèr yǒu huì jiǎng yīngyǔ de dàifu ma?

SYMPTOMS

I have (a/an) ...	wǒ ...
diarrhoea	lādùzi
fever	fāshāo
headache	tóuténg

Index

See also separate indexes for Eating (p125), Entertainment (p126), Shopping (p126), Sleeping (p127) and Sights with map references (p127).

FEATURES

🏮	Fangshan Restaurant	*Eating*
🎭	Beijing North Theatre	*Entertainment*
🍸	No-Name Bar	*Drinking*
🏯	Dongyue Temple	*Highlights*
🏠	Rongbaozhai	*Shopping*
🔭	Ancient Observatory	*Sights/Activities*
🏨	Wangfujing Grand	*Sleeping*

AREAS

	Market
	Building
	Land
	Mall
	Other Area
	Park/Cemetery
	Sports
	Urban

HYDROGRAPHY

	River, Creek
	Intermittent River
	Canal
	Swamp
	Water

BOUNDARIES

	State, Provincial
	Regional, Suburb
	Ancient Wall
	Cliff

ROUTES

	Tollway
	Freeway
	Primary Road
	Secondary Road
	Tertiary Road
	Lane
	Under Construction
	One-Way Street
	Unsealed Road
	Mall/Steps
	Tunnel
	Walking Path
	Walking Trail/Track
	Pedestrian Overpass
	Walking Tour

TRANSPORT

	Airport, Airfield
	Bus Route
	Cycling, Bicycle Path
	Ferry
	General Transport
	Metro
	Monorail
	Rail
	Taxi Rank
	Tram

SYMBOLS

	Bank, ATM
	Buddhist
	Castle, Fortress
	Christian
	Confucian
	Embassy, Consulate
	Hospital, Clinic
	Hindu
	Information
	Internet Access
	Islamic
	Lookout
	Monument
	Mountain, Volcano
	National Park
	Parking Area
	Petrol Station
	Point of Interest
	Police Station
	Post Office
	Ruin
	Shinto
	Taoist
	Telephone
	Toilets
	Zoo, Bird Sanctuary
	Waterfall

24/7 travel advice
www.lonelyplanet.com